The power of the centre

Manchester University Press

European Policy Research Unit Series

Series Editors: *Simon Bulmer, Peter Humphreys* and *Mick Moran*

The European Policy Research Unit Series aims to provide advanced textbooks and thematic studies of key public policy issues in Europe. They concentrate, in particular, on comparing patterns of national policy content, but pay due attention to the European Union dimension. The thematic studies are guided by the character of the policy issue under examination.

The European Policy Research Unit (EPRU) was set up in 1989 within the University of Manchester's Department of Government to promote research on European politics and public policy. The series is part of EPRU's effort to facilitate intellectual exchange and substantive debate on the key policy issues confronting the European states and the European Union.

The power of the centre

Central governments and the macro-implementation of EU public policy

Dionyssis G. Dimitrakopoulos

Manchester University Press
Manchester and New York
distributed exclusively in the USA by Palgrave Macmillan

Copyright © Dionyssis G. Dimitrakopoulos 2008

The right of Dionyssis G. Dimitrakopoulos to be identified as the author of this work has been asserted by him in accordance with the Copyright, Designs and Patents Act 1988.

Published by Manchester University Press
Oxford Road, Manchester M13 9NR, UK
and Room 400, 175 Fifth Avenue, New York, NY 10010, USA
www.manchesteruniversitypress.co.uk

Distributed in the United States exclusively by
Palgrave Macmillan, 175 Fifth Avenue,
New York, NY 10010, USA

Distributed in Canada exclusively by
UBC Press, University of British Columbia, 2029 West Mall,
Vancouver, BC, Canada V6T 1Z2

British Library Cataloguing-in-Publication Data is available

Library of Congress Cataloging-in-Publication Data is available

ISBN 978 0 7190 9003 5 paperback

First published by Manchester University Press in hardback 2008

This paperback edition first published 2013

The publisher has no responsibility for the persistence or accuracy of URLs for any external or third-party internet websites referred to in this book, and does not guarantee that any content on such websites is, or will remain, accurate or appropriate.

Printed by Lightning Source

Του Άλκη

Contents

	List of figures	viii
	Acknowledgements	ix
	List of abbreviations	xi
	Introduction	1
1	Institutional capabilities and the dynamics of implementation	17
2	Patterns of institutional change	30
3	EU public procurement policy	58
4	Transposition	76
5	Macro-implementation	93
6	Conclusion	135
	Bibliography	149
	Index	173

Figures

6.1 Value of public procurement contracts advertised as part (%) of the estimated total public procurement value in 2002 figures, 1995–2002   137
6.2 Public procurement advertised in the Official Journal as part (%) of GDP, 1993–2003   138

Acknowledgements

This book originates from the doctoral dissertation that I wrote and defended at the University of Hull too long ago. I am grateful to Edward C. Page who – initially informally, then formally – provided *pistes de réflexion*, advice, encouragement, patience and constructive criticism while supervising the dissertation. His help has been invaluable. Thanks are also due to Juliet Lodge for enabling me to commence the project. The financial support provided by the EU through TMR fellowship ERBFMBICT 960756 is gratefully acknowledged.

Since the decision – taken later on, to start work on it with the, as reality demonstrated, distant aim of using it as a basis for a monograph, I have inevitably accumulated a number of debts. Indeed, thanks are due to the Hellenic Observatory at the European Institute of the London School of Economics and Political Science both for awarding me a National Bank of Greece Senior Fellowship that enabled me to take time off my routine duties at Birkbeck and for providing a singular combination of intellectual stimulation, excellent research facilities and convivial environment for my research. Its staff played a central role in turning an often solitary experience into a joyous one. The School of Politics and Sociology at Birkbeck funded part of my research and its then Head, Robert Singh, kindly agreed to grant me leave to take up the fellowship. Though the usual disclaimer applies, my work has benefited greatly from Kevin Featherstone's perceptive and insightful comments, challenging discussions with Hussein Kassim, testing comments made by my graduate students at Birkbeck and participants in the research seminar of the LSE's Hellenic Observatory, the frankness of the officials who granted confidential interviews for my research and – at Manchester University Press – Tony Mason's patience. I am also grateful to Blackwell and Taylor & Francis for allowing me to use in this book parts of articles published in the *European Law Journal*, the *Journal of Common Market Studies* and the *Journal of European Public Policy*.

Argyris G. Passas' inspiring lectures during my years as an undergraduate student at Panteion University (Athens) and subsequent friendship, veritable *encadrement intellectuel*, encouragement, imaginative comments and advice on previous drafts of the book amount to a debt that I can only hope to repay. The support provided by my father Yiorgos and mother Theodora is simply incalculable. Last, but by no means least, Alkis A. Passas is certainly too young to know much about implementation but, as many a three-year old, he already knows a hell of a lot about steering people towards his desired result. This is but one of the reasons why this book is dedicated to him.

Bloomsbury

Abbreviations

CCM	*Commission Centrale des Marchés*
CCTA	Central Computer and Telecommunications Agency
CIJAP	*Cellule d'information juridique aux acheteurs publics*
CMPE	*Commission des Marchés Publics de l'État*
CPD	Central Procurement Directorate
CSM	*Commissions spécialisées des marchés*
CUP	Central Unit on Purchasing
DAJ	*Direction des Affaires Juridiques*
DEFRA	Department for Environment, Food and Rural Affairs
DTI	Department of Trade and Industry
EID	European Integration Department
ENYEK	Special EC Legal Service
EQ (O)	European Questions (Official) Committee
EQO (L)	European Questions Official (Legal) Committee
FCO	Foreign and Commonwealth Office
GGHR	Gazette of the Government of the Hellenic Republic
HMSO	Her Majesty's Stationery Office
JORF	*Journal Officiel de la République Française*
MAFF	Ministry of Agriculture, Fisheries and Food
MIEM	*Mission Interministérielle d'Enquête sur les Marchés*
MOPADIS	Tenders and Contracts Monitoring Unit
ND	Nea Dimokratia
NSK	State Legal Council
OEEC	Organisation for European Economic Co-operation
OGC	Office of Government Commerce
PASOK	Pan-Hellenic Socialist Movement
QMV	Qualified majority voting
SGAE	*Secrétariat Général des Affaires Européennes*
SGCI	*Secrétariat Général du Comité Interministériel pour les questions de coopération économique européenne*
SGG	*Secrétariat Général du Gouvernement*
SOE	Council of Economic Advisers
UKRep	UK Permanent Representation to the EU

Introduction

In spring 1990 Greece had a new conservative government after eight years of socialist rule. One of the electoral pledges of the conservative party (Nea Dimokratia) concerned the radical improvement of the country's poor record in the implementation of European legislation.[1] The pledge of the conservative party had a wider symbolic significance because it was a previous conservative government that had taken Greece into the then EEC in January 1981.

Nevertheless, what they actually meant was a rather different story. The basic idea behind this new political priority concerned the adoption of legislative measures for the transposition of European legislation into national law. In other words, the rapid and timely adoption of national legislation was the tool that was going to be used for the improvement of the country's implementation profile. However, if transposition was the only or even the most important source of the problem, what had impeded any Greek government from doing something about this problem earlier?

Most post-accession single-party Greek governments had enjoyed the support of robust parliamentary majorities. Moreover, political dissent was almost completely absent from the Greek Parliament in the post-dictatorial era. The presence of numerous lawyers in Parliament, the Athenian bureaucracy and consecutive cabinets was overwhelming. In other words, there was not much that could impede previous governments from achieving their objective. Furthermore, one could, perhaps, use PASOK's anti-EC rhetoric as an explanation of the country's poor implementation record only between 1981 and 1985 because the end of its first period in office marked a quite clear change in the direction of a much more positive, albeit quite critical, stance. Moreover, Greece had problems implementing European policies before *and* after 1990 and the electoral victory of the conservative (and traditionally 'pro-European') party. Even if the decision of the conservative government to focus on the legislative dimension of the problem went in the right direction, it was not a sufficient step for the improvement of the country's implementation profile. This begs the question: what can national governments do to resolve this problem? Are there any tools that may be used in that respect? Furthermore, during the same period (early 1990s) the EU's implementation deficit was beginning to emerge as a key issue in the development of European integration. If the attitude of the government was a powerful explanatory factor of this systemic phenomenon, why did a country with an unquestionably defining input to European integration, such as France, contribute to the collective so-called 'implementation deficit', whereas an 'awkward partner' such as Britain did much less so?

Placing emphasis on the transposition of EU legislation into national legal orders and – more specifically – focusing on the capacity of governments to push these reforms through parliaments would be surprising since modern parliaments in Europe are not exactly the hotbed of political dissent. Moreover, reducing the issue of implementation to one of producing laws that appear to give effect to European legislation ignores the fact that effective transposition is just a part of a wider process. Getting a legislative act through parliament is one thing. Preparing this act and, above all, ensuring that it accurately reflects the spirit of the European policy that it embodies, is another. Consequently, a *dynamic* rather than static view of the transposition process must be adopted. This means that, on the one hand, we should examine the links between this stage of the process and what precedes it. Does the formulation of policy contain evidence that may illuminate problems in the subsequent stages of the EU policy process? Does formulation constitute an opportunity for the choice of methods and tools that may at least help us foresee some of the difficulties that may appear later, thus facilitating their timely resolution?

On the other hand, once a law has been passed, turning its provisions into concrete reality is not only a matter of coping with different and often competing interests; rather, it entails first and foremost the involvement of political and administrative institutions. This, in turn, raises once more the issue of the national governments' margin for action. What can they do in order to ameliorate their implementation record? Are there any strategies and tools that can be used to steer post-transposition implementation?

Two broad strategies can be envisaged. First, governments may seek to be more pro-active by taking account of the exigencies of implementation in previous stages of the EU policy process. This would allow them to transpose more effectively and finally set up *national* strategic mechanisms and procedures that facilitate monitoring and problem-solving *during* as well as *immediately after* the transposition phase. Second, they may adopt specific measures such as the recruitment of more and better trained staff, which will seek to ensure better implementation at *street-level* (Lipsky 1971).

Following the second strategy as a platform for the analysis of the implementation process is likely to provide rich insights about the relations between front-line implementers and the relevant target groups and other actors, but would be inadequate for the analysis of the *national* actions regarding a country's implementation profile. Discussing the implementation of the EU's environmental policy in Greece Giannakourou (1996, 7) identified the creation of an independent body for the delivery of 'eco-labels' as a significant innovation. Who assessed the need for this body, who decided to create it and which tools have been used in that process? Street-level implementation analysis is not likely to answer these questions.

This book sets out to examine the first strategy in an effort to draw wider lessons regarding the development of the process of European integration. Specifically, it seeks to examine the way in which national central governments deal with the exigencies of the implementation of EU public policy. Focusing on the central governments of Greece, France and the UK and the case of public procurement, it provides an institutionalist account of the *dynamics* of implementation.[2]

The significance of implementation

There are many reasons why the implementation of public policy – construed as the process of forging links in a causal chain so as to obtain a policy's desired results (Pressman and Wildavsky 1984, xxiii) – deserves systematic analysis. First, the politics of implementation is also an essential aspect of the operation of any democratic system. Citizens assess democratically elected politicians (and the officials who act on their behalf) on the basis of the policies that they make *and* implement. The legitimacy of a democratic polity that enacts but does not implement policies is likely to suffer. Conversely, politics does not end when a law is enacted. Rather, 'implementation is the continuation of politics by other means', as a pioneer of implementation analysis put it (Bardach 1977, 85) and the EU is not an exception (Jordan 1997; Dimitrakopoulos 2001c, 2001b).

Second, implementation can be seen as a credibility test for individual member states, the EU and the integration process as a whole. Indeed, more than six decades after the end of the last destructive war on its soil, the EU (one of the organisations that contributed to post-war lasting peace and prosperity) is assessed not only on the basis of the motives of its creators (peace figuring prominently among them) but, increasingly, on its capacity to contribute to improvements in the daily lives of its citizens. This, in turn, means that we need to have a better grasp of the factors that affect the way in which EU policies are turned into reality. For example, since much of European integration is about market-making, the 'level playing field' which is the purported objective of this process will not come to existence if there is a significant implementation deficit. Moreover, to the extent that European integration involves social regulation, a significant implementation deficit will undermine improvements in social standards. As Guy Peters put it (1997, 200) '[t]he capacity to implement policy is one central defining feature of any political system, and if in the future the EU is to be a functioning government then implementation becomes a crucial question'.

Third, as existing literature points out, the EU is not dissimilar from the member states in that they too have an 'implementation deficit'; there is a gap between proclaimed objectives on the one hand and reality (and process) on the other. Indeed, for the EU[3] this is a systemic issue (Mendrinou 1996; Dimitrakopoulos and Richardson 2001).

Fourth, the presence of robust national institutions capable of coping with the exigencies of membership is one of the criteria for accession to the EU. The initial broad reference to 'stability of institutions guaranteeing democracy, the rule of law . . . as well as the capacity to cope with competitive pressure and market forces within the Union [and] the candidate's ability to take on the obligations of membership' found in the so-called 'Copenhagen criteria' (European Council 1993, 13) has been strengthened with explicit reference to the candidate countries' need to adjust their administrative structures in view of accession (European Council 1995, section III A).

Fifth, new issues and controversies have emerged as a result of the development of the study of European integration. The so-called 'Europeanisation' of the nation state – which is usually construed as domestic institutional and/or policy convergence as a consequence of membership of the EU – features prominently among them. Given that the analysis of implementation entails the systematic discussion of the translation of policies into practice, it can contribute to the assessment of the claims made about the domestic impact of EU policies.[4]

Finally, despite the importance of the implementation stage, relatively little is known about the EU as an implementation structure because EU scholars have devoted overwhelming attention to the formulation of EU public policy. Unsurprisingly, this reflects the development of the study of public policy making in nation states. Implementation began to attract systematic[5] scholarly attention only in the 1970s (Derthick 1972; Pressman and Wildavsky 1973; Hargrove 1975; Van Meter and Van Horn 1975; Hood 1976; Bardach 1977; Rein and Rabinovitz 1977; Berman 1978; Dunsire 1978; Gunn 1978). Although the study of implementation of EU policy has in the past been seen as a 'black hole' (Weiler 1991, 2465), this area has been attracting increasing attention. So, what do we know about the factors that affect the implementation of EU public policy? What are the strengths and the limitations of the existing literature?

Implementation in the European Union

There are two generations of scholarship on what can be broadly construed as the study of the implementation of EU public policy. The first generation has the unquestionable merit of raising[6] implementation to the level of a question that is worthy of the attention of EU specialists (Ciavarini Azzi 1985; Siedentopf and Ziller 1988a, 1988b; Schwarze *et al.* 1990; Schwarze, Becker and Pollak 1991, 1993; Snyder 1993; Pappas 1995). Five general trends can be identified in this literature. First, it is often (though certainly not always) characterised by a degree of terminological confusion[7] since the term 'implementation' is often used interchangeably with the terms 'enforcement' and 'application'. Second, existing studies of the transposition of EU legislation into national legal orders construe this stage rather statically and thus fail to underline the importance of what precedes and what follows it. Third, it has the merit of highlighting (Siedentopf and Ziller 1988a, 1988b) the potential impact of the link between formulation and implementation in line with the wider literature on implementation (Bardach 1980; Mayntz 1980b; Berman 1980; Barrett and Hill 1984). Fourth, it underlines the importance of departmental attitudes in the formulation and implementation of EU policy. Finally, the lessons for the wider integration process that can be drawn from these analyses of implementation and its national dimension have remained relatively underdeveloped despite the comparative nature of some existing studies.

The second generation of the literature appeared after the re-launch of the single market project and the 1992 'deadline' for its completion. In that literature, three kinds of explanation[8] have been put forward in an effort to account for the EU's implementation deficit (Dimitrakopoulos and Richardson 2001). They are interest-based, culture-based and institutionalist explanations.[9] *Interest-based explanations* typically highlight the fact that coalitions of actors whose interests are likely to be affected by a new policy often mobilise at the implementation stage in an effort to promote or obstruct it, for example, because they want to minimise or even eliminate adaptation costs (Dimitrakopoulos and Richardson 2001) or because they agree or disagree with it (Jordan 1997; Falkner *et al.* 2004, 458). *Cultural explanations*[10] point in the direction of the impact of cultural attitudes towards authority in general, or law in particular. Here, implementation is contested not necessarily because of the content of a policy but often as a result of cultural attitudes towards its sources. In a law-intensive organisation (Page and Dimitrakopoulos 1997) like the EU, attitudes towards the law can affect implementation patterns. As a result, implementation patterns can vary as a result of the presence of different attitudes towards the law.[11] Moreover, if one focuses on the narrower concept of legal culture, variation can be expected as a result of the co-existence of different legal cultures within the EU (Sverdrup 2005, 15). Furthermore, aspects of political culture appear to affect implementation. For example, Nordic states 'pursue a more consensus-seeking approach with limited use of courts' (Sverdrup 2004, 23). Although interests and culture play a role in the implementation of public policy, both are mediated by *institutions*, i.e. the focus of the third group of explanatory factors. Indeed, between interest-based and cultural explanations, there is a growing and diverse body of literature that discusses the impact of *institutions* on patterns of implementation. This is unsurprising since both interests and culture are mediated and channelled through institutions.

Institutionalist explanations highlight the importance of not only the EU as an implementation structure (Peters 1997; Dimitrakopoulos 1998, Chapter 2; Tallberg 2003) but, more importantly, the impact of domestic institutional arrangements on patterns of implementation. Unsurprisingly, this literature reflects the diversity of the broader literature on the notion of the 'institution' and the impact of institutions on political outcomes. A wide variety of explanations have been put forward. It has been argued that states with high levels of regional autonomy 'perpetrate more infractions' (Mbaye 2001, 276). Institutional veto points have been found to shape the timing and quality of implementation at the national level: though domestic opposition can be mobilised as a result of pressure for adaptation to EU requirements, 'whether it is successful or not depends on the availability of veto points' (Haverland 2000, 100). More specifically, in a study of the implementation of the EU's Packaging Waste Directive in Britain, Germany and the Netherlands, it has been demonstrated that, despite the presence of different policy legacies, what mattered most was the role of institutional veto points:

> [u]nconstrained by institutional veto points, the British and Dutch government adapted to Europe relatively timely and properly. Germany, facing opposition in the Bundesrat, implemented rather late and inappropriately.
> (Haverland 2000, 100)

Moreover, the extent of the institutionalisation of core executive rules regarding the monitoring of ministers and departments has been found to affect the timeliness of the transposition of EU law into domestic legislation, which is an important aspect of the implementation process (Zubek 2005).

In addition to the use of the notion of an 'institution' in the formal sense of the term, institutionalist analyses of implementation have also relied on a broader meaning of the same concept – one that encompasses, for example, patterns of interest intermediation as well as policy legacies. In this vein, it has been argued that:

> [i]mplementation is driven by the demands that a directive imposes on two domestic institutions that are deeply rooted in the histories of member states: the legal and administrative traditions of a country, and the organization of interest groups. When demands are big, i.e. when the costs of institutional transformation are high, directives are not well implemented. When demands are low, and the directive in fact strengthens the current national institutional landscape, then proper implementation takes place.
> (Duina 1997, 175)

This theme is at the heart of the burgeoning literature on the so-called 'Europeanisation' of the nation state, a topic that is often (though certainly not always) discussed in ways that require an understanding of implementation patterns. European integration is seen as a source of pressure that often challenges both domestic policies and institutional arrangements. For example, it has been argued that 'unification implies or actually requires the partial homogenization of European countries. [...] In a sense, unification requires the rejection of nations' histories' (Duina 1999, 122). As a result, extant literature highlights the centrality of the concept of 'goodness of fit' (Risse, Cowles and Caporaso 2001; Börzel 2002; Bailey 2002): the closer domestic institutions and policies fit with EU requirements, the smaller the pressure for change will be. Indeed, it has been argued that 'even very small misfits may lead to non-compliance' (Falkner et al. 2004, 466).

The first common feature of the two generations of the literature on implementation of EU public policy is that often they do not draw on the significant theoretical literature on the implementation of public policy. This is perhaps, in part, due to the fact that the study of aspects of implementation in the EU is often motivated by an interest in a particular element of the process of integration, i.e. a sector, a member state or even more specific issues such as patterns of territorial governance.[12] From this stems two additional characteristics that inform this book. On the one hand, as a result of their interests in 'compliance', scholars have quite often not made enough of the characteristics of implementation as a *process* – despite the lessons discussed in early work on implementation (see, e.g. Derthick 1972; Pressman and Wildavsky 1973; Berman 1978) – that unfolds over *long periods* of time. Indeed, compliance and implementation are often used interchangeably despite the major differences that exist between them. The former is a state of affairs whereas the latter is a process. The former is static whereas the latter is dynamic.[13] More importantly, compliance is one of the potential outcomes of implementation. From this conceptual distinction flows a key question: assuming that one adopts the 'compliance perspective', what precisely constitutes compliance? Concretely, given that much of the literature on compliance in the EU has focused on (a) the protection of the environment, (b) social regulation and, to a lesser extent, (c) the single market, how do we know that a member state has complied with EU policy? For example, assuming that there are a hundred environment or labour inspectorates in a given member state, how many of them ought to fulfil EU requirements – at a given point in time – for one to conclude that this state complies with these requirements? Moreover, even if one were to identify a defining point of this kind, in how many cases (and for how long) should each of these inspectorates comply for one to conclude that the inspectorate as a whole complies? Crucially, even if a conceptually sound and empirically robust state of compliance were to be defined, how do we get there? This book is couched in the belief that it is much more useful and interesting to examine the implementation process as it unfolds over long periods of time.

On the other hand, despite the focus on institutions – which is a useful characteristic of the existing literature – surprisingly little light has been shed on the impact of the internal operation of national central governments.[14] The impact of both interests and culture is channelled through (and filtered by) institutions that subsequently affect political outcomes. This is a key reason why the emphasis on institutions is likely to produce useful insights. However, institutions possess two cardinal characteristics that have often been ignored in the EU-related literature that touches on the issue of implementation. First, when they are confronted with a novel situation or demand, institutions predominantly rely on standard operating procedures and repertoires – sometimes revised at the margins – in an effort to cope. This means that they often cope by absorbing novel functions or demands in their daily routines.[15] Second, institutional change is a very demanding process whose outcome is – more often than not – uncertain (March and Olsen 1989). Indeed, although many reform efforts remain incomplete, others succeed (even for a brief period of time) or fail and this is one of the reasons why theoretical accounts of implementation have always construed it as a *dynamic process*, one that cannot be captured in terms of the static logic of 'the goodness of fit'.

This book focuses on the comparative longitudinal analysis of the role of central governments. It covers Greece, France and Britain by means of a case study, namely public procurement. These choices are explained in the next section.

Central governments, co-ordination and implementation

There are four reasons (theoretical as well as empirical) that account for the focus on central government institutions. First, implementation theory highlights the crucial importance of the link between formulation and implementation (Majone and Wildavsky 1984, 174). Only central government officials are involved in both of these stages though the nature of this involvement varies (*infra*, Chapter 1). The making of public policy entails the choice of theories that link a given understanding of reality and a desired outcome (Majone 1980), and the implementation of a policy entails the testing of the hypotheses that have been built into the policy (Browne and Wildavsky 1984, 254). Thus, the formulation of policy entails decisions that directly affect the implementation process. Sometimes officials formulate policies whose objectives are so ambitious that they turn a degree of failure into a certainty (Derthick 1972, 90). Moreover, formulation often entails decisions regarding the choice of the organisations that will be involved in implementation. So, making this decision is an important means to shape implementation because 'different agencies have characteristically different approaches to programs in the same subject area' (Rein and Rabinovitz 1977, 26). Second, institutionalist accounts of politics highlight the importance of central governments by underlining the usefulness of the concept of 'state capacities' (Skocpol 1985, 17, 21). The organisational configuration and the instruments at its disposal affect a state's capacity to define and pursue policy objectives. Third, in the context of the study of European integration, a significant part of the theoretical debate concerns the role of national (central) governments.

In terms of 'grand theories', both the liberal intergovernmentalist and the neo-functionalist arguments are based (implicitly or explicitly) on claims regarding the capacity of central governments to participate in the process of integration. Liberal intergovernmentalism highlights the importance of interest aggregation, negotiation at the European level and delegation to supranational institutions (Moravcsik 1993; 1998). These functions are performed by central governments whose credibility (i.e. their capacity to honour their commitments) affects both European integration as a whole and their own involvement therein. Neo-functionalists do not deny (Haas 1968) the significant role performed by central government officials. Rather, they relativise and contextualise it by claiming – rightly – that national governments are one of a *number* of important actors. This is a similarity that they share with multi-level governance and historical institutionalist (i.e. meso-level) approaches that contest the capacity of central governments to perform the Herculean task ascribed to them by liberal intergovernmentalists, especially before and after intergovernmental conferences (Marks, Hooghe and Blank 1996; Pierson 1996). Finally, the EU's institutional configuration places particular importance on the role of central governments. They are involved not only in the formulation of EU policy (especially through the Council's groups) but in its implementation as well[16] (Peters 1997; Dimitrakopoulos 1998, Chapter 2). Most of EU policy is implemented at the national level by the administrations of the member states, in line with the principle of indirect administration. The EU's reliance on national administrations justifies the presence of common arrangements for the regulation of the operation of the latter. In formal terms, the principle of *Bundestreue* (federal loyalty, i.e. the obligation to ensure that commitments made in Brussels are honoured at the national level) enunciated by Art. 5 of the Treaty of Rome[17] governs the relationship between the Union and its members whose wishes are formally expressed by their central governments.[18] Moreover, in the context of 'comitology' (Rideau 1987; Blumann 1993; Pollack 2003) i.e. the executive committees that assist the Commission in the adoption of executive measures, the role of central government officials is predominant. This offers them yet another opportunity to shape the patterns of the broader implementation process. In terms of informal arrangements, the Commission raises issues regarding potential infringements with central governments rather than sub-national authorities, even when the latter are responsible for them. More importantly, given that EU policies (and the legislation that embodies them) are often the result of compromises reached by national negotiators who – in most policy areas, most of the time – are central government officials, only they can provide the guidance that implementing agencies often need when policies agreed on in Brussels are turned into concrete reality.

The increasing diversity that characterises the membership of the EU and differences in terms of implementation records provides the main motive for the use of a comparative analysis. Given that they are involved in the making of EU policies that they are subsequently expected to implement, what accounts for the different implementation records? Moreover, given the importance that has been ascribed to institutional convergence in the literature on the so-called 'Europeanisation' of the nation state, what evidence is there to suggest that this pattern exists and – more importantly – that it has a bearing on implementation? In the light of (a) the aforementioned link between formulation and implementation, and (b) the cardinal role performed by central governments, it is important to examine the way in which the latter have coped with the exigencies of their involvement in the EU policy process. Involvement in the EU policy process has generated significant demands for national central governments and the officials who operate therein.

These demands concern, first and foremost, the imperative of co-ordination. This is important for a number of reasons. The expansion of the scope of European integration has placed significant emphasis on the capacity of central governments to define and promote coherent views across a whole range of sectors and issues. In the past, some sectors (e.g. agriculture or regional development) did not appear to have a developed 'international' dimension. Nevertheless, the involvement of the EU therein has turned intra- and cross-sectoral co-ordination into a necessity, despite (or because) of the tendency towards the establishment and preservation of sectoral logics that is inherent in modern governments. In addition, EU policy in a given sector cannot be streamlined easily through the traditional functional lines that characterise the division of labour between the various parts of the national administrative machineries. For example, elements of the common agricultural policy concern external trade, financial affairs, food safety and food production, i.e. issues that are often dealt with by different national ministries. This further enhances the need for co-ordination. Furthermore, the imperative of co-ordination at the intra-ministerial level has been enhanced dramatically. The participation of a wide range of ministerial actors in the committees that meet under the auspices of the Council of the European Union generates the need to improve co-ordination between, as well as within, the political and the administrative level in each government department.[19] Moreover, central administrations must cope with the exigencies of the involvement of national parliaments in the EU policy process because of the increasingly explicit politicisation of European integration,[20] the operation of national parliaments as arenas for political debate, and their potential involvement in the transposition of EU legislation into national law. Finally, in many cases, EU policies have led to significant policy changes at the domestic level. The involvement of central government officials in the negotiations that led to these changes increases the pressure on them for the provision of guidance in the implementation stage. As a result, the way in which national central governments have dealt with these issues – that is (i) the adaptation of the politico–administrative structures, (ii) executive–legislative relations, and (iii) the exigencies of transposition – can be expected to affect their capacity to shape implementation patterns.

Given the aforementioned patterns of internal differentiation and the exigencies of policy formulation and implementation, the imperative of co-ordination indicates that it is important to examine the extent to which national central governments are integrated (March and Simon 1958; Timsit 1987; Hood 1976; Berman 1980, 219). When the centre of a centralised system is 'divided', 'paralysed' or 'inept', the system as a whole becomes dysfunctional (Wright 1996, 161). In the opposite case, it is more likely to provide the basis for the co-ordinated operation of the system. This, in turn, is mirrored by the steering capacity of the system. Although in many cases implementation is quite unproblematic, the total absence of problems is neither a realistic expectation, nor is it useful for the assessment of a system (Berman 1978, 160). Rather, it is more useful to discuss implementation in terms of the steering capacity of the system (Lundquist 1972; 1987). It is expected that the greater the degree of a system's integration – as indicated by the presence and operation of co-ordination machinery, timely and effective problem detection and problem solving through the deployment of appropriate tools of government – the greater its capacity will be to steer implementation in the desired direction.

In the light of the conceptual link between formulation and implementation, the capacity of the central government of a member state to steer the latter can be expected to reflect its involvement in the former. In other words, problematic involvement in formulation marked by the lack of co-ordination is expected to be followed by problematic involvement in implementation. However, the way in which central governments participate in the formulation of EU policy can be expected to reflect the way in which they have responded to the exigencies of membership of the EU (Kassim *et al.* 2001; Kassim, Peters and Wright, 2000; Laffan 2006). States where the central government apparatus has managed to handle the exigencies of membership in an effective manner are more likely to be able to cope with the exigencies of implementation. Therefore, it is important to assess this response prior to the discussion of the dynamics of implementation. Has the pattern of the operation of a national central government remained unchanged despite a country's involvement in European integration (or at least the most advanced stages thereof) or has it been reformed as a result of this critical juncture?

Historical institutionalism offers a flexible framework for the discussion of this question because it provides the tools for the analysis of both continuity and change (Krasner 1984). In a historical institutionalist framework, the expectation of long periods of institutional stability (*stasis*) is coupled with the expectation of change when a critical juncture is reached.[21] To what extent did membership of the EU alter existing patterns of organisation and operation in national central governments? This line of reasoning that links patterns of implementation with formulation and the capacity to cope with the exigencies of membership generates two constraints regarding the choice of (a) the member states and (b) the policy that will be examined.

First, the central governments of Greece, France and the UK have been chosen because they have responded in different ways to the exigencies of membership, and have different implementation records, despite their initial similarities. These similarities concern the (sectoral) patterns of ministerial responsibility and the predominantly internal mobility of most career civil servants. Ministerial responsibility facilitates sectorisation. Low external mobility (coupled with the tendency to rely on generalists, as opposed to specialist civil servants) facilitates the emergence of an administrative ethos. The combination of these two characteristics enhances the need for co-ordination (the first between sectors, the second between the political and the administrative level).[22] When Greece joined the then European Communities in January 1981, the reform proposals regarding the management of membership-related issues by its central government centred on the British and the French systems as a result of (a) their perceived effectiveness in terms of the handling of EC policy (especially formulation) and (b) the similarities of the Greek, French and British central governments (*infra*, Chapter 2). Nevertheless, only a small part of the reform proposals were adopted and even fewer became part of the actual operation of the Athenian bureaucracy. Thus, accession to the EC did not serve as a critical juncture for institutional reform. As a result, of the three states examined here, Greece has the least integrated central government whilst the UK occupies the other extreme of the continuum and France is in the intermediate position where the presence of a robust system of co-ordination intensifies the pressure for and indicates the need for co-ordination. Arguably, the same can be expected in terms of their implementation records.[23]

Second, public procurement has been chosen for a number of reasons. Most important of all is the fact that the EU's policy in this domain has introduced significant changes in all three states. Moreover, this policy has remained constant over time: it essentially relies on a small number of *procedural* requirements. This allows the discussion of the way in which their central Greek, French and British governments have coped with the exigencies of implementation. In addition, its economic importance was and remains very significant,[24] and this is one of the reasons why it is a key part of the effort to establish the single European market. Finally, it is a classic example of regulation on the basis of directives, which is the main way used by the EU in its effort to shape policy outcomes.

Unlike most existing studies, which usually cover a short period of time and focus on compliance with individual directives, this book covers a 25-year period (1981–2006)[25] in an effort to capture the dynamics of implementation. This also reflects the need to capture the dynamics of institutional change (where it occurred) not only in terms of the emergence of new structures but also in terms of their capacity to become a fully functioning part of the

Introduction 13

institutional terrain in which they were initially established. This reflects the view that institutional change is a process that unfolds over long periods of time (March and Olsen 1989; March, Schulz and Zhou 2000).

The research reported here is based on documentary evidence and 48 strictly non-attributable interviews with officials based in Athens (Ministry of Development; Ministry of Foreign Affairs; Ministry of Health, Welfare and Social Security; Ministry of National Economy; Ministry of the Environment, Spatial Planning and Public Works; Secretariat General of the Cabinet; Special EC Legal Service/Ministry of Foreign Affairs), Paris (Commission Centrale des Marchés; Commission des Marchés Publics de l'État; Ministry of Agriculture, Fisheries and Food; Ministry of Economy and Finance; Ministry of Equipment, Housing, Transport and Tourism; Ministry of Industry, Post and Telecommunications; Ministry of Foreign Affairs; Ministry of Employment and Social Affairs; Secrétariat Général du Comité Interministériel pour les questions de coopération économique européenne; Secrétariat Général du Gouvernement), the UK (Department of Trade and Industry; European Secretariat/Cabinet Office; Foreign and Commonwealth Office; Kingston upon Hull City Council; Treasury; Office of Government Commerce; Scottish Procurement Directorate) and Brussels (European Commission, DG Internal Market and Financial Services; Permanent Representation of Greece to the EU; Permanent Representation of the UK to the EU). Semi-structured questionnaires have been used in the interviews which were conducted initially between March 1996 and June 1997 and then in December 2006 and January 2007.

The argument and the structure of the book

This book draws on the theoretical literature on implementation and historical institutionalism and seeks to demonstrate that national central governments can – indeed *do* – shape the patterns of implementation. These patterns mirror the way in which these actors participate in the formulation of EU public policy. In turn, the involvement of the Greek, French and British central governments in the formulation of EU public policy reflects the way in which these institutions have dealt with the exigencies of membership. More specifically, it will be demonstrated that the impact of key characteristics of the institutions of central governments – in particular, the capacity to co-ordinate their activity – extends beyond formulation to the stage of policy implementation. Governments that have difficulty dealing with formulation, also have problems when EU policy is implemented – in particular, their capacity to detect the need for and subsequently effect change through the use of the tools of government will suffer as a result of difficulties in co-ordinating their action.

The book also demonstrates the dynamic nature of patterns of implementation. They change over time and change is driven by learning and fixing at the national level. As a result, the confirmation of the initial expectation (i.e. that implementation would be particularly problematic in Greece and much less so in France and Britain) in terms of the specific case of public procurement highlights only one facet of this complex process. Indeed, empirical evidence indicates that, despite initial problems, sector-specific reforms aiming to improve the capacity of the centre to steer implementation have (in spite of their fragility) borne fruit.

Chapter 1 outlines the framework upon which this study is based. Drawing on implementation theory, the concept of *macro-implementation* is introduced in an effort to give more specific meaning to the involvement of central governments in the implementation stage of the EU policy process. Given the extent of horizontal and vertical differentiation that characterises modern governments, it would be wrong to ascribe to central governments the Herculean role of implementing public policy. This means that a more refined definition of the concept of 'implementation' is required – one that captures the role of central governments. This is why the concept of macro-implementation (Berman 1978) is introduced. Their steering capacity is discussed on the basis of their vertical and horizontal integration. This capacity is then linked to a historical institutionalist account of the way in which national central governments have been organised in an effort to cope with the exigencies of membership. Chapter 2 examines the patterns of institutional change in the concrete cases of Greece, France and the UK. Chapter 3 presents the EU's public procurement policy and maps the institutional terrain in the three central governments with a focus on the handling of public procurement policy. Chapter 4 discusses the transposition of EU public procurement directives in Greece, France and the UK and Chapter 5 discusses their macro-implementation between 1981 and 2006. The concluding chapter examines the empirical findings in the light of the overall argument, discusses alternative explanations as well the implications of the argument presented here for our understanding of European integration and its impact on the nation state.

Notes

1 This idea reflected the political will to remedy what had become a major problem for the Greek state. The fraudulent use of European subsidies (Mendrinou 1994, 86) by the Greek state had made a significant contribution to the national political turmoil that led to the downfall of the socialists in the electoral contests of 1989 and 1990.
2 For an institutionalist discussion of compliance with EU environmental policy see Knill and Lenschow (2000).
3 The systemic importance of this issue is demonstrated by the fact that this deficit has contributed directly to institutional development at the European level. Indeed, the Maastricht Treaty endowed the EU with the capacity to impose sanctions (fines) on member states that fail to implement judgements of the European Court of Justice.

4 Indeed, it has been claimed that '[t]he implementation of EU Directives is but an example of the wider phenomenon of Europeanisation' (Falkner *et al.* 2005, 11).
5 Of course, it is important to add that concerns regarding implementation were present in other classic works – Selznick's book on the Tennessee Valley Authority ([1949] 1966) is a good example.
6 It is important to note that Puchala (1975) was the first scholar to use the term 'postdecisional politics' in his discussion of 'episodes of non-compliance in the EEC system'.
7 Up to a certain extent this characteristic is shared by the second generation of literature in this area.
8 They vary significantly in terms of the extent to which they have been used or discussed in the literature.
9 For an alternative classification of explanations of 'compliance' with international agreements see Underdal (1998). For excellent discussions of compliance with international agreements see Chayes and Chayes (1993) as well as Zürn and Joerges (2005).
10 For example, Falkner *et al.* refer to a 'world of law observance', a 'world of domestic politics' and a 'world of neglect' (2005, 319, 322).
11 For example, as the House of Lords Select Committee on the European Communities put it 'there are Member States that seem to treat their obligation to translate Directives into national law by a certain date as little more than an indicative deadline' (cited in Weiler 1991, 2465 fn. 178).
12 The literature on the 'Europeanisation' of the nation state is a good example of this trend.
13 As Neyer and Wolf rightly argue, compliance should not be confused with implementation (which they construe as the process of administering authoritatively public policy directives and the concomitant changes that they undergo during that process) and effectiveness which they construe as the 'efficacy of a given regulation to solve the political problem that preceded its formulation' (Neyer and Wolf 2005, 41–2). Rather, they define the focus of compliance research as the degree to which the provision of an accord and the implementing measures that have been instituted are adhered to by the addressees of a rule. Thus, perfect compliance, imperfect implementation and zero effectiveness may well co-exist (Neyer and Wolf 2005, 42).
14 Zubek's article (2005) is an exception.
15 For example, discussing the impact of membership of the EU on Whitehall's legislative output, Page demonstrates that '[t]he ongoing Whitehall process continues to be a Whitehall process' (1998, 808).
16 This structural characteristic mirrors the important role that national administrations play in the formulation stage thus establishing what has been accurately called 'bureaucratic interpenetration' or 'intermingling' (Scheinman 1966, 751; Wessels 1985, 17).
17 Blanquet (1994) provides an excellent legal analysis of the wider implications of this provision for the EU legal order.
18 This is much more than the enunciation of a principle or a declaration of intent. The most frequently used expression of this obligation is the clause, almost invariably incorporated into EU directives, stipulating that the member states must communicate to the Commission the texts of the national implementing measures that they have adopted. This is a *conditio sine qua non* for the successful fulfilment

of the Commission's role as guardian of the Treaty. The importance attached to this function is demonstrated by the ECJ's acknowledgment (case C-96/81) that failure to fulfil this obligation may of itself justify recourse to the procedure under Art. 169/226 of the EC Treaty. This positive obligation to facilitate the control of the implementation process is mirrored by a symmetrical obligation focusing on the national level. This obligation involves the creation of the mechanisms for control and the wider *obligation de diligence*, a concept which is frequently used by the ECJ. This entails the obligation to organise the controls (administrative or judicial) and the obligation of the relevant (implementing) authorities to actively utilise them in the pursuit of the *effet utile* (Blanquet 1994, 52). Despite these obligations, the member states maintain a significant degree of autonomy with regards to the way in which they fulfil common objectives. This is the essence of the *principle of institutional autonomy* that has been acknowledged by the ECJ (Rideau 1972; Dimitrakopoulos 2001c). This autonomy is not unfettered. Indeed, the ECJ ruled that when it comes it implementing EU policy, mere administrative practices do not necessarily constitute an appropriate way to meet EU objectives because they may be altered at the whim of the administration (case C-96/81). The ECJ has also ruled that 'national institutions' (as opposed to sub-national institutions) have a duty to ensure the co-ordination of the implementing measures so as to avoid jeopardising the operation of the market (case C-240/78).

19 In some sectors one can also add the need to co-ordinate the action taken by government ministries on the one hand with quasi autonomous non-governmental agencies on the other.
20 This includes institutional and policy-specific issues as well the question of a state's membership of the EU.
21 For an application of this argument to the national Parliaments of the UK, France and Greece see Dimitrakopoulos (2001a).
22 Of course, this is not to deny that there are differences between the two systems. For example, the French executive is often described as 'bicephalous' because the French President is responsible for foreign policy and defence. However, he is usually not directly involved in the daily management of issues regarding the formulation and the implementation of EU directives. By contrast, the President is directly involved in more 'heroic' moments of the process of integration, e.g. in IGCs.
23 For example, in 2005 the ECJ issued a total of 136 judgements concerning failure of member states to fulfil their obligations. Twenty of them concerned Greece, thirteen concerned France and only seven concerned the UK (European Court of Justice 2005, 197). For a discussion of the extent of the problem of 'non-compliance' see Börzel (2001).
24 The European Commission estimates that in 2002 public procurement accounted for about 16% of the EU's GDP (http://ec.europa.eu/internal_market/public procurement/index_en.htm)
25 More specifically, analysis covers the period until the end of January 2007, i.e. a year after the deadline for the transposition of Directive 2004/18 that consolidated, simplified and updated existing public procurement directives (excluding procurement in utilities which is not examined in this book).

1

Institutional capabilities and the dynamics of implementation

The objective of this chapter is threefold. First, it seeks to discuss the concept of 'implementation'. Second, it does so in a manner that highlights (a) its complexity and dynamics, and (b) the role of institutions therein. Third, it draws on theoretical work on implementation in an effort to identify the precise role of central governments therein and the crucial requirement of the co-ordination of its activity.

Implementation mirrors the dynamics of the entire policy process: it is complex, dynamic, political (in the sense that it is dependent on the support of coalitions of actors) and directly affected by the institutional landscape in which it unfolds over time. Irrespective of the degree of political support that it enjoys, a policy is implemented in a context that is characterised by the presence of politico-administrative institutions. These institutions typically endure for much longer than the coalitions that support or oppose an individual programme or policy. This is why an institutional focus is likely to produce important insights regarding the development of implementation over time; after all, the fact that the analysis of implementation originated from the USA, a federal polity, is not a coincidence (see *infra*). The first section of this chapter illustrates the centrality of institutions by means of the discussion of the complexity of implementation; the second section explores the dynamics of implementation; and the final section specifies the level of analysis on which this book is focused, and discusses the role of central governments and the means at their disposal.

The concept of implementation

Implementation analysis stems from the study of federal systems (Derthick 1972; Pressman and Wildavsky 1973; Bardach 1977). This is unsurprising since, as the pioneering work of Martha Derthick, Jeffrey Pressman, Aaron Wildavsky and Eugene Bardach has demonstrated, the complexity of this part of the policy process in these institutional systems is such that, in fact, one should be surprised if federal programmes work at all.[1] Indeed, implementation is the process of forging links in a causal chain in an effort to connect the theory that is embodied in a policy to the desired results (Pressman and Wildavsky 1973, xv). Construed in this way, there are many reasons why implementation is a complex process.

Defining its beginning and end is an extremely difficult endeavour. This means that it is difficult to define accurately the boundaries between the stages of the policy process for they are not entirely self-contained (Hogwood and Gunn 1984, 10). For example, formulation can be based on the unintended consequences produced by the implementation of an existing policy. More importantly, many choices that are made when policy is formulated – including the vertical and horizontal distribution of roles, the choice of target groups and the distribution of resources between the various actors who are involved in implementation – are major determinants of patterns of implementation as well as their outputs and outcomes (Mayntz 1980a; 1983, 17). The causal chain identified by Pressman and Wildavsky cannot be constructed without having the others in view.[2] Indeed, '[t]he separation of policy design from implementation is fatal. It is no better than mindless implementation without a sense of direction' (Pressman and Wildavsky 1984, xxv).

Complexity is a typical characteristic of implementation even when one attempts to define it in terms of the actors who participate in it. The identity and the number of participants and the nature of their input depend on a number of parameters, including the policy that is being implemented. The number of actors involved is directly linked to the complexity of implementation. One of the main contributions of Pressman and Wildavsky's seminal book is the argument that links the length of the causal chain that must be forged once a policy has been adopted with the complexity (and the output) of its implementation: the greater the length of this chain, the larger the number of reciprocal relationships that affect implementation.[3] Put in a different way, when policy is being implemented, acts of agreement have to be registered at various points; otherwise the programme will not continue. Each of these points is a 'decision point' where a 'clearance' is required for the implementation of a programme to continue (Pressman and Wildavsky 1973, xvi).

The multiplicity of actors involved in implementation and the presence of diverging or even competing organisational logics and institutional repertoires among them highlights the need for co-ordination. Indeed, in his discussion of 'perfect administration' Hood argued that one of its conditions is that 'the administrative system has to be unitary, like a huge army with a huge line of authority' (Hood 1976, 6).

Of course, this degree of integration is more an aspiration or an objective than a reality but the key point here is that, since implementation entails the involvement of various institutional actors, *co-ordination* is both a *core requirement* for its success and, as a consequence, a factor that accounts for *variation* between states. There is no ideal way of achieving this objective because government departments (like virtually all organisations) are involved in carrying out multiple tasks at any point in time. Policies or individual programmes will always cut across departmental jurisdictions and there is no way to minimise clearances for all programmes (Pressman and Wildavsky 1984, 162). This is one reason why a *sectoral* approach is required.

Implementation is complex also because there is always a discrepancy between the typically abstract theory upon which a policy is based and the rather concrete (and multi-faceted) reality or context in which it is implemented over time. The function of a theory[4] within implementation analysis is of crucial importance for it is a pre-condition for the definition of the object of implementation. Policies combine the examination of an existing situation, a desired outcome and a way to achieve it. The latter is of cardinal importance because '[a]ny policy or program implies an economic, and probably also sociological, theory about the way the world looks. If this theory is fundamentally incorrect, the policy will probably fail no matter how well it is implemented' (Bardach 1977, 250).

If the theory is correct, then it combines an accurate understanding of the existing situation, the desired outcome and the choice of the appropriate methods and tools to achieve it. On the contrary, a flawed theory might start with an appropriate understanding of the existing situation and a clear view of the desired outcome, but it is bound to fail due to the choice of the wrong methods and tools. It is the direct link between the theory and the choice of the method and tools necessary for the achievement of the desired outcome that underlines the importance of the theory incorporated in a given policy (Berman 1978, 163). This theory defines the paths that ought to be followed in order to achieve the desired outcome.[5]

Finally, the complexity of implementation is even greater in the EU because it entails a significant number of sub-stages and actions (Kovar 1973) that are reminiscent of Bardach's definition of implementation as the process of assembling a machine and then making it run (Bardach 1977, 36). The adoption of a legislative measure[6] at the level of the EU can be considered as the beginning of this stage of the EU policy process.[7] In many cases, the adoption of a directive[8] in Brussels and Strasbourg is followed by the adoption of executive measures at the European level. This is often done in the context of the so-called 'comitology' committees that 'assist' (in various ways)[9] the Commission.[10] Once this has happened, EU directives are transposed into national legislation. Transposition entails not only the incorporation of the spirit and letter of a directive into national legislation but an additional important (and neglected) aspect,[11] namely the elimination (or prevention) of conflict between a new directive and existing (as well as future) national legislation. This cannot be achieved without a significant degree of co-ordination at the national level. Finally, transposition is followed by the action that gives concrete meaning to these provisions and the policy that they embody. Despite its complexity and far from being static, implementation is a dynamic process. This notion is discussed in the next section.

The dynamics of implementation

Implementation is inherently dynamic because it is the pursuit of an objective or set of objectives, or a struggle to realise ideas (Majone and Wildavsky 1984, 180). This pursuit unfolds over time (Lane 1983, 26). It is both open-ended and pre-ordained. It is open-ended, in the sense that there is uncertainty over its final outcome, and it is pre-ordained as a result of choices made when policy was formulated. There are many additional reasons why implementation is dynamic. For those reasons it should be conceptualised and analysed as a process, rather than an event (Mayntz 1980c, 246; Mazmanian and Sabatier 1983, 39).

Implementation typically involves a significant number of actors each with their own tasks, priorities, standard operating procedures and institutional repertoires. As these actors interact with their environment, their priorities may change and the balance of their resources may improve or deteriorate. Second, implementation is dynamic because it is inherently political.[12] It is not the linear continuation of formulation (Hogwood and Gunn 1984, 20, 217; Jones 1984, 29). This is so because actors who were defeated when policy was being formulated often attempt to defeat their opponents when policy is implemented.

In addition, implementation also illustrates two contradictory characteristics that are reflected in the institutions that human beings create, namely the problematic allocation of attention[13] on the one hand, and their capacity to learn, on the other (Cohen, March and Olsen 1972; March and Simon 1958; March and Olsen 1979; March 1988; Olsen and Peters 1996; Argyris and Schön 1996). Indeed, attention is limited. Individuals, organisational units and organisations as a whole cannot attend to everything all the time. Moreover, within a given organisation there is more than one issue competing for attention at any point in time. Efforts to improve the implementation record in the EU (by reducing the implementation gap) offer an excellent example. Rather neglected – or even taken for granted until the late 1970s, improving implementation became an objective of the Jenkins-led Commission and, after having being over-shadowed by the euphoria and policy activity that accompanied the re-launch of the single market project in the mid-1980s, it took centre stage in the run-up to the signing of the Maastricht Treaty.

Learning is one additional reason why implementation (construed as a process) is dynamic. Learning is not only a way in which organisations rationalise the allocation of attention but also an important way in which organisations involved in implementation (and decision making more generally) cope with competing claims and the exigencies of the tasks entrusted to them in the environment in which they operate. Organisational learning is construed here as 'an organization's acquisition of understandings, know-how, techniques and practices of any kind and by whatever means' (Argyris and Schön 1996, xxi).

It entails the improvement of an organisation's performance over time and relies on observations and inferences from experience that create fairly enduring changes in structures and procedures (Olsen and Peters 1996, 6). Organisational learning involves change in an organisation's theory of action that is implicit in its activity. Such changes may stem from conflicting views, shifting organisational environments, the analysis of the potential and the limits of alternative strategies as well as images of desired outcomes (Argyris and Schön 1996, 17). Therefore, learning can be construed both as a process *and* an outcome.

Learning can take three forms. *Single-loop learning* is instrumental (i.e. it focuses on effectiveness) and entails changes in the strategies of action or assumptions underlying them without affecting the values of an organisation's theory of action. *Double-loop learning* entails changes both in an organisation's strategies of action as well as the values that underpin them (Argyris and Schön 1996, 20–1). Finally, a third form of learning, *deuterolearning*, entails acquiring the capacity to learn (Argyris and Schön 1996, 28–9). Learning can be attributed to an agent who is either within or outside an organisation and deliberately seeks to improve performance. Hence, learning (as defined above) and change are inextricably intertwined. However, change is conditional since it depends on the availability of resources, the willingness and capacity of its promoters to overcome opposition and may well be based on *single but critical events*, especially in conditions of ambiguity and uncertainty. Such events are significant because they (a) are branching points which affect subsequent developments and (b) 'evoke meaning, interest and attention for organizational participants' (March, Sproull and Tamuz 1999, 140) and, most importantly, they focus the attention of decision makers. The pace of change that is associated with learning is not linear. Rather, the more radical change is, the more likely it is to activate opposition (Olsen and Peters 1996; Argyris and Schön 1996, Chapter 1; March, Sproull and Tamuz 1999). Hence, single-loop learning, and the incremental pace of change that is associated with it, is less controversial than double-loop learning which is usually combined with radical change.

Finally, implementation should be construed as a dynamic process because it often involves fixing (Bardach 1977). Many of the problems that occur when policy is being implemented cannot be foreseen – in part because of the policy makers' bounded rationality (March and Simon 1958; Simon 1976; Simon 1997). In addition, the formulation of policy involves a balancing act that is tested only when policy is implemented, namely the need to combine uniformity with a degree of autonomy that implementers need (and inevitably use) when abstract arrangements are put into effect in specific contexts. In other words, since discretion is both inevitable and necessary (Majone and Wildavsky 1984, 177), the presence of 'fixers' is a condition for successful implementation. This is particularly important in the growing and increasingly diverse EU.

Fixing is a concept that incorporates two meanings, namely (i) 'repairing' and (ii) 'adjusting' certain elements of the system of games that constitute the implementation process (Bardach 1977, 274–83). Fixing is a multi-faceted notion and activity. It connotes a degree of covertness – since much of it takes place away from the public view. In addition, it indicates that conflict and the use of a degree of coercion may accompany it. Although it is an inherently political activity,[14] it is not limited to the exercise of power. Powerful fixers will not be effective if they do not know when, where and how they should intervene but this will not happen unless they possess the relevant information. The uncertainty that surrounds fixing is further highlighted by the fact that it is often associated with the incentives and the resources of those who can perform this role. Senior civil servants who operate in central governments and their political masters are in a relationship of inter-dependence. The former need the political support of the latter. In turn, the latter need the technical expertise of the former.

In addition to the fixers that exist at the national level, there are two institutional fixers at the level of the EU, namely the European Commission (Mendrinou 1996) and the ECJ.[15] In addition to its role of 'guardian of the Treaty' and its power to refer member states to the ECJ when they fail to fulfil their duties, the Commission has established a number of informal procedures in an attempt to reinforce its monitoring actions. These procedures include mainly the so-called *réunions-paquets* (package meetings) where Commission officials and national civil servants meet in the capital of the interested member state and discuss specific cases of alleged infringements (Thomas 1991, 890). The success (Dewost 1990, 79) of these procedures is partly due to their informal nature and the prevailing spirit of co-operation as opposed to the necessarily adversarial nature of legal proceedings. The Commission has also provided a focal point for the decentralised control of transposition and implementation (Ehlermann 1987, 217) by affected individuals.[16]

The preceding analysis highlights not only the complexity and the dynamic nature of implementation but also the centrality of institutions that operate at the national and the European levels. One of the sources of complexity in implementation is the involvement of various actors whose roles vary considerably over time across sectors and states. In other words, implementation is a process that typically involves multiple organisations that operate at different levels (O'Toole and Montjoy 1984; O'Toole 1986). This is why the level of analysis must be specified. In addition, given the centrality of institutions in the implementation process it is important to give more precise meaning to the notion of institutional capacities since it is a source of considerable variation between member states. Both of these tasks are undertaken in the next section of this chapter.

Macro-implementation, steering and the tools of government

Efforts to implement policy take place in a historically defined context that is marked by the presence of a set of politico–administrative institutions. These institutions shape the pattern of implementation and, in the course of the process, they are also affected by it. Consequently, it is necessary to analyse the linkages between these institutions in an attempt to identify the way in which the institutional setting affect this process. The same applies to the attempts of national governments to improve their implementation record since institutions take centre stage in this effort.

As mentioned earlier, the study of implementation emerged from the USA. This is not a coincidence. The institutional framework of a federal polity coupled with the principle of separation of powers (Singh 2003) creates two fundamental problems, namely the horizontal and the vertical division of power and the inherent need for co-ordination between and within each level of government (Mayntz 1980c, 246). In terms of the study of implementation, this is a recipe for problems. This has not escaped the attention of the pioneers of implementation analysis (Derthick 1972, Pressman and Wildavsky 1984, 133). In fact, the impact of the institutional setting on the implementation of public policy is a key contribution of that literature.

Indeed, Martha Derthick's pioneering work ascribed to the position of central government within the federal system of the USA many of the problems encountered in the implementation of the 'New towns in town' federal programme (Derthick 1972, 83). Although she underlined the importance of the absence of power of coercion, her assessment is explicit about *other* important factors (or resources) that the central government lacked. These included limited knowledge of the situation beyond the centre, the limited capacity of the federal government to utilise even the modest incentives that it possessed, the extremely ambitious nature of policy objectives – which, in turn, further highlight the link to policy formulation – as well as, crucially, President Johnson's inability to co-ordinate governmental action (Derthick 1972, 84–102). Of course, these problems are not uniquely found in federal systems. Rather, they can be expected in any internally differentiated system (Hood 1976, 7; Wolman 1981; Barrett and Fudge 1981; Toonen 1985).

Both the centre of a polity and the entities that operate beyond the centre will always be involved (directly or indirectly) in the implementation of policy but their roles differ from each other. This is why it is important to distinguish between the role of the centre and the role of remainder of the 'implementation structure' (Mayntz 1980c, 245; Hjern and Porter 1981) in the course of the implementation process. Given the focus of this book on the role of central governments, it is important to conceptualise the role of the *centre* in the implementation process. For that purpose, existing theoretical work on implementation, again, provides a useful tool.

Although the distinction between transposition and administrative implementation can be a useful organising principle for the discussion of implementation in the context of the EU, it does not resolve[17] the problem of the definition of the level of analysis. For that purpose Berman's distinction (1978, 164) between *macro-implementation* and *micro-implementation* is both useful and important (see also Mayntz 1980c, 245). In his discussion of the implementation of public policy in the federal system of the USA, Berman defined macro-implementation as the execution of policy by the federal government with the aim to influence local delivery organisations to behave in desired ways and *micro-implementation* as what the local organisations do in response to the federal actions. This book sets out to examine the action taken by national governments in the stage of macro-implementation from the moment of the adoption of a policy at the European level. In other words, the objective is to examine the role of those who seek to direct the activity of 'street-level' or 'front-line' implementers (Lipsky 1971; 1980; Sorg 1983).

The differences between micro-implementation and macro-implementation are significant in terms of their functional exigencies as well as the interactions between actors who are involved therein. While micro-implementation is likely to focus on numerous examples of one aspect of a policy, macro-implementation concerns entire sets of such examples or even policy sectors and sub-sectors. For example, in the area of social policy, micro-implementation would entail the assessment of applications submitted by potential beneficiaries while macro-implementation would involve the provision of resources and guidance to those who actually perform this assessment. The difference between these two facets of implementation is not only one of scale or quantity. Rather, it is also qualitative. While micro-implementation concerns cases of limited (i.e. narrow) importance, macro-implementation deals with individual or clusters of cases whose ramifications are far wider. In other words, *macro-implementation is of systemic importance*. Also, it can be linked to transposition. In addition to the transfer of rights and duties and, possibly, the abolition of pre-existing arrangements that contravene EU policy, transposition can be construed as an opportunity for national governments to make choices (such as the establishment of institutions, the allocation of resources, etc.) that affect the subsequent stages of the policy process, especially macro-implementation. In other words, the latter can be construed in a narrow as well as a slightly broader sense.[18]

Given the multiplicity of actors involved therein, the extent to which macro-implementation achieves its objectives depends on the ability of the system to co-ordinate them – this is the central question examined in this book. The horizontal and vertical integration of a system (Timsit 1987) reflects its ability to avoid redundancies, internal contradictions, lacunae (Peters n.d.) in its pursuit of policy objectives, i.e. the *ability to co-ordinate* its actions. Without the ability to co-ordinate, there is little hope for successful implementation. Co-ordination entails the presence of a purpose and ethos that are shared[19] by participating actors as well as the ability and willingness of those who are located higher up in the hierarchy to use coercion, detect and resolve problems by gathering and distributing resources (Peters 1998).

This is particularly important in the context of macro-implementation. The fact that macro-implementation entails manoeuvring various semi-autonomous actors (Bardach 1977, 51; Berman 1978, 166; Mayntz 1980c, 245; Timsit 1987) and the concomitant expectation of problems – especially when a policy entails (or is meant to produce) change – raises two questions. First, how do central governments – macro-implementers *par excellence* – steer this process? Second, what kind of tools do they utilise? Steering is 'the conscious attempts of the decision-maker to influence implementation in the desired direction' (Lundquist 1972, 36).

There are four types of steering. In *direct* steering implementers are given goals and/or means to determine their output. *Indirect steering* influences the ability and/or will of the implementer to carry out direct steering; *specific* and *general steering* respectively involve a decision-maker's attempt to shape *some* or *all* of implementation decisions or all decisions of a certain type (Lundquist 1972, 36–7). Steering affects three properties of actors, namely 'understand', i.e. their perceptions; 'will', that goes beyond their capacity to understand or act and refers to norms, goals, values, preferences and priorities, i.e. their motives for action; 'can', that is their capability which depends on the availability of the requisite resources (Lundquist 1987, 77–8). Hence, steering is a key 'integration-furthering factor' (Lundquist 1987, 74) of particular importance in any internally differentiated structure or cluster of organisations.

For the discussion of the action undertaken by governments in an effort to steer the process of implementation, it is useful to borrow[20] Christopher Hood's 'N.A.T.O. scheme' (1983, Chapter 1). N.A.T.O. stands for nodality, authority, treasure and organisation. *Nodality* entails 'being in the middle of an information or social network', which means that actors can use it not only for symbolic purposes[21] but also as a way of collecting and diffusing information; *authority* entails the power officially or legally 'to demand, forbid, guarantee, adjudicate' both when it comes to solving problems and regulating conflict; *treasure* denotes the possession of funds or other 'fungible chattels' that can be exchanged while *organisation* entails the possession of not only people with various skills, but also 'land, buildings, materials and equipment somehow arranged' (Hood 1983, 4–6). The use of these terms allows us to think about the availability (and combinations) of alternative tools – the choice of which is very often as politically salient as the choice of policy objectives (Lascoumes and Le Galès 2007), and facilitates the discussion[22] of the tools used by different governments or by the same government at different times (Hood 1983, 7–10).

Central governments steer macro-implementation through the use of these tools. Given the link between formulation and implementation, it is expected that the latter will be problematic – i.e. marked by conflict, inconsistencies, contradictions, redundancies and lacunae – in states where central governments do not cope well with the exigencies of the former. However, this capacity is historically defined. Central governments are institutional structures whose core characteristics – especially the capacity to co-ordinate their action – have developed over long periods of time. This is why it is important to examine the manner in which these structures have dealt with the exigencies of membership in the first place. Has a state's involvement in the process of integration – the EU challenge – led to converging responses or have these responses remained decidedly national? Given the link between formulation and implementation, if national patterns continue to prevail in the 'domestic' stage of EU policy formulation, they can also be expected to prevail when EU policy is implemented at the national level. This is the central hypothesis that this book seeks to discuss. More specifically, if co-ordination is problematic when EU policy is formulated at the national level, this will lead to problematic implementation as well.

The next chapter discusses the way in which the Greek, French and British politico–administrative structures have responded to the challenges of dealing with the exigencies of membership. This question is discussed with reference to (i) organisational developments in the political and the administrative echelons of central governments, (ii) relations between executives and legislatures in EU policy making and (iii) arrangements regarding the transposition of EU and the handling of infringements.[23] Subsequent chapters (Chapters 4 and 5) will demonstrate that although the differences between the Greek, French and British cases confirm the expectations generated by the direct link between formulation and implementation, this is only a part of the 'story'. Indeed, patterns of implementation can – indeed do – *change over time* as a result of learning and fixing (*infra*).

Notes

1 Of course, this statement was part of the very telling sub-title of Pressman and Wildavsky's path-breaking book (1973).
2 Formulation affects implementation in other ways as well. Different types of policies are conducive to different theories, entail different stakes for participants, focus on different institutional settings and target groups. In a more general sense, patterns of political interaction are shaped by policies (Lowi 1964; 1972). The logic of Lowi's typology of public policies (which includes regulatory, distributive, re-distributive and constituent policies) highlights the fact that this is so because what is at stake, and the mobilisation of interests, vary across types of public policy. Moreover, time is an important factor because it alerts us to the possibility of shifts of the focus of policies (European and national) from one type to another. This could result from a number of factors such as political majorities, policy paradigms, etc.

3 It is important to stress that it would be misleading to focus exclusively on the number of these points and ignore their relative importance.
4 Based on the problem of testing their correctness, Majone (1980, 152) draws the analogy between a policy and a scientific theory.
5 The degree of complexity varies according to the extent of change introduced by a new policy (Sabatier and Mazmanian 1983, 159). Change can be analysed in terms of the specific provisions of the relevant legislative measures (both national and European) and in terms of the relations between and within the relevant actors and the resources needed for its implementation.
6 One should not underestimate the importance of 'soft law' (Wellens and Borchardt 1989) which is used extensively in the EU as a means for the clarification, specification or even analysis of hard law provisions. Soft law is issued by the institutions of the EU and carries their authority.
7 Discussing policy implementation in the federal system of the USA, Sabatier and Mazmanian (1981, 6) argue that the process starts with the passage of the statute.
8 This is the EU's most frequently used legislative instrument which is binding as to the objectives that it sets and, in theory, allows member states the freedom to choose how they will do so. This mirrors the fact that the Treaty of Rome is a framework treaty that sets out objectives and methods for their achievement in addition to the institutional framework which is meant to give precise meaning to them (Louis 1990, 74).
9 On the one hand, *consultative* committees must be consulted by the Commission, but their opinion has no binding effect on the content of the implementing measures. On the other hand, *management* committees, used extensively in the context of the Common Agricultural Policy (Bertram 1967; Schindler 1971) discuss and decide on the implementing measures submitted by the Commission. In case of a negative opinion of the committee, the measures are notified to the Council which can rescind or vary the measure (using QMV). Finally, *regulatory* committees, used extensively in the harmonisation of national legislations, customs and veterinary controls, can block the measures proposed by the Commission.
10 For example, once the EU's R&D programmes have been adopted, comitology committees define the conditions for funding. A useful categorisation of their functions has been proposed by Schaefer who identified i) rule-interpreting, ii) fund-approving and iii) rule-setting functions (Schaefer 1996, 16).
11 The importance of this aspect will be demonstrated empirically in Chapters 4 and 5.
12 Eugene Bardach captured this reality when he appositely claimed that 'implementation is the continuation of politics by other means' (Bardach 1977, 85; see also Scharpf 1978, 16). On the notion that the factors that shape formulation also shape implementation see Barrett and Hill (1984).
13 Of course, this concerns target groups and other interested parties as well (Sabatier and Mazmanian 1979, 496).
14 In Bardach's words (1977, 278), 'it is a job for a coalition of political partners with diverse but complementary resources. It is therefore no different from any other political task'.

15 One could also add the European Court of Auditors. Its role is similar to the role of the ECJ in that both are passive and *post hoc*.
16 Although a large number of problems are resolved in these informal meetings or even in the administrative stages of the procedure of Art. 169/226, others reach the ECJ. This is the most visible part of the ECJ's involvement in the implementation process. The ECJ facilitates this process by issuing judgements relating to all aspects of implementation and has thereby been able to identify fundamental principles of this implementation structure. However, the primarily *passive* role of the ECJ is illustrated by the inability of the EU to implement judgements. Until 1993 and the entry into force of the Treaty on European Union, the non-implementation of a judgement could only trigger another procedure under Art. 169 (or Art. 170) of the Treaty of Rome, due to the initial weakness of the provision of Art. 171 (regarding compliance with judgements of the ECJ). As it was not an effective deterrent, a number of member states had accumulated a significant backlog of judgements which they had not implemented. The post-Maastricht version of Art. 171/228 – which has received positive comments in the light of the previous intransigence of the member states – enables the Commission to bring the case (after having opened a dialogue with the state in question) before the ECJ by specifying a lump sum or penalty payment. This may then be imposed on the member state in question. Apart from this *post hoc* function, the ECJ also exerts its influence *during* the implementation process through the procedure of Art. 177/234, which organises a dialogue with national courts (Craig and de Búrca 1995, 399) aiming at the *uniform interpretation* of (primary and secondary) legislation through the so-called preliminary rulings. This is the mechanism that it has used in order to establish and develop the principles of supremacy and direct effect of EU law. The significance of this function of the ECJ is illustrated by the *obligation* of national courts of last instance to submit questions relating to the interpretation of EU law to the ECJ.
17 Rather, it exacerbates it.
18 This is why it would be a mistake to ignore the stage of transposition in the context of the analysis of the dynamics of implementation.
19 For example, the Treasury in Britain and the Ministry of Economics and Finance in France have traditionally been seen as very powerful actors in Whitehall and the French central government respectively (Timsit 1987, 75–6). This is so in part because their role and vision cut across the dividing lines between ministerial departments.
20 The scheme was initially devised in an effort to discuss the ways in which governments interact (how they 'detect' and 'effect') with society and was not aimed at being used for the discussion of action within governments. However, it can be used for that purpose as well as the discussion of the way in which fixers intervene in the implementation process. It is useful also because it reflects fundamental characteristics of the EU construed as an implementation structure (Dimitrakopoulos 1998, Chapter 2). Authority reflects the importance of law in the integration process (Joerges 1996; Charrier 1996; Weiler 1982), treasure mirrors the fundamental importance of economics in the process of integration, organisation and nodality reflect the EU's reliance on the national politico-administrative structures for the implementation of its policies.

21 Here the centre acts as a figurehead.
22 It is important to note here that theorising about the choice of tools is beyond the remit of this study. Rather, the objective here is to illuminate an important aspect of the capabilities of central governments.
23 Mechanisms that deal with post-transposition issues will have clear sectoral characteristics. This is why they shall not be discussed here. Rather, they will be discussed in the context of the case study (*infra*, Chapters 4 and 5).

2

Patterns of institutional change

The purpose of this chapter is to examine the way in which the exigencies of membership of the EU have been dealt with at the domestic level. This discussion will focus on the patterns of institutional development within the three central governments, executive–legislative relations and national mechanisms used for the transposition of EU legislation. There are five factors that link these core aspects of the operation of central governments to the broader theme of this book. First, EU business challenges the traditional distinction between domestic and foreign policy. The unpredictability of the pace and direction of EU policy making and the involvement of numerous other actors pose a major problem for all national governments whose aim is to maximise the benefits of membership whilst reducing the costs of adaptation to new policies. Second, all modern governments face the problem of segmentation; membership of the EU exacerbates it. Ministerial departments (such as the ministries of agriculture) that have traditionally had little (if any) 'international' business, now engage in frequent and intensive negotiations at the level of the EU. The implications of the outcome of these negotiations are rarely limited to one sector. This increases the need for co-ordination at the domestic level (Wright 1996; Kassim, Peters and Wright 2000; Kassim *et al.* 2001) throughout the entire policy making process. Third, choices that are made when policy is formulated are likely to have an impact on implementation. As a result, the stakes are very high for all national politico-administrative structures: no member state (or, more accurately, no central government) can afford to ignore the challenge of dealing with the co-ordination of EU policy. Fourth, although this book focuses on the way in which central governments macro-implement EU policy, ignoring the potential impact of national parliaments would be a misleading omission. EU policy making is, to a great extent, law making because the EU is a community of law whose main means of action is the legally binding legislative measures that it adopts – in other words, it is a law-intensive organisation (Page and Dimitrakopoulos 1997). However, law-making at the domestic level has traditionally been seen as one of the key functions of national parliaments.

More importantly, in member states – such as Britain – where the issue of membership was and remains politically salient, parliaments often provide a forum for debate that may affect the government's EU policy as well as the transposition of EU legislation. Finally, since transposition is the first step in the domestic part of the implementation process, and it entails not only the creation of new national rules but also the elimination (and, even, the prevention) of others that conflict with EU policy – it is important to examine how it is managed by national governments. Is it managed centrally, as an extension of the formulation of EU policy, or does it display strong sectoral characteristics? In the latter case, how (if at all) is it co-ordinated? In the light of the links between formulation and implementation discussed in Chapter 1, if the three member states examined here vary in terms of the way in which they have dealt with these challenges, variation between them can also be expected in terms of the way in which they deal with macro-implementation. A central government's inability to co-ordinate its involvement in the formulation of EU policy is expected to affect its capacity to steer macro-implementation. The more problematic co-ordination is in the former, the more problematic it will be in the latter. So, has the involvement in the process of European integration altered long-standing patterns of central government operation? Both the expectations of continuing variation and convergence are informed by the historical institutionalist understanding of institutional change (Krasner 1984). Here, long periods of institutional stasis are punctuated – when a critical juncture is reached – by short outbursts of rapid change until a new equilibrium is found, which in turn, is followed by another lengthy period of stability marked by small, timid steps which conform to a broader pattern. As Krasner notes (1984, 240) 'institutions generated by functional demands of the past can perpetuate themselves into a future whose functional imperatives are radically different'.

Institutions reflect historical experience that is encoded into standard operating procedures, structures and practices that endure beyond a given historical moment or condition (March and Olsen 1989, 167). The aim of this chapter is to establish that accession to the EU was *not* such a juncture and it has not unsettled domestic patterns of policy making (Page and Wouters 1995; Harmsen 1999).

Greece: unfinished business

Organisational reform

Two distinct periods can be identified. The first started in the early 1960s and ended in 1980 while the second began in January 1981 when Greece became the tenth member of the then EC. Law 4226/1962 that was passed for the ratification of the association agreement also served as the legal basis for both the adaptation of central government structures and the establishment of the framework of the domestic policy formulation process on EC affairs. At the political level, the Minister of Co-ordination[1] – now Minister of Economy and Finance – had overall responsibility for relations with the then EC including the adaptation of the Greek economy, the co-ordination of government action in this area and negotiations with representatives of EC institutions and member states. However, the management of 'political issues' remained under the responsibility of the Ministry of Foreign Affairs. Implicit in this arrangement was the predominantly economic aspect of membership and the notion that most of European policy was, essentially, part of domestic policy. After the submission of the application for full membership in 1975, two basic trends emerged. First, although the new framework laid down by Law 445/1976 reflected, by and large, the framework established in 1962 (including the key role ascribed to the Ministry of Co-ordination) significant limitations were established. First, this ministry no longer possessed the monopoly of representation in negotiations – this role could now be performed by the Prime Minister, the Minister of Foreign Affairs or technical ministers. Second, a junior minister responsible for European affairs was appointed at the Ministry of Foreign Affairs (Presidential Decree 1141/1977). This decision indicated the pronounced *diplomatic* element in negotiations for accession.[2]

Change at the administrative level took two forms. New administrative units were created within central government departments in order to manage European policy. The ministries of Co-ordination, Foreign Affairs and Agriculture rapidly created new specialised units to deal with this policy area. In 1962 the Permanent Representation to the European Communities was established in Brussels. It was a small part of the administrative machinery of the Ministry of Co-ordination although the Permanent Representative came either from the Greek diplomatic *corps* or was a specialist in European economic affairs. New inter-departmental bodies were created in an effort to promote co-ordination. At the administrative level, the European Co-operation Committee was established at the Ministry of Co-ordination. It included senior officials from the ministries of Co-ordination, Foreign Affairs, Economy, Trade, Agriculture, Industry and Labour as well as up to four experts. The involvement of these experts was indicative of a chronic problem of the Athenian bureaucracy, namely the lack of specialised staff.[3] Nevertheless, the role of the Ministry of Co-ordination remained pivotal. The European affairs units of other departments had to consult it in the course of the policy formulation process. In turn, they were responsible for information gathering, the conduct of negotiations as well as the adaptation of domestic legislation to the EC regime. Finally, the Consultative Committee on the Relations with the EC (established in 1976 within the Ministry of Co-ordination) was responsible for the formulation of the Greek negotiating positions. Nevertheless, the appointment of a senior official of the Ministry of Foreign Affairs as Chairman of the Central Negotiating Committee in 1977 underlined the increasing role of this ministry

(Makridimitris and Passas 1994, 39). This was a prelude to the formal shift of power towards this ministry after the Greek accession. As regards co-ordination at the political level, during the 1960s and 1970s, the lack of a specific forum for discussion between ministers dealing with EC policy meant that when problems arose, either the cabinet or the Prime Minister performed this role.

Once membership had been secured, the government sought to organise the management of European affairs on a new basis. Law 1104/1980 introduced three changes, namely the distinction between domestic co-ordination and external representation, the reinforcement of the role of the Minister and Ministry of Foreign Affairs and, finally, the formalisation of the distinction between political and technical issues as a criterion that determined the distribution of roles between departments involved in the policy process. The Minister of Foreign Affairs took over the responsibility for European affairs but it was clear that – at least as a result of his sheer workload – there was a need for a European affairs minister. The formal status[4] of this minister (junior or alternate minister) changed over time in part as a result of the personalities involved and their political clout within the ruling party (Makridimitris and Passas 1994). The same pattern has been followed in the Ministry of National Economy that retained responsibility for the management of European funds.

At the administrative level, institutional change continued throughout the 1980s. New specialised units were established in order to deal with specific parts of the policy process or specific significant aspects of European integration. The establishment of the Special EC Legal Service (ENYEK) in 1986 (Law 1640/1986) within the Ministry of Foreign Affairs was the result of the need to deal with the increasing number of infringement cases. The establishment of the Council of Economic Advisers (SOE) in 1987 (Law 1682/1987) reflected the need for specialist advice on economic aspects of membership. At the same time, the increasing involvement of technical ministries (such as the ministries of Industry, Energy and Technology; Health, Welfare and Social Security; Finance; Transport and Communications) in European affairs as a result of the expansion of the EC/EU's competence and agenda, led to the establishment of new European affairs units as well as the diffusion of the responsibility for these issues to technical units within departments. These departments quickly developed their own links with Brussels often by-passing the formal channel, i.e. the Ministry of Foreign Affairs which, in the meantime, had taken over the Permanent Representation[5] (Stephanou 1992, 16). Moreover, the importance of party allegiance – a key characteristic of the Greek administrative system (Makridimitris 1992, 45) – affected the ability of the administration to develop its own expertise; changes at the ministerial level after each general election resulted in changes in the senior staff that dealt with European affairs. This was the dominant pattern throughout the 1980s and most of the 1990s.

As regards collective bodies operating under the Cabinet, patchy changes occurred that have little to do with the management of European policy – except the period between 1996 and 2004. Rather, they reflect the style and the priorities of each Greek Prime Minister. Indeed, these changes (Xiros 2006, 170–1; see also Loverdos 1991) reflected domestic considerations – such as the conduct of economic policy – and, to a lesser extent, the need for better co-ordination of foreign policy. The most important change concerns the re-establishment in 1994 of the Government Committee – effectively the inner Cabinet – as the only collective political body dealing specifically with European affairs.[6]

Throughout the 1980s (Tsatsos 1993, 265; Spanou 2000, 172) and the first half of the 1990s, the Cabinet met rarely[7] – unlike the inner Cabinet in its various permutations. This changed in 1996 when Costas Simitis became Prime Minister (Spanou 2000, 173). Although he initially re-invigorated the Cabinet as a key collective decision making body between 1996 and 2000, after 2000 he made more extensive use of the inner Cabinet and specialised Cabinet committees in an effort to co-ordinate policy making.[8] He established a number of collective political bodies whose main[9] or secondary[10] role was the co-ordination of EU policy. His successor made even less use of the Cabinet, preferring instead to rely on the inner Cabinet (Xiros 2006, 174). This trend led to the reinforcement of the role of the Prime Minister as ultimate arbiter within the government, in line with the broader pattern of his role in the post-dictatorial era (Loverdos 1991, 252; Makridimitris 1992, 21).

Perhaps the most striking characteristic of the *formal* arrangement is the continuing distinction between the formulation of policy at the domestic level (where the Ministry of Economy and Finance is formally dominant) and external representation, which is the responsibility of the Ministry of Foreign Affairs. In addition, the former is responsible for the adaptation of the Greek economy and administration to EU policy. In *practice*, units tend to work autonomously, in a manner that reinforces fragmentation. Although in some cases this trend is counter-balanced by ministerial circulars, these are implemented only for a short period following their publication. This is reflective of a broader pattern. Although Law 1104/1980 stipulated that inter-departmental committees would be established to co-ordinate policy formulation, this system has – in practice – been abandoned since the early years of Greek membership. Co-ordination is exercised in a piecemeal manner through irregular *ad hoc* meetings or through personal contacts (Makridimitris and Passas 1994, 74). Thus, 'co-ordination at the administrative level relies on the quality of personal contacts between the ever-mobile officials in a manner that ends up being uncontrolled, opportunistic and above all personalised' (Passas 1993, 251 – author's translation).

In addition, the distribution of information after meetings at the level of the EU is often problematic since it relies primarily on the professionalism of the relevant staff, rather than an ethos of information diffusion and the quest for co-ordination.

The Greek Parliament
The law that ratified the Treaty of Accession (Law 945/1979) stipulates that the government ought to submit to Parliament annual reports on developments in the process of integration. However, the first report was submitted eight years after Greece's accession. This was a clear indication of the pattern that followed. Indeed, until 1990 the Greek Parliament did not have an EC-specific mechanism for scrutiny. The establishment of the Greek Parliament's European Community Affairs Committee in June 1990 (Hellenic Parliament 1990) – almost ten years after the Greek accession – was primarily an attempt to fill a significant gap regarding the provision of information on European integration. This was reflected in the composition of the committee – it included twelve Greek MEPs and twelve MPs. This was the only innovative characteristic of the committee. In reality, it proved to be a mixed blessing.

Indeed, the participation of MEPs was designed to improve the channels of information between the Greek Parliament and Brussels. However, this has contributed to the committee's weakness. The committee's objective was to monitor developments and express a view on the process of integration and the actions of the Greek government. Its opinion could not have a binding effect on the Greek government precisely because the committee included MEPs, i.e. members of a body that can have no formal link with the Greek government. Moreover, mixed membership became a major source of problems. MEPs and MPs reportedly (*To Vima* 17 October 1999) found it very hard to agree on whether to meet on Fridays (so as to enable the former to return from Brussels) or during other working days of the week (in order to allow the latter to return to their constituencies for the weekend). The committee focused mainly on institutional issues; co-operation between the Greek and the European Parliaments; European policies and texts that required ratification by the Greek Parliament; and the decisions of (permanent) parliamentary commissions regarding European affairs. When invited by the committee, ministers were obliged to give evidence. Its opinion was transmitted either to one of the permanent commissions or to the Floor of the House. The amendment in 1993 of the Parliament's internal rules of procedure transformed the committee into a permanent one without, however, increasing its powers.

The wider rubber-stamping role of the Greek Parliament was confirmed during the 1990s. From October 1993 until June 1995 the European Community Affairs Committee spent about 30 hours in meetings – 1.4 hours on average per month (*Kathimerini* 16 July 1995) – while only eight laws stemmed from initiatives taken by MPs out of a total of 2,740 new laws passed between 1974 and 1999 (*To Vima* 27 September 1999). Moreover, even new mechanisms, such the 'Prime Minister's time', declined rapidly (*Ta Nea* 30

December 2000). The amendment in spring 2001 of the Constitution of 1975 (as amended in 1986) led to the indirect constitutionalisation of the right of the Parliament to be informed by the government about EU legislation, which in the domestic arena falls within the domain of the law. Despite the symbolic importance of this development, the pattern of incremental and path dependent change remained evident and did not enhance the role of the Parliament in the process of EU policy formulation. Though its membership changed over time,[11] the committee remains unable to go beyond the adoption of an opinion which is not binding on the government (Art. 41B of the Parliament's rules of procedure; Dimitrakopoulos 2001a).

Transposition
The Greek Constitution of 1975, as amended in 1986 (esp. Art. 43, 44 and 78) and primary legislation (Laws 4226/1962; 445/1976; 945/1979), provide the formal framework for transposition. In practice, Parliament has routinely delegated to the government the power to adopt decrees that transpose EU legislation covering areas that normally require primary legislation.[12] As a result, the typically tame Greek Parliament was further marginalised. Actual responsibility for the timeliness and the effectiveness of transposition remains squarely in the hands of the government.

In organisational terms, since the conclusion of the association agreement in 1962, the Ministry of Co-ordination was responsible for transposition by virtue of its responsibility for the adaptation of the Greek economy.[13] The responsibility of the same ministry for this substantive and co-ordinating role was made more explicit in 1976 (Law 445/1976). In terms of horizontal arrangements, ENYEK (the special European affairs legal service, a part of the Ministry of Foreign Affairs) was established formally in 1986 to deal specifically with infringements, including those that concerned transposition. Despite the promising start made through the appointment of highly qualified staff, ENYEK subsequently became the victim of party politics. The decision of the conservative government to limit ENYEK's role by transferring to the state's legal council (NSK) the responsibility to represent Greece to the ECJ had much more to do with ENYEK's alleged proximity and allegiance to Theodoros Pangalos, the socialist minister who established it, than any operational consideration (Makridimitris and Passas 1994).

Given the cross-departmental nature of much of the *acquis*, interministerial committees were established to prepare the transposing legislation (Law 992/1979). An effort was initially made to concentrate responsibility for transposition in the European affairs units at departmental level. Though this arrangement was limited to the submission of proposals, it also reflected the notion that EU business could be handled not as part of departmental policy but as a separate or, in any case, 'special' part of government business. The establishment of these committees reflected awareness of the need for co-ordination. The centrality of the formal role attributed to the Ministry of

Co-ordination – which was responsible for the preparation of the relevant texts – also reflected the high profile of this ministry (and minister) under both conservative and socialist governments. This could have positive implications in cases of inter-departmental tensions, in the light of the lack of active collective bodies. However, the actual operation of the system was characterised by the rapid abandonment of the inter-departmental committees in the wake of accession without the establishment of a clear alternative mechanism. Rather, during the 1980s and much of the 1990s, much was left to the initiative of European affairs units or their technical counterparts. Moreover, the preparation of the relevant legal texts by either the legal affairs units or, more alarmingly, ministerial advisers is a frequent occurrence (Passas 1993, 251). They are political appointees who leave the ministry after a ministerial re-shuffle (Sotiropoulos 2004, 410; Laffan 2006, 700). Moreover, this practice was ineffective in the short term as well, because these individuals had not necessarily participated in the formulation process. This goes against the key lesson highlighted by the literature on implementation (*supra*, Chapter 1).

Despite the efforts of a small number of very experienced officials[14] who were, until 2006, responsible for monitoring (on behalf of the Ministry of National Economy) the transposition of EU legislation throughout the 1980s and 1990s, the process was problematic, at least in terms of the timely adoption of national measures, in part because of the exigencies of inter-departmental co-ordination. Yet, significant problems have persisted because their calls for the timely and co-ordinated transposition of EU law were often ignored. The same applies to their recourse to the ministers whose circulars are equally ineffective. Officials in other ministerial departments often complain about the lack of specialised staff (lawyers) but even if that were true, it would not explain the fact that very often the same departments fail to send to the European Commission (*To Vima* 3 December 1995) the transposing measures. The already unclear lines of authority are further blurred by chronic problems such as the mobility of ministerial advisers who are not members of the administrative hierarchy. This undermines the ability of the administration to learn by establishing and developing its own memory. These weaknesses often lead to ineffective and belated transposition. The frequent use of lengthy transition periods often contributes to the lethargic attitude of the Greek central government in terms of transposition. The absence of a high profile co-ordinator means that far too much depends on the unpredictable sensitivities of individual officials as opposed to the routine and reflective operation of institutional arrangements.

This is demonstrated by the fact that the efforts undertaken between 1996 and 2004 ceased to bear fruit as soon as the promoters of reform lost the general election. Indeed, while Prime Minister Simitis was in power, a significant part of his overall political strategy was based on the need to improve the credibility of Greece as an EU partner. This was a key reason why a centralised system was set up by the then Secretary General of the Cabinet. This system involved one official in each ministerial department who was responsible for transposition and a central database (maintained within the Secretariat General of the Cabinet), which recorded (i) the directives that had been adopted but not transposed, (ii) the directives that were under negotiation and (iii) the relevant judgements of the ECJ that condemned Greece. Although the operation of the system (Yiombré and Kapitsina 2008) and the importance that PM Simitis[15] attached to membership of the EU gradually led to the reduction of the outstanding cases regarding transposition, the momentum was not maintained after the general election of 2004. As a result, the situation deteriorated rapidly and the new government was forced to act. It introduced two changes (*To Vima* 1 October 2006; 7 January 2007). First, the Ministry of Economy and Finance is no longer responsible for the transposition of EU legislation.[16] Second, the new Secretary General of the Government set up a unit (under his authority) to monitor the timely and accurate transposition of EU legislation. The unit relies on a new electronic system devised with the help of an academic lawyer. Nevertheless, her efforts were initially unsuccessful as individual ministerial departments remained unresponsive. This reflects the government's wider co-ordination problems after 2004 (*infra*, Chapter 5).

France: the elusiveness of co-ordination

Organisational reform
A significant part of the structures that deal with EU affairs today stem from France's involvement in the implementation of the Marshall Plan and the creation of the OEEC/OECD. This entailed the establishment of the post of Minister for European affairs[17] without a corresponding separate administrative basis, the Inter-ministerial Committee for European Economic Co-operation as a result of the need to co-ordinate the implementation of the Marshall Plan, and the *Secrétariat Général du Comité Interministériel pour les questions de coopération économique européenne* (Secretariat General of the Inter-ministerial Committee for European Economic Co-operation), i.e. a small secretariat which became known as SGCI (Décret 48–1029, Art. 3).

The Committee was chaired by the Prime Minister and it comprised the Foreign Minister and the Minister of Economy and Finance. Other ministers attended on an *ad hoc* basis. It was responsible for the preparation of the guidelines to the French negotiators for the programme of European reconstruction, the decisions of the French Council of Ministers on these issues and the implementation of the required measures. The SGCI supported the committee in these tasks. Its Secretary General was initially chosen from the ranks of the Ministry of Economy and Finance (Décret 52–1016, Art. 7) and he was also a member of the French delegation in OEEC negotiations. The appointment of Secretaries General who simultaneously worked either in the President's *cabinet*, or for the Prime Minister (Gerbet 1975, 391) gradually enhanced the status and authority of this post during the 1960s.[18]

After the ratification of the Treaties of Rome in August 1957 (Loi 57–880) the committee's remit was extended to cover EC issues but its membership was restricted to the ministers of Foreign Affairs, Economy and Finance, Industry and Trade. In addition, two technical inter-departmental committees took over the responsibility for co-ordinating the implementation of the Treaties (Décret 58–344).

De Gaulle abolished the post of Minister for European affairs and streamlined this policy through his close personal friend Couve de Murville, then Foreign Minister. This is due not only to de Gaulle's wish to downgrade the importance of European integration but also his firm belief in the need to centralise mechanisms and procedures dealing with foreign policy, a part of the President's prerogatives.[19] His successors (Pompidou and Giscard d'Estaing) followed the same pattern until 1980.

In contrast, developments at the administrative level reflected the view that EC affairs ought to be handled as part of the 'domestic' dimension of each policy (Gerbet 1969, 196). In technical ministries, this was coupled with the reinforcement of the structures that dealt with international affairs in an effort to ensure a co-ordinated approach to EC policy.[20] In the two important horizontal ministries, namely the Ministry of Economy and Finance and the *Quai d'Orsay*, this function was entrusted to existing structures (Gerbet 1969, 198–201).

After 1981 two important developments took place. The first entailed the re-establishment of the post of Minister for European affairs after the electoral victory of the socialists in May 1981 (Décret 81–665). Though its status has changed since then (Hayward and Wright 2002, 141) this post became a permanent[21] feature of the institutional structures that deal with European affairs in France (Lequesne 1993; Menon 2000). This post often mirrored the profile of its holders and their proximity to (or distance from) President Mitterrand. In many cases, the appointees were close friends[22] or collaborators[23] of the President.[24] Second, responsibility for the SGCI was transferred back to the Prime Minister in 1984. This underlined not only the importance attached to European affairs but also the need for co-ordination in the centre of the French government.

In terms of the formulation of policy, until 1980, the absence of a European affairs minister and the gradual abandonment of the Elysée committees meant that the dual French executive played a central role in policy formulation at the political level. Under the Constitution of 1958 the President ensured the continuity of the state through his *arbitrage* (Art. 5) while the Prime Minister directed the government's action (Art. 21) which was responsible for determining and conducting policy (Art. 20). In practice, issues that could not be resolved at the administrative level, ascended to the political level, where the Prime Minister or even the President of the Republic (who chairs the meetings of the Cabinet) took the decisions. In general terms, the President defined the general lines of French policy on European affairs, while the Prime Minister co-ordinated ministerial action. Substantive discussions took place in the Cabinet, though many decisions had been prepared by various committees (Quermonne and Chagnollaud 1991, 200).

Despite the wide use of various types of Cabinet-level committees since 1958 (Fournier 1987, 224) the pattern of the involvement of the Interministerial Committee for European Economic Co-operation has been inconsistent, fluctuating between inactivity before (Achard 1972, 43) and operation during periods of *cohabitation*. The reinforcement of the Council of Ministers as a collective body and the role of the Prime Minister as co-ordinator of government action have contributed to this development. After the *débâcle* of the referendum of May 2005, Prime Minister de Villepin created the *Comité Interministériel sur l'Europe* (Inter-ministerial Committee on Europe). It is chaired by the Prime Minister and includes the Foreign Minister, the Minister for European affairs, the Minister of Finance on a permanent basis, and other ministers on an *ad hoc* basis (Décret 2005–1283).

Despite the instability that characterised the political echelon, the important role of the SGCI – *Secrétariat Général des Affaires Européennes* or SGAE since October 2005 – has been confirmed throughout the Fifth Republic (Gerbet 1969, 204; 1975, 392; Lequesne 1993; Menon 2000). Being at the interface of the political and the administrative levels, it is responsible for co-ordination on European issues and acts as the official channel for communication with Brussels. Since its establishment the SGCI has become the neutral *locus* where departmental views confront each other in the quest for a coherent national position. It benefits from its organic link to the Prime Minister. Placed under the Prime Minister's authority, it appears to be above inter-departmental tensions. The meetings that it convenes are the *loci* of confrontation of sectoral views but the fact that ministries do not always respond rapidly to the Secretariat's initiative as a result of tensions between various directorates is an indication of a broader trend. The SGCI intensifies the pressure for intra- as well as inter-departmental co-ordination but its presence reflects not only the existence of this pressure but also the *need for it*[25] despite the fact that it is respected as an institution (Wright 1996, 157–8; Hayward and Wright 2002, 139). This is demonstrated by the circulars that emanate from the top echelons of the hierarchy. They underline the need for the ministries to communicate with the institutions of the EU through the SGCI and the permanent representation in Brussels (Lequesne 1992, 2:685; République Française 1994a). The latest decree that organises the role of the SGAE is indicative of the constant need for co-ordination[26] within the French central government. It stipulates that the SGAE 'prepares', 'instructs' and 'transmits' the French positions that are subsequently presented in meetings at the level of the EU (Art. 2 par. 1 al. a). It is also responsible for 'ensuring' the co-ordination of the French views to that effect.

The role of the French Parliament

The French Constitution of 1958 restricts the role of the French Parliament as a reaction to the problems that stemmed from the operation of the Constitution of 1946 (Cot 1980, 11). The response of the two chambers to the challenge of the French involvement in European integration follows the broad pattern established by the Constitution of 1958 that limits the number of permanent commissions to six in order to ensure that they do not 'shadow' ministerial departments as they did until 1958 (Burdeau, Hamon and Troper 1993, 573). The prevailing view within the French Parliament was that European affairs were an aspect of foreign policy, that was scrutinised by a specialised dominant parliamentary commission in each House. However, the first direct election of MEPs in 1979 created a competitor to both chambers. In response, one *délégation* was established in each House (Loi 79-564) but the commissions remained the dominant players within the parliamentary sphere.[27]

The objective of the two *délégations* was to inform the two chambers about the activities of European institutions. The government was obliged to provide European documents regarding negotiations in Brussels prior to the adoption of formal decisions and covering issues in the domain of the law which, under Art. 34 of the French Constitution of 1958, primarily concerns civil rights, penal law, taxation, national defence and the nationalisation of industries – i.e. issues in which the then EC had little, if any, involvement. The *délégations* could then present their own conclusions to the relevant permanent commission of each chamber. As a result, the role of the *délégations* within the two Houses remained weak throughout the 1980s. They can be depicted as two clearing houses. They had the power to propose non-binding resolutions to a permanent commission which, in turn, could impose its own amendments or even reject the proposal altogether (Cottereau 1982, 46). In addition to these inherent weaknesses, scrutiny was further undermined by the government, which only partly fulfilled its obligations regarding the transmission of documents (Dimitrakopoulos 2001a).

After the entry into force of the Single European Act, further marginal changes were introduced (Loi 90-385) focusing primarily on the more balanced representation of permanent commissions in each *délégation*, the expansion of their membership, and the widening of the range of documents that came under scrutiny. In addition, the *délégations* were granted the right to invite – but not to oblige – ministers to give evidence.

After the adoption of the Treaty on European Union the French Parliament enhanced the profile of the scrutiny mechanism without increasing its powers. The 'constitutionalisation' of this mechanism through the amendment of Art. 88 of the French Constitution was merely the 'price' the socialist government had to pay to ensure the ratification of the treaty (Alberton 1995, 922). The two chambers won the right to pass resolutions on EU policy but the new constitutional provision limited the scope of scrutiny to the pre-1990 arrangements by referring only to proposals involving provisions of legislative nature.

The constitutionalisation of parliamentary scrutiny re-produced the logic of path dependent, incremental change. It led to the establishment by the French government of a procedure aiming to ensure compliance with the new constitutional provisions (République Française 1994b; 1999; 2005). This procedure ensures that the government not only remains the dominant player but can also use parliamentary procedures as a bargaining tool in Brussels. When Parliament intends to pass a resolution but is unable to do so prior to the meeting of the Council of Ministers, a distinction is drawn between two cases. In the first case, when the relevant piece of draft EU legislation is placed on the agenda of the Council of Ministers up to fourteen days before a Council meeting and there is no 'urgency' or 'special motive', the French member of COREPER is instructed to declare that the French government opposes the inclusion of this issue on the agenda. In the second case, when draft EU legislation is placed on the agenda of the Council of Ministers more than fourteen days before the meeting of the Council, the internal rules of procedure of the Council do not allow national representatives to block its inclusion on the agenda of the Council. Nevertheless, if there is no 'urgency' or 'special motive', the French representative will attempt to postpone a formal decision without abstaining from discussions in the Council.

The development of the French mechanism for the scrutiny of EU policy confirms the argument that change has been both incremental – i.e., it has proceeded by means of small, marginal modifications based on existing institutional repertoires – and path dependent, in that it has neither altered nor challenged the balance of power between the Executive and Parliament. The French government has retained a free hand[28] in negotiations, though in 1999 and 2005[29] it further expanded the categories of documents that the two chambers can expect to receive (République Française 2005).

Transposition
The role of the government – that has the power to determine and conduct the nation's policy (Art. 20) – is both very extensive and intensive in transposition, as a result of the Constitution of 1958 and the practice that followed. The Constitution severely restricts the areas in which the parliament plays a significant legislative role. Moreover, the government has the power to (i) adopt *ordonnances*[30] to implement its programme even in fields that are normally covered by the law (Art. 38) and (ii) determine the agenda of the two chambers. It also shares the right of legislative initiative (Art. 39). Thus, the government remains the predominant actor in transposition.[31]

At the organisational level, one of the most important powers of the Inter-ministerial Committee for European Economic Co-operation was the responsibility for the implementation of measures relating to the participation of France in the programme of European economic reconstruction (Décret

48–1029, Art. 2). For that purpose, the SGCI had to co-operate with the relevant parts of the French administrative apparatus in an effort to draw on the expertise of specialised units in the relevant ministries. The subsequent expansion of the remit of the inter-ministerial committee extended the role of the SGCI to cover ECSC and, later, EEC matters (Décret 52–1016, Art. 6; Décret 58–344, Art. 1). The mild terminology used in the aforementioned provisions reflected an attempt to establish a horizontal role for the SGCI without limiting the number or the role of other actors. In practice, neither the SGCI nor any other body played an active role in transposition until 1986 (Sauron 1995, 56). This was reflected at the political level even after the establishment of the post of the Minister for European affairs.[32]

Since the mid-1980s and the re-launch of integration, awareness grew about the challenge of transposition and implementation more broadly (Délégation du Sénat pour l'Union européenne 2001, 15). Jacques Chirac's prime ministerial circular of May 1986 (see Lequesne 1992, 2:681) reflects this awareness. The process that it organised involved the SGCI, the SGG (*Secrétariat Général du Gouvernement* – Secretariat General of the Government) and the relevant ministerial departments not least because – as the *Conseil d'État* noted three years later – problems stemmed in part from the tendency of individual departments to use transposition as an opportunity to engage in more wide-ranging policy reforms (cited in Délégation du Sénat pour l'Union européenne 2001, 15). Once a directive had been adopted, the SGCI would inform the SGG about its content, objective, transposition deadline and the lead department, and one of its own officials would be designated as a contact point. The Secretary General of the government would then request from the lead ministry a detailed plan (including a specific timetable) concerning transposition, a copy of which was to be sent to the SGCI and to the Prime Minister's *cabinet*. The responsibility for the implementation of this plan (and timetable) rests with the SGG. This is important given its position at the heart of the French government which enables it to have direct recourse to the Prime Minister or his *cabinet* in case of inter-departmental tensions. The effectiveness of the procedure outlined in Chirac's circular was mitigated by the lack of staff in SGG who would keep up with the deadlines for the transposition by putting pressure on the relevant ministries (Lequesne 1993, 128) despite an 'alert procedure' that enabled the SGCI[33] to be informed by the European Commission of any problems relating to the process of transposition (Carnelutti 1988, 17).

The link between formulation, transposition and implementation was highlighted (albeit indirectly) in another prime ministerial circular of March 1994 (République Française 1994a). It stipulated that a study of legal impact should be prepared by the lead ministry – ahead of negotiations in Brussels – comprising, *inter alia*, a list of the national legal texts that would have to be amended or abolished, the issues posing a problem from the point of view of national law and a comparative legal analysis (if necessary). This study had to be submitted to the SGCI within a month from the submission of the EU legislative proposal with a view to organising inter-departmental meetings involving the *Conseil d'État*[34] as well.[35] Monitoring was ensured through a *fiche de suivi juridique* maintained by the lead ministry and the detailed database of the SGCI.[36] The fact that at the *intra*-departmental level the units that formulate policy and then negotiate in Brussels are also responsible for transposition is considered as a major strength of the French system.[37]

The role of the SGCI in transposition is more subtle when compared to its intensive presence in formulation. It is more active in cases of conflict. In these cases it is the mechanism that may trigger the intervention of the other – politically powerful – actors such as ministerial *cabinets*, the PM or even the President, thus maintaining what may be termed as a political review procedure (Lequesne 1993, 132). This has given rise to the argument that it is the capacity of the departments to transpose, rather than the lack of a co-ordinator, that explains transposition-related problems in France (Lequesne 1993, 132). Whilst not denying the role of the SGCI/SGAE, its presence arguably reflects the need for co-ordination rather than its routine occurrence. Three facts support this view. First, in addition to Chirac's circular of 1986, successive Prime Ministers issued further circulars regarding transposition and one (Raffarin) even mentioned the need to improve the French transposition record in the government's *déclaration de politique générale* (République Française 1990; 1998; 2004; Raffarin 2002). However, inter-departmental co-ordination remained problematic to such an extent that disagreements[38] led to enduring blockages and – as the French Senate discovered – the efforts to improve the situation have remained a 'lettre morte' (Délégation du Sénat pour l'Union européenne 2002, 5). These circulars emphasise the importance of the link between formulation, transposition and implementation – including the need to ensure that the definitions adopted at the European level do not create interpretation problems in subsequent stages of the process. Second, the decision was taken in November 2002 to discuss the issue of transposition every six months at Cabinet level (République Française. Conseil des Ministres 2002; *Le Monde* 10 November 2002). Finally, Prime Minister Raffarin decided in October 2004 to enhance the co-ordination of transposition through quarterly meetings of departmental officials under the joint responsibility of the heads of SGG and SGCI. He also requested that any remaining problems be submitted to his *arbitrage*.

The UK

Organisational reform

The extension to European affairs of pre-existing methods of handling policy is the most significant characteristic of Whitehall's response to the exigencies of membership (Bulmer and Burch 1998; Kassim 2000). This concerns primarily the administrative level. The impact of the political salience of membership on institutional development at the political level was evident since the 1950s. The first Cabinet minister with special responsibility for European affairs was appointed in 1957, i.e. prior to the British accession, but it did not prevent the involvement of other departments. Initially, the handling of these issues was confined to a handful of departments such as the Department of Economic Affairs, the Foreign Office and the Cabinet Office. The first major change came with Prime Minister Edward Heath's decision to centralise to the Cabinet Office the responsibility for the co-ordination of European policy. This reflected his view that European policy is part of domestic rather than foreign policy, his willingness to avoid its confinement to a small part of the Whitehall and the political salience of membership.[39] After the British accession, the sheer workload of the Foreign Secretary led to the appointment in March 1974 of a European affairs minister at the Foreign and Commonwealth Office (FCO). Since then, this post has become a permanent feature of the British system despite the fact that the FCO has never had (with the exception of a short spell under Wilson) overall responsibility for European policy. Over the years, the Cabinet has remained the most senior political mechanism dealing with Britain's European policy. A permanent 'EC/EU slot' in its weekly meetings serves as the basis for a report by the Foreign Secretary on recent developments in this area.

Below the Cabinet a web of committees deal with European policy. Until 1974, the Ministerial Committee for Europe was the *locus* of policy formulation at the political level (Sasse 1975, 59). It was chaired by the Chancellor of the Duchy of Lancaster and membership varied according to the issues that were under discussion. This role was subsequently performed by ODP (E), a sub-committee of the powerful Overseas and Defense Policy Committee that was chaired by the Prime Minister. More recently, this role was taken up by two sub-committees, namely European Union Strategy (EUS) and European Policy (EP). The former is chaired by the Prime Minister, includes a small number of ministers (including the Foreign Secretary, the Chancellor, the Home Secretary and the Minister for Europe), and oversees the government's European strategy and the presentation of its European policy. The latter is chaired by the Foreign Secretary, includes almost the entire Cabinet and determines the UK's policy on the EU.

At the administrative level, changes were gradual and mirrored the increasing involvement of various departments in negotiations. The FCO[40] developed gradually its own EC-related machinery (*The British Imperial Calendar and Civil Service List 1967, 1969, 1971*) that initially took the form of the European Economic Organisations Department that was subsequently re-named European Integration Department (EID) in 1970. In 1974 the EID was divided into an 'Internal' department dealing with the internal working and development of the EC, parliamentary as well as legal aspects of membership and an 'External' department dealing with the EC's external relations with third countries and European Political Co-operation (United

Kingdom. Civil Service Department 1974, cols. 343–4). The UK's Permanent Representation to the EC/EU (UKRep) grew[41] gradually as a result of the intensification of the negotiations and in 1971 it had twenty-nine staff (including eighteen diplomats) and trainees from various departments (Wallace 1973, 91; Kassim 2001). Most of the main Whitehall departments – like MAFF – quickly established divisions responsible for relations with the EC, as a result of the competence and activity of the EC in the policy areas that they covered.

Prior to accession, a small secretariat in the Cabinet Office gradually grew and became a distinct 'European Unit' (Wallace 1973, 91) – subsequently renamed European Secretariat, responsible for Cabinet-level discussions on British accession. Its staff is seconded from various Whitehall departments for a period of two years thus ensuring that knowledge of European affairs (and the exigencies of co-ordination) is constantly disseminated within Whitehall. In technical departments EU policy is handled as part of domestic policy. However, the creation of horizontal co-ordinating units was intended to limit the negative effects of this functional diffusion. This trend appeared in departments that were heavily involved in EU policy, such as the Treasury, the Department of Trade and Industry (DTI) and Ministry of Agriculture, Fisheries and Food (MAFF).

A web of committees comprising senior officials from various departments has also been created. Initially, the function of collective co-ordination was taken up by the Official Committee for Europe (Sasse 1975, 59). More recently, this role was absorbed by the European Questions (Official) Committee.[42] It deals with the many run off the mill issues (Stack 1983, 129) mainly by ensuring that an individual department's view does not contain any points of tension with other departmental views – and the provision of advice on procedure, tactics and strategy for forthcoming negotiations (Spence 1993, 59). Its membership is determined by the agenda, thereby creating an extensive network of participants who also receive copies of the minutes. Due to the committee's workload, informal co-ordination meetings are also arranged – whenever necessary – either on the initiative of the European Secretariat or the lead department. The spirit of inclusion of any department that may have an interest in a given policy proposal is the prevailing characteristic of the administrative ethos in Whitehall in terms of the handling of EU policy. This is illustrated by the wide circulation of minutes and participation in these meetings.

The European Secretariat is at the heart of the British system of co-ordination. It is a powerful co-ordinating body that performs various roles (Kassim 2000, 34–7). It manages overall co-ordination on all EU proposals (including major policy initiatives), ensures that the UK's EU policy is consistent with the broad policy objectives of the British government,[43] monitors parliamentary scrutiny and offers advice on EU institutions, procedures (including the Luxembourg compromise) and protocol. More importantly, it also supervises the practical follow-up of decisions. Technical departments are required to (and routinely) signal to the European Secretariat the issues that are likely to cause interdepartmental tensions. Its position above these tensions and at the heart of government – under the responsibility of the Prime Minister – ensures that it is a neutral basis for the quest of co-ordination. Over the years, it has accumulated knowledge, experience and institutionalised memory on EU issues which is accessible to all Whitehall departments. The Head of the Secretariat[44] briefs the Prime Minister before the meetings of the European Council, attends Cabinet meetings when required and chairs the weekly co-ordination meetings that bring together officials from UKRep (including the Permanent Representative) and Whitehall.

Prior to devolution Whitehall's territorial departments provided input in policy making. Since devolution the British government retains overall responsibility on EU matters but officials of the devolved administrations are involved in the formulation of policy on EU issues that fall in their responsibility. Issues that cannot be resolved at the administrative level are dealt with by the Joint Ministerial Committee on Europe. The entire arrangement and its operation are couched in terms – such as the 'principle of no surprises' – that highlight the primacy of consultation, co-operation and co-ordination (Bulmer *et al.* 2006, 79–80). This reflects the wider culture of consultation, diffusion of information and sustained quest for a co-ordinated position that prevails in Whitehall.[45] The devolved administrations have absorbed most of the staff of Whitehall's territorial departments (Bulmer *et al.* 2006, 79). Arguably, this has contributed to the success of the new system because this change ensured the diffusion of expertise and the ethos of consultation across levels of government.

The role of Westminster
Westminster was quick to react to the accession of the UK because the issue of erosion of the principle of parliamentary sovereignty was at the heart of the debate regarding accession (Taylor 1975, 279). However, the response of the government was both carefully defined and firm. Even before accession, the Chancellor of the Duchy of Lancaster had noted that:

> the Government are deeply concerned that Parliament, as well as United Kingdom Ministers should play its full part when future Community policies are being formulated, and in particular that Parliament should be *informed* about and have an opportunity to *consider* at the formative stage those Community instruments which, when made by the Council, will be binding in this country.
> (House of Commons 21 December 1972, col. 1743, added emphasis)

The House of Commons established a select committee to consider draft European legislation and other documents, to report on whether they raise 'questions of legal or political importance' and to make recommendations for further consideration of these documents by the House. The principal criteria used were the effect on UK law, contentiousness and financial implications (Norton 1995, 96). Prior to 1991, once a document had been recommended for debate by the select committee, the debate could take place either on the Floor of the House or in a standing committee. Yet debates on the Floor of the House took place after 10pm and were poorly attended (Bates 1991, 123). As a result, in 1991 the House established two permanent standing committees where debates could take place. The development of the Commons' internal rules regarding relations with the government has been consistently incremental (Dimitrakopoulos 2001a). The modification adopted in 1980 – i.e. immediately after the first direct election of MEPs – was consistent with the symbolic value attached to Westminster. The new arrangement formally recognised the obligation of British ministers *to avoid* giving their agreement in Brussels before the completion of scrutiny. This arrangement is the most important procedural 'constraint' on the government and is widely envied by other parliaments in the EU (Norton 1995, 107). The relevant Resolution obliged ministers to withhold agreement when:

> a proposal for European legislation has been recommended by the Select Committee on European Legislation for consideration by the House before the House has given it consideration unless (a) that committee has indicated that agreement need not be withheld, or (b) the Minister concerned decides that for special reasons agreement should not be withheld; and in the latter case the Minister should, at the first opportunity thereafter, explain the reasons for his decision to the House.
> (House of Commons 30 October 1980, col. 843)

Paradoxically, this arrangement was not only consistent with Margaret Thatcher's criticism of the then EC, but also a powerful argument in negotiations in Brussels. In fact, it is more useful to the government than the Parliament because the latter maintained a significant margin for action by stating that ministers can overcome this negative procedural constraint if 'special reasons' render it necessary. The very broad criteria used in this assessment include the need to avoid a legal vacuum; the desirability of permitting a particular measure of benefit to the UK to come into force as soon as possible and the difficulty, especially in the case of protracted or difficult negotiations, of putting a late reserve on a measure which will have little effect on the UK or which is likely to be of benefit to the UK. More importantly, assessing whether these criteria are satisfied remains firmly the responsibility of the government. This arrangement was confirmed by resolutions adopted in 1990 (House of Commons 24 October 1990, col. 399) and 1998 (House of Commons 17 November 1998, col. 778; Dimitrakopoulos 2001a). This resolution further extends the right of ministers not to withhold agreement for proposals that they consider to be 'confidential'.

Institutional adaptation in the House of Lords followed the basic select committee model (House of Lords 10 April 1974, col. 1229). The committee operates in a rather decentralised manner. It has appointed specialised sub-committees and, following a double 'sift' (one by its chairman of the committee and one by each sub-committee), scrutiny focuses on a small number of documents that are then analysed in greater detail. This underpins one of the committee's most important strengths, namely the scrutiny of policy trends rather than specific pieces of draft legislation. Post-1990 arrangements used in the House of Commons – obliging ministers to withhold agreement if scrutiny has not been completed – were extended to the House of Lords in 1999 (House of Lords 6 December 1999, cols. 1019–20).

Thus, institutional change at Westminster followed an incremental and path-dependent logic (Dimitrakopoulos 2001a). The two Houses have essentially used existing mechanisms and procedures to respond to pressures for change stemming from the process of integration. More importantly, change failed to challenge the established patterns of interactions between the Parliament and the Executive whereby the accountability of the latter to the former has declined over time (see Dunleavy and Jones with Burnham, Elgie and Fysh 1993; Burnham and Jones with Elgie 1995).

Transposition
The laconic provisions of the European Communities Act 1972 (especially section 2 § 1 and § 2) served a clear political purpose, namely the need to avoid the perpetuation of the debate on the very principle of membership. This political debate would have continued if the Heath government had decided to create a detailed set of legal provisions which would include legal instruments that transpose EC legislation on an *ad hoc* basis. The former transposed the *acquis* while the latter provided the basis for the transposition of legislation in the future. The same Act stipulated that statutory instruments would be the main means used for that purpose. Subordinate legislation such as this was made by executive bodies such as the Crown, ministers, some departments, public corporations and local authorities (De Smith and Brazier 1994, 359–64). Despite the fact that the great bulk of subordinate legislation is made by virtue of parliamentary authority, this type of legislation is characterised by the willingness to limit the parliamentary input in this process. Nevertheless, Westminster is not totally excluded from this process because some statutory instruments adopted on the basis of the European Communities Act are subject to the affirmative resolution procedure which requires a parliamentary resolution (adopted by both Houses) approving the instrument (De Smith and Brazier 1994, 374). However, the importance of this provision should not be over-estimated for it is used only in a small[46] number of cases. This is so because many orders that practically implement EU legislation are made under other legislative instruments (Collins 1990, 121) which do not necessarily contain a similar procedural requirement.

Indeed, successive British governments have used powers previously delegated by Parliament (Butt Philip and Baron 1988, 650). Thus, the government remains the dominant actor in transposition.[47]

In general terms, the British administrative apparatus is characterised by the absence of mechanisms that deal exclusively with transposition. On the contrary, the units that have the responsibility for transposition are, as a rule, those that formulate national policy and then negotiate at the European level (Butt Philip 1985, 97; Drewry 1995, 457). This reflects awareness of the fact that the units and the officials who have participated in the formulation and negotiation stages know what the relevant actors want, how the final compromise was reached as well as its purpose. However, this does not mean that mechanisms that deal only with a part of the implementation process are totally absent. Legal issues are discussed in EQO (L) that is chaired by the legal adviser to the Cabinet Office. This committee also discusses issues regarding implementation and infringement cases (Drewry 1995, 470; Kassim 2000, 35), despite the existence of departmental legal advisers. Furthermore, a specialised unit (Single Market Compliance Unit) in the DTI handled complaints by British firms regarding implementation of EU policy in other member states.

The significant role of the European Secretariat in the formulation process is mirrored by its involvement in transposition. It keeps an eye on the process, provides guidance to individual departments and intervenes in problematic cases. The ethos of wide consultation within Whitehall is at the heart of this process. In cases of interdepartmental tensions, the European Secretariat seeks a compromise. This means that occasionally issues have to ascend to the political level. The European Secretariat assesses the need for this form of action although the intensity of a particular department's pre-occupations is another important factor. Moreover, the European Secretariat keeps track of measures that have been or need to be transposed, and does so on a pro-active basis.[48] The tables that it prepares are then circulated within Whitehall.

Although the cases of its intervention in day-to-day transposition are rather limited, it does intervene in cases of interdepartmental conflict relating to implementation styles. Indeed, the main source of conflict seems to be the strong tendency of some departments, like the DTI, to prefer codes of practice and administrative circulars as a reflection of their strong deregulatory culture. These pre-occupations need to be balanced by the traditional administrative willingness to have everything 'cut and dried'. The need to balance effectiveness-seeking 'gold-plating', i.e. the tendency of some sectoral departments to add requirements during transposition, with the avoidance of over-implementation (the imposition of unnecessary regulatory burden) is often the focus of the European Secretariat's input to the implementation process.

The input provided by the Cabinet Office-based unit in charge of deregulation is a major aspect of that tension. It tends to promote copy-out as a method that minimises regulatory burden on industry. It entails the word-by-word incorporation of EU legislation into British law. This minimises each department's margin for discretion in transposition but it must be balanced with the traditional British emphasis on specific texts which, in turn, reduce the need for and the margin of judicial interpretation. Assessing which formula should prevail is a part of the functions performed by the European Secretariat. Prominent among these is the assessment of the likelihood and the potential outcome of a legal challenge by the European Commission. Finally, the devolved administrations consider – in bilateral consultation with the relevant Whitehall department – how to transpose and implement EU policy including whether they should transpose by means of UK or separate legislation – and how to do so. The principles on the basis of which they participate in formulation continue to inform their involvement in transposition (United Kingdom Government 2001).

Conclusion: *plus ça change* ...

Despite facing similar pressures, the three member states examined here have responded in ways that reflect pre-existing patterns. This confirms the basic premise of historical institutionalism that highlights long periods of stasis that are punctuated by bursts of rapid change. Accession to the EU has not been a punctuation of that kind. Rather, the similarities[49] and the differences between the three systems reflect their broader, historically-defined, long-standing characteristics.

Three key similarities can be identified. First, all central governments have created new units in an effort to deal with EU business but the main premise on which the handling of policy has been based, has remained unchanged: technical units remain responsible for the EU dimension of their brief. Though European or international affairs units had to be created initially, their role has declined in line with the reduction of their comparative advantage: as awareness about the European dimension of national policy and knowledge about the operation of the EU increased in technical units, the need for 'EU specialists' declined. This is important not only because it facilitates the crucial linkages between formulation and implementation but also because it highlights and reinforces the need for co-ordination. Second, the status of the three national parliaments has remained unchanged in the sense that their role in both formulation and transposition is of secondary importance. The proverbial ball is squarely in the hands of national governments, even in Britain where the principle of membership has remained controversial. Party discipline, the structure of incentives that ambitious backbenchers face and broader characteristics of the political system have played a central role in this respect. The traditional 'fusion' of the executive and the legislature in Britain (Bagehot [1867] 1963) and the lessons from the unhappy experiences of the Fourth Republic in France and the pre-dictatorial period in Greece, have all contributed towards the marginalisation of the three parliaments. In addition, the institutionalised capacity of executives to control the internal operation of these parliaments and the structure of incentives of ambitious backbench MPs[50] have further contributed to this trend. This extends to transposition since national governments tend to resort primarily to secondary legislation for that purpose. Third, EU-specific committees have been created at the political and the administrative levels in an effort to promote co-ordination. However, the *actual* operation of these committees is, in fact, a significant part of the differences between these systems.

Indeed, although the three governments have established committees (be they EU-specific or not) in an effort to achieve co-ordination, their operation differs in the sense that it has been very patchy in Greece (where they appear to have been abandoned), less patchy in France and quite consistent in Britain. In the case of Greece, this is unsurprising since it reflects a pattern that has characterised the entire period after the restoration of the democratic regime in 1974: collective bodies are established but are quickly abandoned (the Simitis era being a partial exception) in a system that is marked by the dominance of the Prime Minister – not as a *primus inter pares* but as a *primus solus* – at the political level and fragmentation at the administrative level. Although the occasional establishment of collective bodies indicates awareness of the need for co-ordination, their quick demise is an indication of the prevailing ethos of segmentation. In France the operation of the system confirms the constant *need* for – as opposed to the consistent presence of – co-ordination (Délégation du Sénat pour l'Union européenne 2002, 5). This is clearly indicated by the repeated attempts to enhance or refine the system. As two prominent observers of French politics noted, this reiteration is an indication of frequent failure (Hayward and Wright 2002, 257). Finally, the British system – often seen as the most effective system of co-ordination in EU matters – is marked by the dual presence of strong co-ordinating mechanisms (both at the political and the administrative levels) and an *ethos* that is conducive to the dissemination of information and the collaborative quest for a co-ordinated position on the, almost inevitably, inter-departmental issues that arise in the course of policy making. As a seasoned observer put it, '[t]he smooth running of the system is due principally to its "fit" with the wider polity, which its objectives and *modus operandi* embody, reflect and project' (Kassim 2000, 45).

Moreover, these differences, and the way in which they are illustrated in the domain of EU affairs, reflect historically defined patterns of institutional development and the politico-administrative cultures of the three states. For example, the extensive and intensive use of political appointees as ministerial advisers who by-pass the traditional channels of operation within the Athenian bureaucracy mirrors the chronic lack of qualified staff which, in turn, is the result of the patronage system that has prevailed since the establishment of the modern Greek state. Although reliance on ministerial advisers (some of whom are academics) may resolve problems regarding the lack of expertise in the short term, it also prevents the administration from developing contacts with the administrations of other member states in an effort to improve intelligence-gathering ahead of meetings in Brussels, its own expertise and even perhaps the most elementary of administrative functions, namely institutional memory.[51] This contrasts markedly with the British system where the presence of a permanent, independent and politically 'neutral' civil service allows the administration to inject a significant degree of continuity into the handling of EU business. This directly affects the capacity of a given system to draw lessons from experience and to subsequently implement change. The Greek system is, again, the outlier. Indeed, unlike its British – and, to a lesser extent, French – counterparts, it is not endowed with the pro-active attitude at official level that is required for effective lesson-drawing and fixing. As a result, it relies much more on the willingness and ability of the promoters of change to sustain their interest in reform.

Another important difference concerns the co-ordination of transposition. Unlike the British and French cases where the European Secretariat and the SGAE are active – though to different degrees – the Greek system does not, in fact, involve a sustained quest for co-ordination in transposition either at the political[52] or the administrative levels. The similarities between the French and the British system should not be over-estimated in that respect. The fact that successive French Prime Ministers have felt the need to remind ministers (and departments) of the need to (a) reflect on the potential impact and implementation-related exigencies of new EU proposals ahead of negotiations in Brussels and (b) ensure the timely and co-ordinated transposition of EU legislation indicates the difference between the two systems: what is routinely done in Whitehall has to be actively sought in Paris despite the direct link between the SGG and SGAE on the one hand and the French Prime Minister on the other.[53]

This leads to the expectation of variegated implementation records.[54] Fragmented systems can be expected to have a more problematic implementation record than integrated systems. Integrated structures are more likely to be stake-sensitive (Elmore 1978). This is an inherent element built into the implementation structure that encourages prospective thinking. The detection of implementation problems is easier in integrated structures and the same applies to problem-solving, at least in the short term. Given that EU policies often introduce enduring changes at the national level, implementation is likely to be problematic in fragmented systems because these systems are less likely to take into account EU requirements when they make policy in these or even neighbouring policy areas. Finally, demand for fixing is likely to be greater in fragmented politico-administrative structures because of the increased likelihood of problematic implementation.

Although the preceding discussion has led to the formulation of tentative general insights, it is important to note that the dynamics of implementation are likely to differ across areas or types of public policy (Lowi 1964; 1972). This is why a case study is necessary. The liberalisation of public procurement will be examined in the next three chapters. Chapter 3 presents the EU's public procurement policy and maps the institutional terrain in the three central governments with a focus on the handling of public procurement policy. Chapters 4 and 5 discuss the macro-implementation of this policy in Greece, France and Britain.

Notes

1 This Ministry was later re-named Ministry of National Economy and, since 2004, Ministry of Economy and Finance.
2 The remit of this post was very broad since the minister was responsible for the whole range of relations with the EC (Decision of the Prime Minister 565/1977).
3 Specialised training programmes for civil servants and judges were created in an attempt to resolve this problem.
4 The powers of these ministers remained unchanged throughout the 1980s and 1990s and included the *de facto* power to co-ordinate the formulation of policy and the formal power to represent Greece in EC/EU institutions assisting or standing in for the Minister of Foreign Affairs.
5 Nevertheless, most of its staff stemmed from technical ministries.
6 This body had already operated in the late 1970s and was subsequently abandoned when the Government Council was established in the 1980s. The Committee was re-established initially informally in the early 1990s and subsequently formally in 1994 (Xiros 2006, 170–1). Currently, it is chaired by the Prime Minister and includes six ministers, namely the Ministers of Foreign Affairs, National Economy, Home Affairs, Defence, Environment and Education (Presidential Decree 63/2005).
7 Collective decisions were often seen as superfluous after the presentation of the government's programme in parliament (Athanassopoulos 1986, 92).
8 During Simitis' eight-year tenure (1996–2004), the Cabinet met 175 times. The inner Cabinet held 64 formal and 34 informal meetings (Simitis 2005, 458).
9 The Committee for the Co-ordination of EU Policy (Act of the Ministerial Council 288 of 23 December 1996) was chaired either by the Minister of Foreign Affairs or his Deputy and normally included as full members the Ministers of National Economy, Finance, Development, Agriculture, Employment and Social Security, Merchant Shipping, Transport and Communications.
10 Moreover, the Committee for the Organisation and the Co-ordination of International Economic Relations also dealt with economic aspects of EU affairs.
11 Currently the committee has thirty members, all of whom are members of the Greek Parliament.
12 In 1979 Parliament gave very broad powers to the government for the transposition of the *acquis* and future EU legislation (Law 945/1979). This arrangement was extended repeatedly. Examples include Laws 1440/1984 and 2367/1995. Moreover, the scope of the delegation of legislative power was extended in 1990 (Law 1880/1990, Art. 2).

Patterns of institutional change 55

13 This also included the supervision of the measures taken by other ministries.
14 Their unit reports directly to the Minister. Since 2003 the Head of the unit was appointed national co-ordinator for the transposition of EU legislation and the notification of national measures to the European Commission (Yiombré and Kapitsina 2008).
15 The activity of the Secretary General of the Simitis-led Cabinet and the hands-on approach of individual ministers has contributed to the improvement of Greece's record (Yiombré and Kapitsina 2008).
16 This is so, in part, because after 2004 the Ministry of Economy and Finance had ceased monitoring systematically the transposition of EU legislation into national law (*To Vima* 1 October 2006).
17 It has been occupied by a number of already important or future prominent members of the French political *élite*, like Mollet, Pflimlin and Mitterrand.
18 Since 2002 the senior official who occupies this post is also the Prime Minister's European affairs advisor.
19 This was also illustrated by the gradual abandonment of the so-called Elysée committees that he had created. They also included the Prime Minister, the principal ministers and senior civil servants. There were four Elysée committees dealing with Algeria, foreign affairs, European affairs and economic policy (Gerbet 1969, 205).
20 The development of the administrative structures dealing with EC policy after 1980 followed (in general terms) the patterns of the 1960s and 1970s. Despite the differences concerning their status, the services dealing with international affairs within technical ministries, continued the handling of EC policy. For detailed discussions see Lequesne (1987, 281–9; 1993, 39–42), Le Vigan (1990), Carnelutti (1992) and Lequertier (1994).
21 This post ceased to exist only during the first six months (March to August 1986) of the first *cohabitation*. It was restored (Décret 86–1029) at the request of Jean-Bernard Raimond, then Foreign Minister, who was overwhelmed by the functional pressures produced by this 'dual' portfolio. This request was backed by President Mitterrand's policy on European affairs.
22 Roland Dumas (Décret 83–1135) and Edith Cresson (Décret 88–724) are two examples.
23 Elisabeth Guigou is the case in point (Décret 90–980).
24 Edith Cresson's terms of reference demonstrate this point for they included the responsibility for the implementation of the single market project and the adaptation of the French economy, in collaboration with economic and social actors. Since the second half of the 1990s, the terms of reference changed this post into a specialised foreign affairs minister (see, e.g. Décrets 97–724; 2002–908; 2005–715).
25 Anand Menon's perceptive distinction between apparent and effective co-ordination (2000, 97) further supports this view.
26 The *Quai d'Orsay* retains responsibility for the EU's common foreign and security policy.
27 Prior to the establishment of the *délégations*, the chairman of the foreign affairs commission was very keen to underline their subordinate status. He therefore stressed the fact that the *délégations* were no more than an *intermediary* between the government and the commissions; the latter alone had the responsibility for issues of substance (Laporte 1981, 133).

28 For a different assessment see Rizzutto (2004).
29 Since 1999 the SGCI provides government ministers with information that allows (but does not compel) them to inform the two Houses how their resolutions were taken into account in the course of negotiations at the level of the EU (République Française 1999, annex, VII).
30 Their adoption requires authorisation from Parliament and the President's assent. The latter is more than a formality. Between 1986 and 1988 socialist President Mitterrand refused to sign a number of *ordonnances* embodying the privatisation programme of Chirac's conservative government (Burdeau, Hamon and Troper 1993, 623). The French government uses this method despite the fact that the members of the two assemblies have voiced their concerns about it (Délégation du Sénat pour l'Union européenne 2002, 4).
31 Law 2001-1 is one relatively recent example of a law that allowed the government to use *ordonnances* in order to transpose EU legislation into French law.
32 Even the aforementioned case of Edith Cresson was exceptional in that, first, the emphasis on the completion of the internal market (Décret 88-724, Art. 1) was the result of her status as minister (whereas most of her predecessors and many of her successors had junior status) and second, this division of labour lasted only for two years.
33 The SGCI also promoted contacts between other parts of the French central government with the European Commission (Lequesne 1993, 128).
34 The *Conseil d'État* is consulted in order to determine the nature of the required national text and the route that has to be followed (through the government or the French Parliament).
35 The *Direction des Affaires Juridiques* (DAJ – Directorate for Legal Affairs) of the *Quai d'Orsay* and the legal unit of the SGCI have horizontal competence for legal issues. DAJ acts as a think tank on legal issues involving the interpretation of EU legislation and represents France in the ECJ (Lequesne 1993, 92–6).
36 In addition to the EU directives in force, the database indicates the stage of transposition that they have reached and the specific administrative units that deal with each directive.
37 The *intra*-departmental element of the issue of co-ordination has also been highlighted when Prime Minister Jospin asked his ministers to ensure that each ministry has one focal point in charge of co-ordinating transposition (République Française 1998). Prime Minister Raffarin's circular of September 2004 further enhanced this arrangement by requesting ministers to appoint two officials – including a member of their *cabinet* – to act as contact points for all issues regarding transposition (République Française 2004).
38 In addition one can note the extreme case of Directive 2000/26 on insurance against civil liability in respect of the use of motor vehicles where officials of the Ministry of Economy and Finance refused to attend co-ordination meetings intended to resolve a disagreement with the officials of the Ministry of Justice (Assemblée nationale. Délégation pour l'Union européenne 2003, 27).
39 It was too important to be left in the hands of one ministerial department.
40 It is perceived as a 'pro-European' department and as a result, it has attracted criticism from politicians (Young and Sloman 1982, 80; Clarke 1992, 107).
41 The Ambassador who heads UKRep is always drawn from the ranks of the FCO. Desk officers are staff seconded from Whitehall departments. UKRep staff ensure

Patterns of institutional change

that the system of same day reporting provides a regular flow of information to Whitehall.
42 It meets at official – EQ(O) – and senior official – EQ(O*) – level (Kassim 2000, 35).
43 It also ensures that the briefing provided by the Prime Minister's Policy Directorate takes account of EU aspects.
44 Since 2000 the Head of the European Secretariat (a senior diplomat) is also the Prime Minister's advisor on European affairs. Sir Stephen Wall was the first simultaneous incumbent of these two posts.
45 The pattern of policy making may change when different parties prevail in Westminster and the Scottish and Welsh administrations (Bulmer *et al.* 2006, 88).
46 The remainder are subject to the negative resolution procedure. In this case, the instrument becomes effective automatically unless it is annulled by a resolution (Greenwood and Wilson 1989, 276).
47 Quasi-legislative devices such as administrative circulars and codes of practice are also used by the government for that purpose (Drewry 1995, 457).
48 In addition, in 2003 all ministerial departments were asked (with the Prime Minister's backing) to designate one official in charge of transposition and those that had to improve their performance were supported and monitored (Assemblée nationale. Délégation pour l'Union européenne 2004, 29).
49 It is important to note here that instead of being the result of pressure for convergence, these similarities mirror historically defined (i.e. pre-existing) characteristics of the three systems in question.
50 Arguably, the prospect of a ministerial career of majority MPs is rendered less likely if they systematically vote against the government.
51 Though they often take official files with them when they depart from their posts after government re-shuffles, they – perhaps unsurprisingly – leave files that concern alleged infringements of EU legislation.
52 Prime Minister Simitis' tenure (1996–2004) was an exception in the 25-year period covered by this study.
53 In more general terms, although both the French and the British systems have been construed as tightly organised systems – in contrast to the Greek loosely coupled system (Metcalfe 1988) – subtle but important differences persist between them (Metcalfe 1987, 19–21).
54 For example, between 1973 and 1998 forty-one cases have been brought to the ECJ against the UK and 188 against France (Bulmer and Armstrong 2003, 399–400). For a discussion of 'non-compliance' and different national records see Börzel (2001).

3

EU public procurement policy

The purpose of this chapter is twofold. First, it seeks to examine the emergence and the development of the European Union's public procurement policy, especially the changes that it was meant to bring about at the national level. Second, in the light of the institutionalist argument that forms the basis of this book, it presents the national institutional structures (at the level of central governments) that deal with public procurement policy in Greece, France and Britain.

Public procurement is an interesting case study for a number of reasons. EU policy in this area has introduced significant changes in the three states examined in this book. This policy has remained constant over time: it essentially relies on a number of procedural requirements. This allows the discussion of the way in which their central governments have coped over time with the exigencies of implementation. In addition, its economic importance was and remains very significant and this is one of the reasons why it is a key part of the effort to establish the single European market. Indeed, it is a cornerstone of the single market and promotes its logic by placing emphasis on liberalisation. Finally, it is a classic example of regulation[1] on the basis of directives, which is the main way used by the EU in its effort to shape policy outcomes and an area where the distinction between micro-implementation (i.e. the actual award of contracts) and macro-implementation (i.e. the action taken by central governments in their effort to steer micro-implementation) discussed in Chapter 1 can be established.

In the light of the fact that the EU's policy in this field focuses on the regulation of the behaviour of awarding entities, the analysis of micro-implementation would require the examination of the award procedures used by them. Given the number of entities[2] that are covered by the directives, this is a Herculean task.[3] Although only part of these entities are located in the three member states examined in this book, one cannot aspire to examine the behaviour of every single one of them and cover every single advertised contract.[4] After all, focusing on the award of the advertised contracts would necessarily be based on the assumption that all awarding entities have actually

EU public procurement policy

implemented a fundamental aspect of the policy, namely the obligation to advertise (at the level of the EU) every contract that falls in the remit of the relevant directives. In other words, this approach takes for granted that a fundamental objective of the policy has been achieved. Clearly, this is an unrealistic assumption. So, how did the EU become involved in this policy area and which form did its involvement take?

The early days

Until the beginning of the 1970s the provisions of the Treaty of Rome (Articles 7, 30, 52 and 59 in particular) were the only possible legal basis for the action of the EU. They incorporated basic principles of the EU such as the prohibition of discrimination on the basis of nationality, the free movement of goods, the freedom of establishment and the freedom to provide services that individuals and companies enjoyed.

It is precisely the abstract character of these provisions that is deemed to have rendered them insufficient for the liberalisation of public procurement. The adoption of a minimalist strategy would mean that the correct implementation of the policy would place substantial emphasis on the ability and the willingness of private actors – i.e. potential suppliers, the policy's target groups – to actively employ the concept of direct effect[5] as the basic method leading to the liberalisation of the market. The rejection of a minimalist legal strategy indicated, indirectly but unambiguously, the recognition of the inability of these provisions to promote liberalisation in the domain of public procurement.

Thus, at least a minimum of European legislation was necessary in order to open the hitherto protected markets. From the perspective of implementation analysis, the exclusive use of directives constitutes a clear political choice because it automatically creates a *two-tier system*. This, first, entails the adoption of national measures for the transposition of these directives into national legislation. This, in turn, entails the involvement of an *increased number of actors* with different – and possibly conflicting interests – and the subsequent possible creation of tensions between them. The potential for delays also means that a window of opportunity is created for various actors who may try to protect interests that have not been taken into account 'sufficiently' in the formulation process, by attempting to steer it in the direction that suits them.

The logic of the EU's public procurement policy

The logic of EU policy in this domain is based on three fundamental elements, namely selectivity, the principle of transparency and the equal treatment of tenderers. First, the EU's policy is *selective* and it is not meant to abolish national systems. This characteristic of the EU's policy is illustrated through the use of *quantitative thresholds* for the definition of its scope. In other words, the directives cover contracts whose value equals or exceeds the thresholds. Secondly, the basic means used for the liberalisation of the market is the principle of *transparency*. The awarding entities that are covered by the directives are obliged to advertise the contracts across the EU[6] if their value equals or exceeds the threshold. The scope of this obligation covers a number of awarding entities whose definition is integrated into the directives. It is believed that the principle of transparency enables potential tenderers from other member states to submit tenders, thus promoting competition. Thirdly, this principle is complemented by the obligation of awarding entities to treat European tenderers *equally*, irrespective of their nationality. Indeed, objective criteria aim at the limitation (if not the elimination) of discriminatory practices used by awarding entities, thus enhancing competition between tenderers. Moreover, these criteria operate both at the level of the initial selection of viable and reliable companies and the award of contracts to them. Consequently, the EU's policy mix focuses mainly on the allocation of the contracts through the regulation of the behaviour of the awarding authorities.

Given that EU funds are very often used by national authorities for public procurement (mainly works) projects, there is a risk that the EU may end up funding projects that are carried out in a way that violates the principles of its own procurement policy. This is why the Commission instituted a system of monitoring the compatibility of national award practices where EU funds are used with the EU's public procurement policy (Commission of the European Communities 1989a). The system is based on a questionnaire which has to be completed by the national authorities that apply for financial assistance from the EU. It contains information about the type of the awarding authority, the purpose, value and duration of the contract, the award procedure, the publication of the tender notice, the technical capacity and commercial standing of the participants. On making the payments, the European Commission assumes that the contracting authority has complied with the EU's public procurement rules. Payment is suspended if no references are given relating to the publication of notices in the *Official Journal of the European Union* and no declaration is made to the effect that the appropriate procedures have been followed. The European Commission makes sample checks[7] mainly in relation to qualitative selection criteria and award procedures. In cases of breaches of EU obligations, both suspension of payments and refunds are used in accordance with the specific rules of each Fund.

The scope of the EU's public procurement policy

The EU-wide regulation of public procurement commenced from the field of public *works* in the early 1970s and went on to cover supplies (late 1970s) and the provision of services (early 1990s). Directive 71/305 became a cornerstone of the then EEC's policy in this field as it contained i) a set of principles guiding the co-ordination of national award procedures, ii) a definition of the awarding authorities that it covered, iii) a definition of an open and a restricted award procedure, iv) a set of obligatory rules regarding the publicity of contracts, v) a set of objective qualitative selection criteria regarding the technical and financial capacity and reliability of the companies and vi) most importantly, two mutually excluding award criteria, namely the lowest price and the most economically advantageous offer. The definition of public *supplies* in Directive 77/62 shifted from a rather vague reference to the 'delivery of products' that included siting and installation operations to a more precise definition (Flamme and Flamme 1988, 456) that covers the purchase, lease, rental and hire purchase with or without option to buy products. The regulation of public supply procedures at the level of the EU has been based on a strong element of commercial policy which directly affects the unity of the single market. This reflects the fact that – unlike works projects – supplies are frequent and repetitive, they concern a wide range of products and practically every public authority. Finally, the regulation of the provision of *services* completed the regulatory framework of public procurement in the EU in the early 1990s. Directive 92/50 defined services by means of a negative sentence, which excludes (among other aspects) supplies, works, arbitration and conciliation, employment, voice telephony and satellite services. This reflected both the very technical and complex nature of the field and the willingness of the formulators to avoid 'loopholes' that could undermine implementation.

The utilities companies – in addition to public authorities[8] – which are active in the fields of water, energy, transport and telecommunications came under the remit of the EU's public procurement regime in the early 1990s. The initial exclusion of these companies from the EU's regulatory framework was mainly based on their legal status.[9] Furthermore, their operation in the marketplace included commercial and industrial activities that had to be taken into consideration. Although it took almost twenty years from the adoption of Directive 71/305 to the final inclusion of utilities in this regulatory framework, their initial exclusion has never escaped the attention of the EC/EU for reasons which finally led to the adoption of Directives 90/531, 92/13 and 93/38. These reasons are twofold. First, attention has shifted from the question of their status to the function that they perform; this led to the indisputable recognition of the fact that they perform public functions by providing goods (water and energy) and services (transport and telecommunications) to the public and private sectors. Secondly, the Commission discovered that they operated in sizeable but closed markets, frequently as a result of the use of their 'exclusive or special rights' in a way that restricted competition (Commission of the European Communities 1988). Defined in Art. 2 § 1 of Directive 90/531 as entities which are *public* authorities or undertakings or (in the opposite case) entities that operate on the basis of *special or exclusive rights granted by a competent authority of a member state*, utilities came – in the early 1990s – under the remit of the EU's public procurement regime only in so far as their activities in the water, energy, transport and telecommunications sectors are concerned.[10] Procurement in the utilities sector is outside of the remit of this book; rather the focus remains on the 'public sector' directives.

The inadequacy of the existing national and European legal arrangements, especially in the light of the speed of award procedures and the unreliability of undertakings for the correction of certain infringements – led to the establishment of a set of minimum *review procedures* in the field of public procurement, commonly known as 'Remedies Directives' (Flamme and Flamme 1990; Arrowsmith 1993). Indeed public authorities are covered by Directive 89/665 and utilities by Directive 92/13. These directives stipulate that national rules must be available to any person having or having had an interest in obtaining a contract. They include i) *interim measures* for the suspension of award procedures or the implementation of any decision taken by award entities, ii) the *setting aside* of decisions taken unlawfully and iii) the award of *damages* to persons harmed by an infringement. The effective implementation of the decisions taken by the bodies that are responsible for the review procedures must be ensured by the member states. Although these bodies need not be judicial in character, their decisions must be legally binding.

Recent developments[11]

By proposing a new legislative package in May 2000, the Commission sought – after a lengthy consultation process – to simplify and clarify existing EU legislation and to adapt it to a changing economic environment, in line with its wider effort to shift attention from the creation to the actual operation of the single market, in line with its SLIM initiative (Simpler Legislation for the Internal Market). More specifically the Commission proposed the merging of the three main EU directives (covering works, supplies and services contracts respectively) into one coherent text, the simplified presentation of the thresholds and (more importantly) the re-drafting of the legislative provisions in a manner that reflects the various stages of the award process (thus making the directives more user-friendly for policy makers, purchasing officers and interested firms).

The proposal of the Commission also entailed the creation of a new (so-called 'competitive dialogue') award process which would apply to complex contracts. In addition, the Commission sought to improve flexibility by allowing awarding bodies to define their requirements not only on the basis of standards but also in terms of performance, and to take account of market developments. Thus, it proposed the exclusion of the telecommunications sector since it was deemed to have made sufficient progress in terms of ownership and market behaviour to merit more freedom.[12]

EU public procurement policy

Directives 2004/18 and 2004/17 of March 2004 mark a significant step in the direction identified by the Commission. While the former covers works, supply and services contracts which were hitherto covered by three separate texts, the latter co-ordinates the procurement procedures of entities operating in the water, energy, transport and postal services sectors. They are the result of a lengthy process in the course of which individual member states sought to reconcile two conflicting needs, namely greater flexibility for their own awarding authorities (usually in markets where competition is already quite strong) on the one hand, and a tighter legislation that would lead to greater accordance with the spirit of EU procurement legislation in other member states whose compliance record is poor, on the other.

More importantly, the new directives explicitly provide for the establishment of central purchasing bodies in the member states. The establishment of these bodies is not compulsory but given that they can – by definition – make purchases on behalf of other bodies, they can help improve the implementation of EU public policy by reducing the number of transactions that individual awarding bodies need to make as well as the need for the provision of training, guidance etc. Moreover, the directives regulate the use of framework agreements for public procurement purposes. These are agreements that establish the terms for the subsequent award of contracts and are used extensively for repetitive purchases.

In addition, the new directives reflect the jurisprudence of the European Court of Justice which ruled that environmental and social considerations (such as emission standards and the needs of disabled people) are not necessarily barriers to greater competition in the sector (European Union 2000; Commission of the European Communities 2001a; 2001b). The final texts incorporate the vast majority of the proposals made by the Commission including a controversial proposal regarding the exclusion of bidders who have been found guilty of corruption, illegal tax avoidance or professional misconduct. Although the final version of this provision was somewhat diluted in that respect, it marks a significant change in the modernisation of procurement practices in Europe.

In line with the proposal of the Commission, the final text also excludes the telecommunications sector, thus acknowledging (or rewarding) progress towards the use of competitive practices by companies that operate therein. The slightly higher thresholds used for the definition of the scope of the new directives also reflect the conflict between the member states (and the European Parliament) which sought to restrict the scope of the new directives (thereby giving greater autonomy to awarding authorities) and the promoters of greater liberalisation. Nevertheless, one must not exaggerate the importance of this distinction. The logic of competition, value for money, transparency and non-discrimination gained significant ground, not only as the direct result of the EU's public procurement policy but also due to other constraints including budgetary restrictions and the emphasis on reduced public spending that characterises the euro zone. Finally, the new directives promote the use of electronic signatures as a means to increase the speed and reduce the cost of cross-border procurement.

Implications for national authorities

Public procurement can be approached from two different angles. In a narrow sense, it can be defined as the attempt of public authorities to use public funds so as to procure supplies, services or works that they need. By contrast, these needs can be fulfilled as part of an effort to achieve wider socio-economic objectives when governments direct the choices made by awarding authorities. These methods may concern segments of the population of a given country (such as the unemployed), sectors of the economy (e.g. information technology), specific firms (for example, 'national champions'), or territorial units, such as regions. These methods appear to contradict the logic of the free market which permeates the EU's public procurement policy, precisely because they entail the use of some form of discriminatory measures.[13]

The second approach to public procurement is known to every member state (Woolcock, Hodges and Schreiber 1991, 28–9). In the past some of them have used discriminatory measures in the field of public procurement in order to achieve wider socio-economic objectives. Indeed part of the ECJ's jurisprudence on public procurement concerns the compatibility of these schemes with EU legislation (Commission of the European Communities 1989b; Bovis 1998, 233–41). In the UK in the past these methods consisted in (i) a price advantage (5%) given to tenderers whose bid had a positive effect on employment in Northern Ireland, (ii) the purchase of home-made aircraft material by British airline corporations and (iii) the purchase of British-made computers when there was no undue price differential (Turpin 1972, 251–3). In the case of Greece, a price advantage of (a) up to 7% over the lowest tender was applied to enterprises established at a distance of more than 50 kilometres from Athens and (b) up to 10% in cases of companies established in the Greek islands. In France public procurement has been a fundamental part of the industrial programmes that led to the establishment of 'national champions' (Hayward 1995).

Public procurement is important in Europe not only because of its potential use, but also because of its sheer size. Companies that are active in fields such as high technology or even traditional heavy industries may depend on public procurement for a very significant portion of their sales (Jeanrenaud 1984, 152). Moreover, the importance of public procurement is also based on its overall volume. Indeed, it has been estimated that between 10 and 20% of government expenditure (excluding public firms) concerns payments for the purchase of goods and services (WS Atkins Management Consultants 1988, 16–9). Furthermore, the total volume of public procurement in the mid-1980s represented around 15% of the EC's GDP. These figures concerned mainly building and construction, equipment goods, services, energy, water, transport and communications, which are areas of economic activity regulated by the EU's public procurement policy. More importantly, the aforementioned report (which covered only France, Germany, Belgium, Italy and the UK) estimated that less than 2% of public purchases came from foreign suppliers, thus illustrating a very low level of import penetration. The potential and actual importance of public procurement for the European economy and its importance for the establishment of a proper single market provided the impetus for the involvement of the EU in this policy area.

The logic of the EU's action in this sector of the economy is characterised by the predominance of the free market model. Its introduction and development (especially during the 1980s) were designed to produce significant changes at the domestic level. The approach adopted at the level of the EU reflects the belief that:

> many benefits ... will accrue from a genuine liberalization of this sector throughout the EC ... First, the introduction of EC-wide competitive tendering ... will greatly increase the opportunities for industry ... to expand both in the Community and the home market. Expansion will enable economies of scale to be realized, thus reducing costs, while the spur of competition will stimulate efficiency. A considerable part of the resultant savings is likely to be put back into developing the businesses concerned through modernization of plant and infrastructure and research and development, leading to the creation of new jobs. Secondly, governments and the users of the services they provide will benefit from a wider choice of goods and services both in terms of quality and price. Substantial savings in government budgets will be possible and the general public's wants will be satisfied at lower cost.
> (Commission of the European Communities 1987, 1–2)

The EU's public procurement policy is a regulatory policy *par excellence* for a number of reasons. It is based predominantly on the use of coercion (by means of legally binding measures) whose objective is i) the elimination of discriminatory practices and ii) the promotion of transparent and objective procedures stipulated in the directives. Hence, the theory that has been incorporated into the policy can be summarised as follows: if awarding authorities advertise opportunities for contracts and then use the explicit and common criteria defined in the directives, competition will be improved and efficiency gains will follow. More specifically, awarding authorities are obliged to advertise contracts above specific (and periodically revised) thresholds[14] and use specific selection and award criteria, namely the lowest price or the most economical offer.

The development of the policy has led it beyond the limits of a mere framework for the co-ordination of national policies which was the initial objective. It is a comprehensive legislative framework covering almost all aspects of this policy area.[15] This view is supported by the use of secondary legislation due to the ineffectiveness of Art. 30 and other 'state-building' provisions (Page and Dimitrakopoulos 1997) of the Treaty. In more general terms, the content of these provisions is characterised by the constant reinforcement of two aspects of the EU's public procurement regime, namely its scope and its density. The scope has been extended from works to supplies and then services and from the public to the private arena. Density has been reinforced by the regulation of an increasing number of policy dimensions, mainly publicity requirements, selection criteria and award criteria. The development of these directives and the changes that have been introduced as a result of EU (or broader international) developments has led to the need for legislative consolidation achieved initially through Directives 93/36 (supplies), 93/37 (works) and 93/38 (utilities) and a decade later through Directives 2004/17 and 2004/18.

Unlike the regulation of the procurement activities in the utilities sector, public authorities face a more robust regulatory framework. Indeed, one could describe the part of the policy that concerns utilities as a mere safety net which is meant to deter them from adopting uncompetitive practices. In that sense the content of the policy is rather negative, unlike the part that concerns public authorities which is characterised by a more resolute and positive drive towards competitive practices.

Coercion is used in order to distribute obligations and rights to awarding entities. The content of the obligations focuses on the constant limitation of their ability to use *discretion* and the drive towards *transparent* and *objective* procedures. This indicates the *extent of change* introduced by the EU's public procurement policy: change is quite extensive. The aim is to liberalise previously protected markets. The increasing intensity of the policy which has been mentioned earlier is orientated primarily towards the allocation of the contracts and concerns the definition of their content only in a subsidiary manner. The efficacy of coercion presupposes the existence of credible sanctions regulated by Directives 89/665 and 92/13.

The EU's public procurement policy does not necessarily lead to the adoption of a centralised or a decentralised procurement system. In other words, it has no direct implications for the allocation of regulatory power at the national level. However, it places substantial emphasis on the role of market players – mainly actual and potential tenderers. The willingness of the member states to entrust market players (rather than public institutions like the European Commission) with the task of monitoring the competition game is illustrated by the adoption of the aforementioned Remedies Directives. This idea emanates from the logic upon which this policy is based, namely the strict economic dimension of public procurement and the subsequent substantial limitation of its scope. However, this choice is not devoid of negative repercussions. Both the use of market forces in general and the specific use of the legal concept of direct effect by market players rely heavily on the willingness of the latter to 'bite the hand that feeds them' (Commission of the European Communities 1990, 25). Clearly, this danger

EU *public procurement policy* 67

of market failure (Woolcock 1991, 128) is an inherent feature of the approach adopted by the EU.

Moreover, one must also underline the direct repercussion of the Remedies Directives upon the institutional autonomy of the member states. Although this is not the policy's most developed dimension, the mere existence of these directives limits the institutional autonomy of the member states by prescribing minimum levels of protection for actual or potential tenderers.[16]

This book focuses on macro-implementation, that is the way in which central governments steer the behaviour of the awarding entities in the desired direction, that is the equal treatment of tenderers based in the EU, irrespective of their nationality. In the light of the approach to implementation analysis outlined in Chapter 1, it is important to map the relevant national institutions, that is describe the division of labour relating to this policy area at the national level. Which institutions deal with procurement policy? What kind of changes, if any, has the EU's policy in this field brought about to the national institutional structures? More generally, have they evolved over time and if so, how? This is important because the emphasis that the policy has placed on market players and awarding entities does not mean that they are the only parts of the implementation structure built into the policy. This structure also includes national and EU institutions, such as ministries, courts and parliaments. This is why the discussion of the implementation process must be preceded by the presentation of the domestic institutional structures that deals with public procurement policy.

Institutional mapping at the level of central governments

Greece

Responsibility for public procurement was (and remains) dispersed within the Greek central government. However, significant changes have occurred, especially during the 1990s in response to issues that concern the implementation of the EU's public procurement policy. These will be discussed in the next two chapters since they constitute the most significant indications of the use of learning and steering in the government's (largely successful) effort to improve implementation. As a result, the presentation that follows will deal with general, as opposed to EU-specific, issues.

Three ministerial departments deal with public procurement policy in the Greek central government. The Ministry of the Environment, Spatial Planning and Public Works, the Ministry of Development (which now incorporates the Ministry of Trade and the Ministry of Industry that used to be separate ministerial departments) and the Ministry of Economy and Finance (formerly Ministry of Co-ordination and Ministry of National Economy) deal with public works, supplies and services respectively. The first two departments have a long experience in their respective parts of this policy area. By contrast, the latter was chosen in the early 1990s – largely as a response to the extension of the EU's public procurement regime to services – to deal with procurement in services for two reasons. First, the lack of obvious alternatives meant that the Athenian bureaucracy did not possess another institutional focal point that could absorb this function. Second, a senior civil servant in the then Ministry of National Economy possessed both long experience and the relevant academic background and this served as a justification for the decision not to allocate responsibility for this sector to the Ministry of Trade whose status was being challenged during the 1980s and 1990s, until it merged with the Ministry of Industry.

Moreover, the repeated transfer of responsibility for public supplies from one ministry to another throughout the twentieth century (Zorbala 1992, 151) can be taken as an illustration of the lack of a long-term perspective in this policy area, especially because the last transfers coincided with the first period of EU membership. The transfer of responsibility for public supplies from the Ministry of Trade to the Ministry of National Economy in 1982 – where it remained until 1985 – coincided with the initial phase of the transposition of the EU's procurement legislation in Greece and is linked to some problems in this process (*infra*, Chapter 4). Each one of the aforementioned ministries deals with policy formulation as well as implementation within its particular remit.[17]

France
The *Commission Centrale des Marchés* (CCM – Central Procurement Commission) has traditionally been the most prominent part of the French administrative structures that deal with public procurement policy. This interministerial body was created in 1959[18] to resolve the co-ordination problems that emanated from the dispersed procurement methods used by various public bodies (Dillemann 1987, 95–8). The *Code des Marchés Publics* (Public Procurement Code) that incorporates most of the French legislation regarding public procurement provided the legal basis for this pivotal structure. The CCM was placed under the authority of the Minister of Economy and Finance, and was responsible for the formulation and the implementation of French public procurement policy. The only changes that are linked to the EU's public procurement policy were the establishment of the international affairs unit along with the recruitment of additional staff absorbed by the existing administrative structures and the creation of a junior post at the SGCI. Furthermore, other ministries were also responsible for some aspects of procurement policy, namely the Ministry of the Interior which deals with local authorities and the Ministry of Equipment, Housing, Transport and Tourism that dealt with some public work projects.[19] However, the authority of the CCM was not contested and, unlike the aforementioned departments, it covered every aspect of this policy area and the whole of the policy process.

Until the end of the 1990s the CCM was composed of three sections (administrative, technical and economic) and an international affairs unit.

EU public procurement policy 69

The administrative section dealt with proposals regarding the content of the Public Procurement Code. The economic section was responsible for promoting the optimisation of public procurement, in particular by means of increased competition. Finally, the technical section dealt with issues regarding standardisation, technical specifications and the harmonisation of technical documents used for procurement purposes in France. The CCM also had powers of enquiry[20] and the right to make policy proposals. In addition to this institution, the Minister of Economy and Finance had the power to create (in conjunction with other relevant ministers) permanent study groups on procurement and draw on their expertise so as to rationalise public procurement in France.

The *commissions spécialisées des marchés* (CSM – specialised commissions for procurement) were an important additional aspect of the institutional architecture (Dillemann 1987, 106). Established in the early 1970s,[21] these were consultative bodies that had the power to object to the way in which particular procurement cases were handled by the awarding authorities but their negative opinions could be (and were actually often) over-ruled. All the official in charge of a procurement project had to do was to explain this decision to their superior.[22] The reform introduced by successive French governments since 1999 led to changes in the institutional arrangements that deal with public procurement policy in France.

The reform was motivated in part by the need to simplify the system, enhance its transparency, improve legal certainty and ameliorate its capacity to prevent corruption, such as the cases that were being investigated when the government initiated the reform (Ministère de l'Economie, des Finances et de l'Industrie 1999, 4–5). The most important institutional aspect of the reform was the establishment of the *Commission des marchés publics de l'État* (CMPE – State Procurement Commission) in 2004 (Décret 2004–1299). This body is mandated to assist both ministers and officials[23] responsible for individual projects, by providing advice. This advice concerns the preparation of the vast majority of procurement projects worth at least six million euros (excluding tax).[24] Its opinions, recommendations and reserves are not binding. Rather, they focus on the definition of the need that a procurement project is meant to satisfy, the choice of procedure, the clarity of the relevant documentation, the technical aspects of competition or negotiation, and the financial aspects of the contract (Commission des Marchés Publics de l'État 2006, 7). Its role in implementation will be discussed in Chapter 5.

The UK
The implementation of the EU's procurement policy in the United Kingdom has not led to the creation of new administrative units. The only significant change concerned, initially, the recruitment of additional staff to the Treasury which has overall responsibility for this policy. The remit of the Treasury covered policy formulation, negotiation in Brussels, transposition

and implementation.[25] Within the Treasury, this policy was handled – until the end of 1999 – by the Procurement Group which was headed by an under secretary and comprised the Central Unit on Purchasing (CUP) and the Procurement Policy Team whose Head also acted as the representative of the UK in the EU's Advisory Committee for Public Contracts. Moreover, the group drew many of its staff (including three of its Heads during the 1990s) from outside the civil service. The intensity of the Treasury's predominance in this policy area was illustrated by the fact that the CUP also advised central government departments on the use of best procurement practice. The Treasury's traditional leading role reflects a view of this policy as a predominantly economic issue focusing on procurement as a fundamental part of public expenditure.

Between the advent of New Labour to power in May 1997 and April 2000 the Procurement Policy Team (a joint unit of the Treasury and the DTI) was responsible for procurement policy (House of Commons 23 July 1997, col. 674). Since April 2000 these roles are exercised by the Office of Government Commerce (OGC) which is an independent office of the Treasury.[26] The OGC is responsible for policy developments in the domestic, EU and international spheres, representation of the UK in EU fora, the transposition of EU legislation into UK law and issues regarding infringements of EU legislation (Office of Government Commerce 2006a; 2006d; 2006e).

Since its establishment in April 2000, the OGC is responsible for the provision of guidance and expertise for the successful implementation of procurement projects. It comprises six directorates. One – the Policy, Practice and Legal Directorate – sets the policy and the best practice framework within which government procurement ought to operate – this is the main source of 'guidance, advice and support to departments' (HM Treasury 2001, 77), and two specialise in IT and construction projects (the IT Directorate, and the Property and Construction Directorate).[27] The specialised directorates are explicitly mandated to generate guidance and advice in their particular areas of activity, in co-operation with the Policy, Practice and Legal Directorate. Similar to the recent reform of the French system, the OGC as a whole reflects the demand within Whitehall for an 'one-stop shop' that aims to provide consistent procurement advice as well as procurement services. A key part of its tasks is the identification and the dissemination of best practice (HM Treasury 2001).

Further changes were introduced as a result of devolution. Although public procurement is a devolved matter, responsibility for EU affairs is not. As regards specifically the handling of EU public procurement policy, concordats[28] have been signed with the Scottish Executive and the Northern Ireland Executive Committee. They provide for timely consultation and exchange of information between the two levels of government. To that effect, senior officials of the devolved and central administrations meet at least twice every year. In addition, other officers are invited to meetings organised at

EU *public procurement policy* 71

both levels of government as and when the agenda includes items of mutual interest. As regards the formulation of EU policy, the officials of the devolved administrations 'have a role in supporting the single UK negotiating line' and may attend meetings of Council working groups on procurement matters. This is decided in bilateral meetings with the lead Whitehall department in accordance with the concordat on co-ordination of EU policy issues (*infra*, Chapter 2). The devolved administrations have the power to choose between (i) transposing EU legislation separately and (ii) UK implementing legislation to be made by the Treasury. In the former case, they must consult closely with UK ministers. Finally, as regards the handling of cases of alleged infringements, the reply is drafted by the devolved administrations when the issue concerns exclusively the conduct of awarding authorities under the responsibility of the devolved administrations but it has to be agreed with the relevant Whitehall department (at official or ministerial level) prior to being submitted by UKRep. Officials of the devolved administrations are also invited to attend 'package meetings' that are arranged occasionally to discuss procurement-related infringement cases (Scottish Executive n.d.; Northern Ireland Executive Committee n.d.).

Conclusion

The striking difference between the three systems is the dispersal of responsibility for public procurement policy in the Greek central government. Given that the EU directives essentially rely on one uniform policy theory – as demonstrated by the consolidation directives of 2004, a single mechanism could, at least in theory, help co-ordinate the notoriously fragmented (Makridimitris and Passas 1994) Athenian bureaucracy. Nevertheless, the absence of such a mechanism at the administrative level is not necessarily a source of problems for two reasons. On the one hand, individual ministerial departments remain responsible for their own part of procurement policy (works, supplies and services). As a result, a degree of co-ordination may be achieved albeit at a sub-sectoral (i.e. *intra*-ministerial) level. On the other hand, unlike the French and the British systems that provide a clear focal point at the administrative level, the absence from the Greek system of such a mechanism means that when problems occur that go beyond the administrative level or the sub-sectoral remit of individual departments, the solution can be sought only at the political level of the Greek central government. However, co-ordination at that level has been a systemic problem even before the country's accession and goes way beyond the requirements of membership of the EU (Loverdos 1991; Xiros 2006; *infra*, Chapter 2). In contrast, the French and British systems are marked by the presence of a powerful central actor within the national central government.

Both structures have changed over time but these changes do not touch on the key features of the system (especially the need for a central mechanism that acts as a focal point for the entire system) nor do they appear to be directly linked to membership of the EU. Despite their common characteristics – especially the fact that they reflect the logic of an *administration de mission* (Pisani 1956), the French and the British systems differ in one important sense: while the role of the OGC (and, in the past, the Treasury) reflects the sustained *presence* of co-ordination as a cornerstone of the entire system, the reform of the French system indicates the *need* (as well as the partial presence) of such an ethos. As in the case of the co-ordination of EU policy more generally, the French system appears to reflect the quest for more (or better) co-ordination whilst the British system indicates its presence. The discussion of macro-implementation in the next two chapters will examine the impact of this factor.[29]

Notes

1 This is the dominant type of EU policy.
2 In the mid-1990s the directives covered 110,000 entities (European Commission 1996, 5).
3 The enormity of this task is further highlighted by the fact that in 2002 alone, 106,346 invitations to tender were published in the *Official Journal* (European Commission 2004, 6, fig. 2).
4 According to Tenders Electronic Daily (the EU's procurement-related data base), in 2005 Greek, French and British authorities awarded a total of 31,627 contracts.
5 The ECJ has acknowledged the direct effect of the aforementioned Treaty provisions (Rideau 1994, 683–4).
6 This was initially achieved through the publication of notices in a supplement of the *Official Journal of the European Communities* and their electronic dissemination through the Tenders Electronic Daily data base. Since July 1998 the printed edition has been discontinued and the supplement is available electronically through the internet. In both cases the EU covers the cost of publication.
7 The increasing role of the European Commission in this policy area has had direct repercussions on the part of its internal administrative structure that deals with this policy area. Responsibility had been distributed to vertical units of DG III until 1984 when a specific division was established although it did not deal exclusively with this policy area. It focused on public procurement between 1985 and 1988 after its upgrading to a separate directorate composed of two units dealing with the formulation and the implementation of EU policy respectively. Additional Commission officials and national experts were recruited thus producing an increase of more than 40% in the staff dealing with this policy area. The directorate lost its autonomy in September 1990 after its integration into a directorate of the DG that deals with the single market. Subsequent changes included the establishment of a separate directorate for public procurement policy. In 2006 it comprised three units, one dealing with e-procurement as well as international and economic issues, and two that deal with policy formulation and implementation, each covering a large group of member states. As regards the institutional arrangements at the level of the EU one ought to also mention the

EU public procurement policy

Advisory Committee for Public Contracts. This is a consultative committee – initially created in the early 1970s through Decision 71/306 to examine problems in the field of public works, in which Commission officials meet with representatives of the member states to discuss issues regarding EU policy, including implementation problems.

8   Public authorities that are covered by the directives are mentioned in lists (categorised by member state) attached to them. Although there is a clear pattern which has led to the continuous extension of the lists through decisions of the European Commission – Decision 90/380 being an example – one is struck by the divergence that characterises the lists relating to different states. While some of the lists are very detailed, others use rather general expressions in order to include *categories* of authorities without mentioning specific names (Rees 1994, 174). The pattern is not consistent along the lines of specific states. It varies from one directive to another.

9   Some of them are bodies governed by public law while others are governed by private law (Berlin 1991, 14).

10 This provision excludes their activities in other sectors where they are active players as a result of their diversification. Special thresholds apply to them for supply contracts.

11 Between 1993 and 2000 the EU adopted directives 97/52 and 98/4 (concerning, respectively, utilities and works, service and supply contracts) so as to harmonise its legislation with the provisions of the agreement on public procurement concluded at the end of the Uruguay Round. None of these directives has altered the fundamental logic of the EU's policy in this area.

12 The same may apply to other utilities in the future. By contrast, the postal services sector is now covered by the revised EU public procurement regime.

13 It is important to note that these are ideal types which are frequently combined in various policy mixes.

14 Commission Regulation No 2083/2005 of 19 December 2005 set the following thresholds: (a) 422,000 euros for supply and services (including design contests) contracts awarded by entities other than utilities, (b) 5,278,000 euros for works contracts awarded by the same entities, and (c) 137,000 euros for most supply and services contracts awarded by utilities (for the remainder the threshold was set at 211,000 euros).

15 However, this regulatory framework does not cover the execution of procurement contracts.

16 This, in turn, illustrates the growing importance of effectiveness which is at the heart not only of the concept of implementation but also the importance attached to Art. 5 of the Treaty of Rome.

17 Utilities' procurement is dealt with by technical ministries.

18 On the origin of this body and the pre-1959 practice in the French central government see Dillemann (1987, 96–8).

19 It has also absorbed some of the new staff.

20 In addition, it provided administrative support to the *Mission interministérielle d'enquête sur les marchés* (the inter-ministerial task force for enquiry into public procurement) which investigates cases of alleged irregularities (Loi 91–3; *infra*, Chapter 5).

21 They had replaced departmental committees that suffered from internal control problems (Commissions Spécialisées des Marchés 2002, 26).
22 In addition, negative opinions were sometimes used by the financial controller (who was present) to block the process for reasons that were not linked to the availability of funds.
23 It is also important to note that the inter-ministerial nature of this body is meant to promote not only the diffusion of best practice throughout the administration, but also the need to draw on the expertise of officials with various backgrounds. In formal terms, it is composed of three procurement specialists nominated (as president and two vice-presidents) by the Minister of Economy and Finance, two specialists chosen by its president from a list compiled by the government, a representative of the ministry under whose responsibility a procurement project is to be devised and carried out, a *rapporteur général* and the heads (or their representatives) of (a) the legal affairs directorate and (b) the directorate general for competition, consumer affairs and anti-fraud of the Ministry of Economy and Finance. In reality, its President and two Vice-Presidents are members (active or retired) of the *Conseil d'État* or the *Cour des comptes* (Court of Auditors).
24 The CMPE actually retains for detailed examination only a part of the dossiers that are transmitted to it. The majority of the remaining dossiers are returned to the relevant awarding body with the comments of the President or one of the two Vice Presidents. Awarding bodies also have the right to involve the CMPE at any stage of award procedures regarding projects of a smaller value. The CMPE also has the right to (and exceptionally does) submit its observations to the relevant ministers if it considers that their involvement would be useful (*infra*, Chapter 5).
25 Moreover, the partial responsibility of the Department of the Environment – now DEFRA – (alongside the three regional departments) for local authorities, has left the primacy of the Treasury intact. This responsibility follows organisational rather than functional lines. In other words, it covers works, supplies and services contracts and the dividing lines concern sets of bodies (local government authorities) rather than aspects of the policy or stages of the policy process.
26 The establishment of the OGC in April 2000 is the result of the Gershon report on civilian procurement (Gershon 1999) commissioned by the Paymaster General in November 1998. Peter Gershon, who was Managing Director of Marconi Electronic Systems when he wrote the report, was also the first Chief Executive of the OGC. The OGC reports to the Chancellor of the Exchequer who, in practice, delegates responsibility to the Chief Secretary of the Treasury. The supervisory board of the OGC is chaired by the Chief Secretary and includes permanent secretaries from major central government departments, two senior industry representatives, the Comptroller and the Auditor General. The OGC has also assumed responsibility for the provision of procurement services that in the past had been offered by other agencies such as the Buying Agency and the Central Computer and Telecommunications Agency (HM Treasury 2001, 76).
27 Two deal with the demand and the supply side of public procurement (the Customer Relations and the Supplier Relations and e-Commerce Directorates). Finally, the Corporate Relations Directorate provides central planning, secretarial and other similar functions to the OGC as a whole.
28 Currently there is no public procurement concordat for Wales.

EU public procurement policy

29 None of these member states can actually be said to object to the liberalisation of public procurement. Even if one assumed the opposite, the assumption would be disproved by their direct and unequivocal acceptance of the *laissez faire* logic of the Treaty (especially the provisions that concern the four freedoms). As it has been argued in this chapter, Treaty provisions and the jurisprudence of the ECJ did not suffice to prevent discrimination. Moreover, the same argument applies to their participation in the formulation of the directives of the 1980s and 1990s when the French and British governments agreed to Greek requests for *temporary* exemptions.

4

Transposition

The purpose of this chapter is twofold. First, it seeks to discuss the way in which EU directives on public procurement have been transposed into national legislation. Second, it seeks to ascertain whether there is a common pattern of EU-induced convergence in terms of the transposition of these directives and, more importantly, to what extent patterns of transposition are related to key characteristics of national central governments.

Greece: conflicting political priorities and the two faces of authority

The process of transposition in Greece has been characterised by three fundamental elements (Dimitrakopoulos 2001b). First, the accession of Greece in January 1981 meant that the EC's policy had already developed its basic characteristics. As a result, Greek policy had to be adapted[1] accordingly. Second, the first four years of Greek membership were marked by the socialist government's reluctance to implement some of the fundamental aspects of the Treaty of Accession. The memorandum that it submitted in spring 1982 reflected the need for longer transitional periods in various aspects of trade relations, including public procurement. The memorandum was consistent with domestic economic realities as well as PASOK's pre-electoral view that Greek firms and producers were not ready to compete in an open European market. However, the memorandum broke with PASOK's previous rhetoric regarding withdrawal from the then EC and the establishment of a 'special relationship'. Indeed, it was an initial indication that the new government was increasingly aware of the new organisational context in which it was operating. The memorandum was the beginning of a process of gradual change in the attitude of the government towards the EC while it realistically reflected the state of the Greek economy (Pangalos 2000). Third, the intensity of protectionist policies that had been implemented in the past (Zorbala 1992) meant that not only was there a need to transpose the relevant rules into Greek legislation, but an important effort had to be made in order to modify or abolish a large number of legislative instruments that incorporated these policies. Although this had been partly achieved through the Treaty of Accession (Zorbala 1992, 217–8), the significant degree of co-ordination that was required was missing and, as a result, transposition was problematic. The adoption of Law 936/1979 was illustrative of these problems.

Between the conclusion of the Treaty of Accession (May 1979) and its ratification by the Greek Parliament (July 1979), Parliament passed this law that facilitated the implementation of discriminatory practices against imported products in the field of supplies (Art. 6 § 6), along the lines of a protectionist policy dating from 1955.[2] Having already missed this opportunity to commence the process of transposition even before the date of accession, successive Greek governments followed the same pattern throughout the 1980s. The problems that have been observed also concerned services contracts and the system of remedies. Throughout the 1980s, laws were used extensively;[3] this was frequently based on the delegation of legislative power from Parliament.

The transposition of legislation regarding supplies has been characterised by the conflict between the EC policy and the overt policy of the so-called 'Hellenisation' of supplies – i.e. preference for domestic products, implemented by the socialist government between 1981 and 1985 not only in concrete, practical terms but also by means of public ministerial declarations (Bernitsas 1987, 188). The conflict involved the *non-transposition* of the directives (that is the lack of any national implementing measures) as well as the use of existing legislation for the protection of the domestic market.[4] As a result, the European Commission initiated the procedure of Art. 169 of the Treaty (case C-84/86). The need to handle this issue and a large number of similar problems regarding other aspects of trade liberalisation led the government to create an EC Affairs Unit in the Ministry of Trade which – despite the existence of a separate Legal Affairs Unit and the recent establishment of ENYEK (a similar unit in the Ministry of Foreign Affairs) in 1986 – was responsible for dealing with problems relating to infringement procedures. In other words, there was a mismatch between the problem (conflict between domestic legislation and practice on the one hand and EU policy on the other) and the response chosen by the government, i.e. the establishment of an administrative unit whose aim was to deal with infringement proceedings. The Greek government managed to convince the Commission not to pursue the case further. This is so because the Greek authorities were about to commence the process of transposition (Dimitrakopoulos 2001b).

The initial result took the form of Law 1797/1988. It did not provide a satisfactory solution because it abolished the distinction between domestic and international competitions only indirectly while it did not abolish the system for the protection of regional and provincial industries at all (Zorbala 1992, 208). It was followed by Presidential Decree 105/1989 that transposed correctly Directive 77/62. This was followed by Presidential Decree 173/1990 containing discriminatory provisions (e.g. Art. 19 § 2) that were subsequently abolished by Presidential Decree 137/1991, both adopted by the conservative government that succeeded the socialists in power. The process was completed by Law 2286/1995 which expressly abolished every remaining discriminatory provision.[5]

The differences between the two parties and the way in which they understood the role of the Ministry of Trade in the area of public procurement was also evident in the decisions that they took about intra-departmental arrangements. The establishment in 1988 of a Secretariat General for State Procurement (within the then Ministry of Trade) with a remit covering every aspect of public supplies – including the European dimension – reflects an effort to modernise the Greek legal framework. The need to end a series of EU-related problems was a major incentive for this effort. The decision of the conservative government to abolish this body four years later (Presidential Decree 304/1992) symbolised its willingness to limit the role of the state in the economy. The end of a cycle of conflict with the European Commission is illustrated by the reinforcement of the role of the Community Affairs Unit in the formulation of policy, negotiation and transposition rather than the preparation for litigation. The return of the socialists to power in 1993 led to the establishment in 1995 (Law 2286/1995) of a Directorate General for State Purchasing.

The transposition of the directives on public works presents a more diverse picture. Those that had been adopted prior to 1981 were characterised by problems regarding the specificity and accuracy of the Greek legislation (Law 1418/1984). The Commission held the view that (a) the mere introduction of the principle of non-discrimination between Greek and European bidders was insufficient for the liberalisation of the market, (b) the use of administrative circulars as a follow-up to legislation was sub-optimal and (c) a number of important provisions, including those regarding the selection criteria, had either been ignored or transposed incorrectly (Spathopoulos 1990, 109–10). The problem was resolved in 1991 with the adoption of Presidential Decree 265/1991. The use of the copy-out technique certainly enabled Greece to avoid a condemnation in the ECJ for non-transposition but created several problems in the stage of administrative implementation (*infra*, Chapter 5). By contrast, Presidential Decree 334/2000 accurately transposed Directive 93/37.

The transposition of the directive on services differed in a number of ways. The fundamental characteristic of the process in this case was the challenge to the responsibility of the Ministry of National Economy for this area of policy. Given the initial absence of transposing legislation, the European Commission initiated the infringement procedure under Art. 169 of the Treaty. The initial action (formal notice of August 1993 and the reasoned opinion of May 1994) had no result thus leading to a condemning judgement issued by the ECJ (case C-311/95). In the proceedings before the ECJ, the representatives of the Greek government – despite not disputing the failure to transpose Directive 92/50 – argued that initial steps had already been taken through the establishment of an inter-departmental committee at official level in November 1994. Its purpose was to prepare the accurate and effective transposing legislation. Moreover, the Ministry of the Environment, Spatial Planning and Public Works had already issued a circular and a draft Presidential Decree for the provisional transposition of Directive 92/50. The activism of this department is at the heart of the problem (Dimitrakopoulos 2001b).

Indeed, officials of the then Ministry of National Economy, which is formally responsible for this aspect of procurement policy, preferred the adoption of a single text because the directive in question covers many different forms of services. On the contrary, officials of the Ministry of the Environment, Spatial Planning and Public Works preferred the adoption of two legislative instruments, one of which ought to cover the regulation of plans and studies prepared for public works projects while the other would cover the remaining forms of services. In essence, this ministerial department sought to maintain the *status quo* which contained many discriminatory clauses that protect domestic planning firms from European competition.[6] In addition, the body that represents Greek civil engineers opposed the liberalisation of the market (Simitis 2005, 411) that would result from the transposition and subsequent implementation of this directive. They did not want to face competition from abroad. Moreover, this conflict is directly linked to the high profile of the Ministry of the Environment, Spatial Planning and Public Works, which is based on the use of significant European and national funds and its concomitant role as a major mechanism for economic development. In January 1998 the Commission initiated proceedings against Greece under Art. 171/228 of the Treaty for failure to comply with the aforementioned ruling of the ECJ (European Commission press release IP/98/6) and six months later it took Greece to the ECJ with a view to imposing a penalty of €39,975 for each day of the duration of the infringement (European Commission press release IP/98/559). The Greek government managed to avoid the fine as a result of the adoption of Presidential Decree 346/1998.[7] In addition to the changes that it introduced in the legislative framework (in line with the directive), it established the Services Procurement Unit (Art. 35) whose role has become instrumental in the subsequent stages of the implementation process (*infra*, Chapter 5).

The transposition of Directive 89/665 (remedies) has been plagued also by a legal dispute regarding the adequacy of the Greek legislation. However, a significant part of the problem was rooted (initially) in the inability of the central government to initiate and co-ordinate the process of transposition. More importantly, it resulted from the unilateral action of the Ministry of the Environment, Spatial Planning and Public Works. The Commission utilised its powers under Art. 169/226 and rightly argued that Greek legislation (Presidential Decree 23/1993) covered only part of the required domain (Koutoupa 1993, CS88).

In the proceedings before the ECJ (case C-236/95) the Greek government admitted not having adopted the necessary measures to cover supplies contracts but argued that the existing system of remedies offered some legal protection to bidders and that the recent jurisprudence of the Council of State[8] made explicit reference to the directive, thus providing adequate protection for bidders. Moreover, it argued that domestic formal and procedural difficulties undermined its efforts effectively to transpose the directive. However, it did not avoid a condemning judgement.

When Prime Minister Simitis took office (in 1996) he realised that the significant backlog of directives that had not been transposed included Directive 89/665 (remedies).[9] Acting in an effort to resolve the problem, the Secretary General of the Cabinet created a committee composed of two members of the Council of State and a member of the Court of Appeal. These were experienced judges who prepared a draft legal text in order to transpose the directive in a manner that would cover the three sub-sectors concerned (works, services and supplies). However, one of the three ministers concerned initially refused to sign the draft decree arguing that the directive would effectively bring all major works projects to a halt across the country. As a result, Prime Minister Simitis convened an ad hoc meeting with the ministers concerned, at the end of which all ministers signed the draft document. Law 2522/1997 transposed the directive, six years after the formal deadline. The new text introduced significant changes to the Greek system of remedies (Marinos 1997) and it is the direct consequence of the aforementioned ruling of the ECJ (Georgopoulos 2000, 86).[10] Clearly, this was an issue that would have been resolved more rapidly and more effectively, if effective alert procedures and co-ordinating mechanisms had existed at the heart of the Greek central government prior to 1996.

Finally, as regards the transposition of Directive 2004/18 that consolidates, simplifies and updates the EU's public procurement legislation, two key characteristics confirm the existing procedural patterns. The perceived specificity of the three sub-sectors has led to the preparation and adoption of separate transposing instruments. Law 3316/2005 deals with the works-related services that concern the design and the execution of public works projects, thereby leaving the remaining forms of public procurement, i.e. those that concern other service-related contracts (e.g. those that concern financial services, legal services, etc), supply-related and works-related contracts to be transposed separately. Its adoption has been delayed both as a result of the inter-departmental consultation and the workload of the Council of State which scrutinised the compatibility of the initial draft with EU legislation. As a consequence, the transposition of Directive 2004/18 had not been completed eleven months after the deadline. Nevertheless, all three ministries concerned have issued substantive circulars[11] that bring the directive to the attention of the relevant awarding authorities (Ministry of Development 2006a; Ministry of Economy and Finance 2006; Ministry of the Environment, Spatial Planning and Public Works 2006).

France: authority, nodality and their limits

The process of transposition in France was – throughout the 1970s and 1980s – one of accurate and, in most cases, swift and timely transposition (see, e.g. Décret 79–98; Décret 81–551; Décret 90–824; Décret 92–311) based on the use of formal and informal authority. Prior to discussing the case of belated transposition, it is worth noting that the French pattern is characterised by the incorporation of the directives into the *Code des Marchés Publics*. This is done through the extensive use of decrees followed by *arrêtés ministériels*, i.e. ministerial decisions, and ministerial instructions prepared by the CCM. They are published in the *Journal Officiel de la République Française* (Official Journal of the French Republic) and integrated into the *Code* whose *Livre V* (Book V) since 1989 concerned the EC's public procurement policy, thus ensuring widespread publicity for these rules. In other words, the French central government utilised authority (since the *Code* is a legally binding text) and nodality (because the rules incorporated in the *Code* are known not only to officials who work for awarding authorities but interested bidders as well). This is important because unlike, for example, their Greek counterparts, officials who work for French awarding authorities have a single authoritative source that contains the relevant legislation. At the same time, the presence of the *Code* facilitates the role of the European Commission as guardian of the treaty. It is much easier for its officials – as well as actual or potential bidders both from France and abroad – to ascertain whether a directive has been transposed or not.[12] Nevertheless, the frequent additions of various provisions to the *Code* has not only increased the number of articles that it contained but also – as a consequence – the complexity of the text (Ministère de l'Économie et des Finances 1999). As a result, the simplification of the *Code* became one of the main objectives of the reform introduced in 2001 (*infra*, Chapter 5).

Two important characteristics of the process as it unfolded in the 1980s deserve to be highlighted. First, while the extensive use of decrees confirms the preponderance of the French government, one must also underline the repercussions of the extension of the EU policy's agenda for the choice of the national implementing measures. Indeed, the modification of the French penal code through the creation of the crime of favouritism which falls in the remit of the French Parliament by virtue of Art. 34 of the Constitution of 1958, necessarily brought the latter into the process of transposition.[13] Nevertheless, the involvement of the Parliament in this process did not produce spectacular results. Rather, it seemed to be a matter of constitutional procedural necessity. Second, the initial use of rather succinct texts that were interpreted by extremely detailed ministerial instructions has been construed as an attempt by the government to keep its hands free through the transposition of just the essential minimum requirements stipulated by the directives (Drago 1975, 864).

In contrast, the intensification during the 1990s of the drive towards the liberalisation of public procurement (and the single market more generally) has been marked by tensions, delays[14] and a pronounced effort on the part of the French authorities to reform the *Code* and the wider system of public procurement in France.[15] The four-year delay that marked the transposition of Directive 92/50 (public service contracts) was indicative of the broader trend of conflict in which the French government explicitly acknowledged the deficiencies of the internal system of co-ordination. When the deadline for the entry into force expired (July 1993), the European Commission brought the case to the ECJ (case C-234/95) under Art. 169 of the Treaty. The French government did not deny that it had not transposed the directive in question, despite the letter of formal notice that the European Commission had sent in August 1993. In the light of the absence of a reply from the French authorities, the European Commission proceeded to the stage of the reasoned opinion in September 1994. At that point the French government argued that a draft law concerning private entities that operate 'in the general interest' had been submitted to the French Senate. This was done in an effort to extend the domestic provisions that apply to works contracts. Moreover, the French government argued that when it comes to contracts concluded by the state and local authorities the precise wording of the relevant decree was in the process of being finalised by means of inter-departmental consultations. This was much more than a tactical device intended to avoid condemnation by the ECJ. This is so for two reasons. First, the French authorities were well aware that, whilst recognising the autonomy of national governments in the choice of the instruments and methods for the transposition of EU legislation into national law, the jurisprudence of the ECJ had repeatedly rejected the notion that this autonomy could be used as an explanation (or excuse) for belated or incorrect transposition[16] (Dimitrakopoulos 1998, Chapter 2). Second, member states had an entire year to organise and complete the process of transposition and – in doing so – overcome the problem of inter-departmental co-ordination posed by a novel, overarching and, arguably, complex directive. The French authorities had not transposed the directive by the time the case reached the ECJ. As a result, the ECJ condemned France for non-transposition. Although the delay may have been due to the general election of 1993, this is only a partial explanation of the problem. The same applies to the argument – put forward within the French central administration – that pragmatism must guide transposition in that it is in nobody's interests to be the first to transpose. However, this fails to account for the fact that the, at least in principle, pro-market government that took office in 1995 took two years to transpose the directive in question. The French authorities finally transposed this directive in January 1997 (Loi 97–50). Although officials of the *Commission Centrale des Marchés* claimed to have instructed the administration to implement the directive in practice, even prior to its transposition, this did not resolve the problem.[17] This is so because, as the ECJ has repeatedly stated in its jurisprudence, administrative practices cannot substitute for transposition. This is because they do not guarantee transparency and legal certainty. In fact, this significant delay was a prelude to the institutional problems that contributed to the reforms that followed later. The case of Directive 92/50 also illustrates the point about the multitude of texts that are used in France for the transposition of EU directives and their impact on the *Code*. Indeed, in addition to the aforementioned law, the French government introduced three decrees (98–111, 98–112, 98–113).

The French government used the same response when the European Commission (press release IP/00/238) brought a case to the ECJ (case C-97/00) for failure to transpose accurately Directive 97/52 which adapted the EU's regime to the Government Procurement Agreement concluded during the Uruguay Round. When the case reached the ECJ, the Commission argued that the French authorities had transposed (Arrêté du 22 avril 1998) only the part of the directive that concerned the thresholds above which notices have to be advertised in the Official Journal of the European Communities. In turn, the French government did not deny the allegations but claimed that the interdepartmental examination of the transposing decree was close to its completion and that it would be submitted shortly to the *Conseil d'État*. Nevertheless, it did not manage to avoid a condemning judgement. The issue was resolved as a result of the reform of the *Code* that took place in 2001 (Décret 2001–210). The *Code* was reformed again in 2004 and 2006 but these reforms have much more to do with the French experience in implementing procurement policy throughout the 1990s, than with the transposition of EU legislation (*infra*, Chapter 5). Finally, Décret 2006–975 transposed into the French Public Procurement Code the directives of 2004 that update, codify and simplify the EU's public procurement rules.[18] Its belated entry in force (by eight months) was the result of (i) the French government's attempts to find a way to promote the involvement of small and medium-sized enterprises in public procurement as well as (ii) the workload of the *Conseil d'État* that scrutinised the compatibility of draft transposing legislation with the said Directive (*Les Echos* 3 February 2006; 14 April 2006; 9 July 2006).

The UK: the changing form of authority

Transposition in the UK has been characterised by the initial use of administrative circulars and guidelines by the administration.[19] These were subsequently replaced by subordinate legislation in the form of statutory instruments since the beginning of the 1990s. The choice of circulars and guidelines issued by the Treasury and other ministerial departments (including the Scottish, Welsh and Northern Ireland Offices) reflects the traditional lack of legislation covering this policy area before the adoption of the directives (Arrowsmith 2006, 89). During that period these issues were dealt with as a matter of administration. This action was based on a number of principles and procedures developed by the Treasury and committees of the House of Commons such as the Public Accounts Committee (Turpin 1989, 62).

The use of directives at the European level in the stage of collective policy formulation certainly constitutes a valid argument in favour of the use of any form of national implementing measures. This is so not only because of its very definition found in the Treaty (Art. 189/249) but also because the content of the directives gives the member states the right to choose the laws, regulations and administrative provisions that are required for their transposition. This, in turn, reflects clearly the principle of institutional autonomy in the broad sense of the term (Dimitrakopoulos 2001c). However, several[20] developments have led the British central government to the decision to abandon the aforementioned practice.

First and foremost, the long and consistent jurisprudence of the ECJ has rejected the use of purely administrative measures for transposition (Labayle 1989, 628). Indeed, on the basis of the jurisprudence of the ECJ an important distinction has been drawn between two situations (Fernández Martín 1996, 103) namely, first, cases in which a directive's intended effect is limited to the internal sphere of the administration and does not create any effects on third parties and, second, cases in which a directive is intended to produce benefits for third parties. The EU's public procurement directives clearly fall into the second category because their objective is the creation of opportunities for potential bidders to bid for public contracts through a set of legal obligations imposed on awarding entities. The effectiveness of these obligations would be undermined if national governments were allowed to transpose the directives by means of administrative measures. This is so in part because of the implications of this practice in terms of legal certainty. Purely administrative measures are, by definition, easy to amend at the whim of the administration. This undermines legal certainty which is important in law-intensive areas of public policy such as public procurement. As a result, the use of circulars and guidelines is deemed to be inappropriate for the purposes of transposition of the directives.[21] The validity of the ECJ's view that circulars and guidelines are not suitable for the transposition of EC policy is also illustrated (*infra*, Chapter 5) by the fact that in the case of the UK they enabled the continuing use of discriminatory practices in pursuit of other policies.

Secondly, the very nature of circulars and guidelines as *internal* administrative instruments defeats the purpose of EU policy in this field. A transparent market where informed players transform rights conferred upon them into business opportunities cannot rely on mere internal administrative measures. This potential fails to be fulfilled when the relevant directives are not brought to the attention of these players through the appropriate transposing measures. Internal documents such as circulars cannot ensure the degree of transparency that is normally achieved through publicly available legislation.[22]

Finally, there is a link between the shift to legislative measures on the one hand, and the completion (and, more importantly, the reinforcement of the regulatory force) of the EU's policy in this area on the other. This is illustrated by the extension to services and the finishing touches added by the consolidation directives of 1993. The significant role played by the Treasury in this process ought to de underlined here. Indeed, it used its authority and nodality in order to bring about change in a framework which was characterised by the absence of any substantive challenges to its views in the domestic phase of the EU policy process. This means that this combination of authority and nodality reduced the number of decision points involved in the transposition process in a way that subsequently reinforced effectiveness.

The form of legislation that was chosen (statutory instruments) reflects the dominant position of the government in the transposition process. The limitation of the participation of Westminster is embodied in the European Communities Act 1972. Section 2 § 2 provides the required enabling basis for the adoption of the legislative instruments (*supra*, Chapter 2) thus justifying the use of the term[23] 'legislation without legislature' (Miers and Page 1990, 104). The broad picture of this stage of the policy process in the UK is one of timely and accurate transposition[24] (The Public Supply Contracts Regulations 1991. Statutory Instrument 2679; Public Works Contracts Regulations 1991. Statutory Instrument 2680; Public Services Contracts Regulations 1993. Statutory Instrument 3228; Public Supply Contracts Regulations 1995. Statutory Instrument 201; Public Contracts (Works, Services and Supply) (Amendment) Regulations 2000. Statutory Instrument 2009).

The shift to legislative measures did not lead to the abolition of the use of circulars and guidelines. On the contrary, they are still used by the Treasury or other departments not only for the implementation of EU public procurement policy but also in order to remind awarding authorities of their EU obligations in case of domestic changes in other aspects of procurement policy as well. Joint circular 5/96–11/96 relating to compulsory competitive tendering provides an example of this practice (Department of the Environment/Welsh Office 1996).

Moreover, the adoption of Statutory Instrument 2009 of 2000 that transposed Directive 97/52 raised concerns because it simply amended existing domestic legislation and, as a result, compelled awarding authorities to consult various texts, in order to determine which applies (Arrowsmith 2000, NA151). The absence of a consolidated text placed more emphasis on the co-ordinating capacity of central government and its ability to steer awarding authorities in the right direction. In contrast, the regulations (Public Contracts Regulations 2006. Statutory Instrument 5) that transposed Directive 2004/18 – which simplifies, codifies and updates the EU's procurement legislation – actually replace the pre-existing domestic legislation (Arrowsmith 2006, 87) in an effort to promote clarity and transparency (in line with the objective of the aforementioned directive). The transposition process was marked by two key developments, namely two consultation exercises and the actual implementation of the arrangements that stemmed from devolution. The two[25] public consultation exercises were organised by the Office of Government Commerce. The first consultation exercise took place between May and August 2004 and concerned the approach that the OGC should take in transposing the new directives. The second exercise took place between June and September 2005 and concerned the draft regulations that the OGC prepared in an effort to transpose the new directives. The draft regulations were prepared by the OGC's lawyers on the basis of instructions provided by the OGC's policy staff who negotiated in Brussels.

Both consultation exercises involved not only awarding authorities (including central government departments), but also the Chartered Institute of Purchasing and Supply, actual and potential suppliers, as well as the legal and academic communities. The purpose of the first consultation was to help inform decisions regarding the transposition of the directives. It covered a wide range of issues including confusing definitions, the time period covered by recurring contracts, the extent of congruence between past UK practice and the new provisions (such as those regarding central purchasing bodies), the scope of arrangements regarding reserved contracts and sheltered workshops,[26] the adequacy of OGC guidance regarding new EU level arrangements (such as framework agreements in the public sector), or views on even completely new arrangements (Office of Government Commerce 2004a). This consultation exercise provided an opportunity for various interested parties to seek specific guidance regarding numerous issues and to highlight the importance of guidance in the post-transposition phase (Office of Government Commerce 2004b, 1). The issues raised were quite specific and varied from definitions of concepts to particular practices and ways to turn specific provisions into practice (such as the coverage of the provisions regarding mandatory exclusions).[27] In each case, the OGC presented the main groups of responses that it received and either offered specific answers to questions or referred to the draft regulations that would transpose Directive 2004/18.

These draft regulations were the focus of the second consultation (Office of Government Commerce 2005a; 2005b). The basic decisions of the OGC were not challenged.[28] These decisions concerned the structure of the regulations (that follows the structure of the purchasing process, as reflected in the directive), the active use of the provisions of the directive that maximise flexibility and, finally, the provisions regarding central purchasing bodies. The issues raised concerned technical clarifications (such as the position of the provisions regarding social and environmental criteria within the draft regulations), as opposed to questions of principle. In its response, the OGC provided answers to the points made and indicated what its guidance would cover.

Transposition

The second important aspect of the transposition of Directive 2004/18 concerned the impact of devolution. Indeed, unlike the devolved administrations of Wales and Northern Ireland, the Scottish Executive chose to make separate regulations (The Public Contracts (Scotland) Regulations 2006. Scottish Statutory Instrument 1) for the transposition of the said directive, in line with the arrangements described in Chapter 3. This followed two consultation exercises similar to those organised south of the border. Despite their similarities with those that apply in the remainder of the UK (Arrowsmith 2006, 89), the decision of the Scottish Executive to make separate regulations was based on (a) the fact that, under arrangements regarding devolution in Scotland, public procurement is a devolved domain and (b) its willingness to include provisions that apply to procurement projects whose value does not exceed the threshold stipulated by the EU directives.[29] Crucially, the public procurement policy officials of the Scottish Executive who were involved in the definition of the UK's negotiating position ahead of negotiations in Brussels, were also involved[30] not only in negotiations that took place in Brussels, but also in the preparation of the Scottish regulations. Throughout this process officials of the Scottish Executive and the OGC maintained close contacts.

Conclusion

Is there a common pattern of EU-induced convergence in terms of the transposition of the EU's public procurement directives (adopted by – lest one forgets – either exclusively or with the direct involvement of representatives of national governments)? More importantly, to what extent are patterns of transposition related to key characteristics of national central governments? Four observations can be made from a comparative perspective.

First, there is clear convergence in terms of the instruments used for the transposition of the EU's public procurement directives. Initially, unlike the Greek authorities that have always relied on legislation followed by administrative circulars that bring new legislation to the attention of individual parts of the administration, the French system relied on a small number of legislative texts that were followed by numerous and substantive administrative documents while the British system entailed the use of purely administrative circulars. The increasing intensity of the EU's involvement in the regulation of public procurement, the inadequacy of purely administrative documents and, more importantly, the jurisprudence of the ECJ have led to a new trend namely the use of *legislative* texts for the purposes of transposition and *administrative* texts for the purposes of informing and steering awarding authorities. This reflects the importance of combining authority and nodality for the purposes of transposition.

Second, unlike the British case, which is characterised by the timely transposition of the directives, transposition in France and Greece has been characterised by delays. Both in Greece and in France, the role of the ECJ has been significant in changing the patterns of non-transposition and incorrect transposition.

Third, these delays were not due to the role of the relevant national parliaments. Indeed, the directives examined here are routinely (or predominantly) transposed by means of *government* legislation (presidential decrees in Greece, *décrets* in France, statutory instruments in Britain) made by the executives concerned. The small number of cases of transposition by means of legislation made by national parliaments (in France and Greece) do not reflect a broader trend, nor were they linked to the delays, in line with the expectations that stem from the fact that majority MPs in both parliaments are – like those in Westminster – usually loyal to their party.

Fourth, the role of central government institutions in shaping patterns of transposition appears to be significant, though this is much more evident in the cases of Greece and France. The fact that the transposition of Directive 92/50 (services) was problematic both in France and Greece is not a coincidence. In both cases the problems stemmed from the inability of the two executives to co-ordinate the activity of ministerial departments. The weaknesses regarding co-ordination[31] were exposed as a result of the fact that the directive in question was novel and did not follow the traditional lines of the division of labour and responsibility between ministerial departments. In terms of the use of the tools of government, one must certainly underline the diffused nature of nodality and authority in a form which contrasts clearly with the British case, even after devolution. Indeed, unlike the case of the UK where only one actor (initially the Treasury, then the Procurement Policy Team and, since 2000, the OGC) had to accumulate the relevant information (need for change) and then take the necessary measures (choice of statutory instruments), the Greek case illustrates the negative effect of the existence of diffused forms of authority and nodality, in a manner that increases the number of decision points involved in the process. Instead of an authoritative decision of the main body responsible for this aspect of public procurement (the then Ministry of National Economy), the Ministry of the Environment, Spatial Planning and Public Works used this window of opportunity in order to promote its sectoral logic, thus undermining the effectiveness of the process through the additional decision point that it created.

One major characteristic of the process of transposition is that, although it can be repeated – it can be boiled down to a small number of discreet acts. In that sense, unlike post-transposition implementation – it cannot provide the sole basis for the assessment of the way in which key characteristics of national central governments affect 'post-decisional' politics, i.e. action *beyond transposition*. A more extensive discussion of this question requires the analysis of patterns of post-transposition implementation. This is what the next chapter seeks to do.

Notes

1 The importance of this point should not be over-estimated because the provisions of the Treaty would have the same effect, although the pace of change would have been slower (*supra*, Chapter 3).
2 Law 3215/1955 established a general preferential scheme, which was characterised by the imposition of a number of taxes and levies to imports. Clearly they were meant to protect domestic products (Zorbala 1992, 206–7).
3 They were followed by presidential decrees that gave more specific meaning to some of their provisions.
4 The second aspect concerns the administrative stage of implementation. Therefore, it shall be analysed in Chapter 5. However, it is mentioned here because it has been facilitated by the *non-transposition* of the directives.
5 It was only because the European Commission used every ounce of its good will that the Greek government managed to avoid an embarrassing judgement of the ECJ.
6 The unwillingness of the interested organisations to accept the opening up of the sector to European competition was a major factor that led to the condemnation of Greece by the ECJ (Spathopoulos 1990, 110).
7 This was subsequently amended (at the instigation of the European Commission) by Presidential Decree 18/2000 that took account of the Government Procurement Agreement concluded in the context of the Uruguay Round.
8 This concerned especially its judgements in cases 355/1995, 470/1995, 471/1995, 473/1995 and 559/1995.
9 He was aware of it as a result of the fact that he served as Minister of Trade right after the electoral victory of the socialists in 1993.
10 The only decentralised aspect of the system that it introduced concerns the collection and provision of information to the European Commission regarding the use of the system of remedies in the fields of works (Ministry of the Environment, Spatial Planning and Public Works), supplies (Ministry of Development) and services (Ministry of National Economy).
11 Substantive circulars go beyond the mere description of a directive and include guidance on its use by the awarding authorities.
12 Indeed, the presence of the *Code* makes redundant the formal requirement regarding the transmission to the Commission of formal texts that transpose EU directives. Of course, the transmission of such texts in *draft* form remains a powerful tool because it allows national and EU officials to avoid mistakes in the process of transposition.
13 The same applies to the regulation of utilities.
14 One example is the transposition of Directive 89/665 (remedies) that took place nine months after the prescribed deadline (Décret 92-964).
15 The institutional aspects of this reform were discussed in Chapter 3.
16 The same applies to the entire range of duties that stem from membership.
17 The situation relating to Directive 92/50 had (at that time) been described as 'alarming' (Commission of the European Communities 1995, 25; Commission des Communautés européennes 1996, 57). The countries that contributed to this situation included, significantly, Greece.
18 It is important to note the recent conflict over the use of *ordonnances* for (*inter alia*) the transposition of EU legislation on public procurement. Members of the

French Senate opposed the government's wish to rely on this kind of instrument and asked the Constitutional Council to oppose the adoption of Law 2003–951, which they deemed to violate various provisions of the French Constitution. Art. 5 of this law stipulates that the government may take the measures required for the harmonisation of French legislation with EU directives on public procurement. However, the directives that the government had in mind (specifically Directives 2004/17 and 2004/18 that codify, update and simplify existing EU legislation on procurement in the utilities' and the public sectors respectively) had not been adopted when the government drafted this law and presented it to the two chambers. As a result, claimed the Senators, the law violated Art. 38 of the Constitution because it was not specific enough (nor could it, presumably, be specific enough since the directives had not been adopted) to satisfy the requirements of the aforementioned constitutional provision. The Constitutional Council rejected their argument although it did not explain why it considers that Art. 5 of this law was specific enough to satisfy the requirements of Art. 38 of the French Constitution.

19 During that time interested parties could rely on the doctrine of direct effect (Arrowsmith 2006).

20 In addition to the factors that are mentioned here, the extension of the remit of the directives to utilities has certainly contributed to the switch to legislative measures. Private ownership of many utilities in the UK meant that circulars and guidelines could not be used precisely because these companies are not part of the British administration. As a result, legislation was needed.

21 Moreover, Treasury officials were aware of the fact that administrative circulars are – unlike statutory instruments -mere administrative devices, not law.

22 This does not mean that legislation guarantees transparency. Rather, it is more likely than internal administrative documents to achieve it. After all, one must not confuse access to information with the capacity to process it. In areas of public policy that – like public procurement – are marked by the presence of highly technical legal rules, interested parties need to possess a significant degree of legal expertise. This concerns both tenderers (be they actual or potential) and awarding authorities. This is one of the reasons why the access of small and medium-sized enterprises to cross-border public procurement remains largely an objective rather than reality (European Commission 2004, 20).

23 Miers and Page (1990, 110) regard section 2 § 2 of the European Communities Act 1972 as the provision that contains the most extensive delegation of law making power. The fact that these legislative instruments had to be laid in the House does not alter the validity of this point, especially in the light of the fact that in this case the statutory instruments in question had *immediate effect* subject only to annulment through a *negative* resolution of the Parliament.

24 Nevertheless, it is important to note the case that opposed the Treasury and BT in relation to the transposition of the first two directives that covered the formerly excluded sectors (i.e. utlities). The significance of this case is based on the fact that it coincides with the shift from administrative circulars and guidelines to legislative instruments and also the extension of the European regulatory framework to utilities. Indeed, the change from administrative circulars and guidelines to statutory instruments for the transposition of the directives into UK legislation has been marked by a challenge relating to their content emanating

from a private company which was covered by the utilities directives. The case opposed BT to the Treasury on the way in which Art. 8 § 1 and § 2 of Directive 90/531 had to be implemented. This provision – which exemplifies the much wider margin for manoeuvre left at the discretion of utilities – stipulates that the directive will not apply to contracts awarded by utilities for purchases intended exclusively to enable them to provide telecommunications services where other entities are free to offer the same services in the same geographical area and under substantially the same conditions. These contracts concern activities described in Art. 2 § 2 (d) of Directive 90/531, namely the provision or operation of public telecommunications networks or the provision of one or more public telecommunications services. Art. 8 § 2 further stipulates that the contracting entities shall notify the Commission (at its request) of any services they regard as covered by the aforementioned exclusion, thus enabling it to publish periodically a comprehensive list of these services. The Treasury, in transposing Directives 90/531 and 92/13 through the Utilities Supply and Works Contracts Regulations 1992, took the view that it had the responsibility to define the services which fall outside the remit of the said directive and so it did in Schedule 2 which was linked to Regulation 7 § 1. Furthermore, the Treasury implemented the procedural aspect of the provision in a way (Regulation 7 § 2) that obliged utilities to notify to it the services provided by them that they consider as services that fall into the remit of the exemption, instead of sending the relevant list directly to the Commission. Thus, BT brought to the High Court an action against the Treasury for annulment of Schedule 2. The High Court's Queen's Bench Division, Divisional Court, in turn, submitted to the ECJ a reference for a preliminary ruling (case C-392/93) relating to the interpretation of Directive 90/531. Basically the questions concerned two issues, namely i) the division of power between the UK government (in this case the Treasury) and the utilities as to who must identify the services falling under the exemption and then submit them to the Commission at its request and ii) whether the UK government must compensate BT if the ECJ found that the relevant national provision implemented incorrectly Art. 8 of Directive 90/531. The Treasury argued that the directive did not preclude the member states from using their authority in order to define the services that are covered by the exemption. This argument was based on the view – also shared by the French, German and Italian governments – that in this way they specify the content of the provision, thus enabling the exercise of judicial review that would otherwise be impossible. Moreover, the Treasury (supported by the German government) considered that this form of action might be necessary in case of a conflict of view with utilities, thus jeopardising legal certainty. The ECJ dismissed the Treasury's argument, following the opinion of the Advocate General, thus accepting that the power to determine which telecommunications services are to be excluded is vested in the utilities, not the national governments. Nevertheless, it did not go as far as to accept that the UK government had to compensate BT. It based its view on the fact that in this particular case, one of the three conditions for state liability in case of incorrect transposition had not been fulfilled because the interpretation of the directive that the Treasury adopted was not manifestly contrary to the wording of the directive itself or to the objective pursued by it. Finally, this ruling of the ECJ rightly underlined the failure of the European Commission to identify this problem when the Treasury communicated the transposing text to it, thereby

fulfilling the national obligation incorporated into the directives which is designed to facilitate the Commission's monitoring function. The case delayed the adoption of the Utilities Contracts Regulations 1996, which implemented through Regulation 7 § 1 and § 2 the necessary changes thus bringing British legislation in line with the ruling and further transposed Directive 93/38. Although the implementation of the utilities-related aspect of the EU's public procurement policy is beyond the remit of this book, this case indicates that the shift from circulars to legislation is far from a mere technical arrangement. Challenging legislation in courts is both costly and time-consuming. This is why the manner in which transposing legislation is drafted and the form that it takes should be problematised (instead of being taken for granted) in the context of the analysis of broader domestic patterns of EU policy implementation. Seen from the perspective of a large and well-resourced firm such as BT, this is not a major problem. However, smaller firms might think twice or even refrain from taking such action. This case also indicates that speed is not always the best way to assess transposition. Directives are often very complex legal texts subject to various interpretations. Institutional arrangements that promote the diffusion of information and the airing of differing views might gain in effectiveness much more than they might initially lose in speed.
25 Directives 2004/17 (utilities) and 2004/18 (public sector) were the first to be adopted and transposed since the establishment of the OGC.
26 These arrangements concern particular sections of the population (such as disabled people or prisoners) and reflect an effort to promote their social and economic integration.
27 One of the important issues raised during the consultation exercise concerned the separate transposition of the directive in Scotland. This was understandable since these were the first procurement-related directives to be transposed after the implementation of the arrangements regarding devolution. In response, the OGC stated clearly that it was 'working closely' with the Scottish authorities (see *infra*).
28 For the purposes of facilitating the task of those involved in the consultation exercise, the OGC consultation document included a useful transposition table that indicated which draft domestic provision corresponded to each provision of the directive.
29 In turn, this was linked to the small size of many purchasing bodies in Scotland, many of which often do not engage in expensive procurement projects.
30 The relevant staff attended a small number of meetings in the Council's working group but this was only due to lack of time and resources.
31 This was confirmed during the transposition of Directive 97/52 in France.

5
Macro-implementation

The purpose of this chapter is twofold. First, it examines the impact of central government institutions (especially their co-ordination capacity) on the domestic patterns of implementation. Second, it seeks to shed light on the dynamics of these patterns over a period of twenty-five years.

Greece: N.A.T.O. in action

Beyond resistance
The process of change that underpins the implementation of EU public procurement policy in Greece has been channelled through central government institutions aiming to produce lasting effects. The Commission has contributed to the process of change that had been initiated in the second half of the 1980s by avoiding the marginalisation of Greece whilst using its powers of guardian of the Treaty. This approach had three important repercussions. First, it contributed to a gradual shift in the implementation patterns facilitated by continuous contact with 'Brussels' and a change in the attitude of the socialist government *vis-à-vis* the integration process, as illustrated by the appointment of a number of pro-European politicians to senior ministerial posts, including the then Ministry of National Economy. Second, the increasing number of infringement procedures initiated on the basis of Art. 169/226 led to the institutionalisation of contacts with the Commission. These *réunions-paquets* produced significant results. Commission officials were informed of changes in national legislation and jurisprudence while they also highlighted outstanding complaints that had been brought to their attention by bidders. Third, Greek officials gradually discovered that the Commission could easily be used as a mechanism for blame avoidance whenever they were faced with pressure or protests from domestic suppliers. This was a crucial development because it diverted pressure away from the Greek central government, thus facilitating change by making it appear practically inevitable. Nevertheless, these informal procedures have not eliminated every problem, as case C-79/94 illustrates (Dimitrakopoulos 2001b).

This case concerned a three-year framework agreement concluded in July 1991 by the then Ministry of Industry and six textile manufacturers for the supply of dressing materials to hospitals. The agreement could be extended to cover the needs of other institutions for these materials, still exclusively supplied by the six manufacturers. The Greek administration admitted that it had not advertised the contract but argued that cancelling it unilaterally would expose the Greek state to claims for damages from manufacturers. Further, the ministry in question abolished a clause stipulating that the manufacturers would use only domestic primary material and stated its intention to organise a public competition before the end of 1993, thus fulfilling EU obligations. Nevertheless, commensurate action did not follow. As a result, the case reached the ECJ, whose condemning judgement was inevitable. This case was indicative of a broader pattern of subtle, incremental and adaptive change. Indeed, the Greek government used substantive arguments based on EU legislation. It argued that Directive 77/62 did not apply in that case, because the value of each contract did not exceed the threshold, and that in the past no foreign supplier had expressed an interest in similar competitions, thus reducing the publication of a tender notice to a mere formality. This line of reasoning illustrates that the central government was becoming more capable and willing to use *substantive* and *procedural* arguments based on *EU rules rather than national policy priorities.*

Until the early 1990s administrative implementation of public works directives relied exclusively on the lowest price as the main criterion for the award of contracts. This was a key choice that produced a number of significant unintended consequences. Constructors used artificially low bids (Kosmidis 1997) in order to beat competition. This meant that they had to find ways to limit construction costs after the award of a contract. This had a direct impact on the quality of the works; some had structural problems, while in other cases the quality of the materials used was poor (*To Vima* 24 November 1996; 12 January 1997). The use of unrealistic bids did not prevent constructors from making a profit. On the contrary, they made extensive use of their legal right to claim a refund (Koutoupa 1995, CS98) for the difference between the initial bid and the final cost of the project *after* its completion, thus falsifying competition. This problem was associated with the incomplete or low quality plans upon which these projects were based (Simitis 2005, 261). This resulted from the lack of specialist staff in the central administration, which was unable effectively to monitor the construction process. Therefore, it relied on *ex post* controls, facing a *fait accompli* every time there was a problem. The Commission and a group of determined ministers were the catalysts that increased the pace of change by means of a number of measures channelled through the central government (Dimitrakopoulos 2001b).

The conditional nature of EU funding gave a *de facto* role to the Commission. Although EU public procurement policy does not regulate the enforcement of public contracts,[1] the role of the Commission was mainly based on this phase and the link to regional policy. The Head of DG XVI and Commissioner Bruce Millan, then in charge of EU regional policy, repeatedly warned the Greek government that the flow of funds from Brussels was going to stop (*To Vima* 16 June 1996). This actually happened in 1993, in a demonstration of specific and direct steering, in the case of the Evinos dam (*To Vima* 2 February 1997) because the conservative government had not used the correct award procedure. This event provided a key incentive for change, especially at the political level, because it enabled the government to better conceptualise what was at stake. This new interpretation of events provided the impetus for change. The first sign was a letter by three ministers of the new socialist government that took office in 1993 to the Commission. The letter contained a clear political undertaking regarding the adoption of all legislative and administrative measures necessary to improve implementation (general steering).[2] These measures were to be channelled through the Ministry of the Environment, Spatial Planning and Public Works, under the supervision of a joint steering committee composed of officials of the said ministry, the Ministry of National Economy and, crucially, the Commission (specific steering).

The most significant legislative measure was the limitation of the right of constructors to re-assess the cost of works projects on an *ex post* basis (Simitis 2005, 261–2). This obliged them to submit more realistic bids.[3] Furthermore, the administration is no longer obliged to accept the constructor's final assessment of the cost. Procedures for the preparation and submission of plans have been simplified, while a register of public works designers has been introduced. Model notices have been established in order to compel awarding authorities to use comparable documents in the course of the award procedures. Competitive procedures for the award of contracts have been extended below the threshold stipulated by the directives.

Moreover, since January 1997 a new unit (the Tenders and Contracts Monitoring Unit – MOPADIS[4]) established within the Centre for International and European Economic Law, an independent academic research centre based in Thessaloniki, provides advice to public bodies that are covered by the directives. This advice concerns both the material and the procedures used by awarding authorities. More specifically, awarding authorities can obtain (i) guidance with a view to avoid mistakes when detailed and summary tender documents are drafted, (ii) corrective measures in cases of errors, (iii) advice regarding complaints[5] prior to the conclusion of a contract, (iv) advice regarding supplementary contracts, (v) supporting statistical information for the reports that national and awarding authorities are expected to submit to the EU, (vi) generic advice regarding common errors and guidance as to how to avoid them, as well as (vii) updates on EU legislation (Ministry of National Economy 1997a; 1999). The creation of this new arrangement by the Ministry of National Economy was explicitly couched in the need for the provision of co-ordinated advisory support to the awarding authorities.[6] Indeed, the relevant circular of the Ministry of National Economy explicitly acknowledged the fact that the main cause of problems regarding 'compliance with EU legislation' was incomplete knowledge of the relevant provisions (Ministry of National Economy 1997b).

Moreover, the importance of the need for various fixing mechanisms has been acknowledged. They go beyond the introduction of new legislation and include the diffusion of information, training and other administrative measures regarding the entire system of public procurement. The extension of the scope of the system – just one year after its establishment, and the fact that about 600 Greek awarding authorities have used it demonstrate the demand for guidance and the importance of the new system. Although the number of written questions submitted to MOPADIS appears to have remained stable between its establishment in January 1997 and March 2005, many queries are submitted informally (e.g. by telephone) and the number of tender documents that have been submitted to it increased from 200 in 1997 to about 1,000 in 2004 (MOPADIS n.d.). In addition, MOPADIS (a) publishes written guides regarding various aspects of public procurement for the attention of awarding bodies and (b) occasionally intervenes on its own initiative by asking awarding bodies to inform it about contracts that they have advertised.

More importantly, since 1999 all major[7] public contracts have to be reviewed pre-emptively (i.e. prior to their conclusion) by the Greek Court of Auditors as a condition of their validity (Art. 8 of Law 2741/1999) despite the ensuing time pressures (Simitis 2005, 371). This arrangement has also been included in the Constitution as amended in 2001 (Art. 98). In a clear instance of specific and direct steering, fines have been imposed by the government on companies that do not fulfil contractual obligations (*To Vima* 12 January 1997), while a number of award procedures have been suspended because incorrect procedures had been followed (*To Vima* 24 November 1996). In addition, major public works now have to be covered by insurance schemes (*To Vima* 11 February 1996).

Further, the focus of the mechanism for control shifted to control during (rather than after) construction work. Monitoring mechanisms[8] have been established (Simitis 2005, 209). External advice has also been sought through a specialist Italian company that has been brought in to monitor quality in major public works projects. New administrative units have been created within the Ministry of the Environment, Spatial Planning and Public Works in order to monitor the implementation process. Apart from the creation of a Directorate-General for Quality Control in Public Works within the Secretariat-General for Public Works (Presidential Decree 428/1995), the most significant institutional change involved the establishment of a Secretariat-General for Jointly-Funded Public Works (Presidential Decree 166/1996) reporting directly to the Minister. This enhanced its profile within the implementation structure and underlined the 'hands-on' approach of the then Minister, Costas Laliotis. Specialist staff has been recruited in order to enhance administrative effectiveness, especially at the regional level (Simitis 2005, 263, 364).

The need for specialist managers in the public sector, some of whom would manage jointly-funded public works projects in the context of regional policy, led to the establishment (Law 2372/1996) of the Management Unit for the Community Support Framework, a semi-independent body under the supervision of the Minister of National Economy (*To Vima* 25 February 1996). It employs officials from the private and the public sectors and is responsible for the assessment of the staffing needs of various parts of the administration. It has the power to recruit new staff from the private sector or second civil servants and to provide technical expertise regarding the management of projects in effort to assist public bodies in meeting EU criteria and obligations for funding. Strong opposition from the officials of the Ministry of National Economy and their union (*Ekonomikos Tachydromos* 8 June 1995), delayed its establishment.[9] Its opponents argued that (a) it would simply establish a new power centre, blurring existing lines of authority, and (b) the recruitment of staff from the private sector did not guarantee success, since the mentality and the methods of the private sector were simply 'inappropriate' for this particular task.[10] Opposition to the establishment of this body was not limited to civil servants; rather, it stemmed from opposition parties as well (Lalioti 2002, 76). Also, ministers in charge of technical departments expressed serious reservations but encouragement provided by the European Commission helped overcome their concerns (Lalioti 2002, 71).

Further proposals regarding the establishment of an independent administrative authority that would have the power to go beyond monitoring the implementation of public procurement policy were rejected by the socialist government. Senior government officials objected to the proposal (*To Vima* 28 September 1997) because they felt that the establishment of this authority in the Greek context would be construed as the unacceptable transfer of political responsibility. Constitutional obstacles have also been invoked. More importantly, the socialist government led by Costas Simitis had already commenced the process of implementing a number of important reforms – including the direct involvement of the Greek Court of Auditors – that effectively dealt with the concerns that motivated the aforementioned proposal (see *infra*).

Change in public works did not stop there but spilled over into public supplies as well as services, i.e. two areas where the risk of losing EU funding did not exist. Indeed, technical standards that are used for the description of supplies are now determined by one public body and controlled by the Ministry of Development. In addition, the income of public officials involved in public procurement is now subject to official scrutiny designed to detect corruption. Finally, Law 3060/2002 extended the power of the Greek Court of Auditors to review (*prior* to their conclusion) all major services contracts as a condition of their validity. As regards specifically services contracts, until the adoption of the relevant legislative measures, the implementation process could rely on the willingness of interested parties to use the concept of direct effect in order to oblige the administration to use the correct award procedures, the possible action of the European Commission under the revised Art. 171/228 of the Treaty for non-implementation of a judgement of the ECJ and, finally, the professionalism of purchasing officers.[11] The author witnessed an incident that demonstrates the point about the professionalism of individual civil servants. This author's interview with a senior official of the then Ministry of National Economy was interrupted by a purchasing officer of an awarding authority who sought guidance regarding the award procedure that he had to follow in relation to a specific contract. He had to have recourse to this ministry – which at that time (1997) was not formally responsible for this aspect of public procurement – as he was unable to find in the other ministries that he contacted an official who could answer his query. Presidential Decree 346/1998 established the Services Procurement Unit (within the then Ministry of National Economy, now Ministry of Economy and Finance) that is in charge of providing guidance to purchasing officers regarding services contracts (Art. 35). In addition to being involved in EU-level negotiations regarding procurement in services, the unit is directly involved in the transposition as well as the implementation of Directive 2004/18. While awarding authorities retain formal responsibility for individual service procurement projects, since its establishment the unit has become a focal point that provides guidance and resolves practical problems (such as responses to questions regarding the appointment of the panels that award contracts, ways to deal with competitions where only one bid is submitted) despite a degree of resistance from some sizeable awarding authorities. Although it initially comprised just one official, its size has grown[12] and its most experienced staff are also involved in training purchasing officers. Part of its capacity to steer awarding authorities lies in the willingness of its staff to provide written responses to requests made by bidders. Though they are not legally binding, the willingness of these officials to 'go on record' is indicative of their confidence in their expertise and views.[13] This provides a major incentive to individual authorities to follow the views of the unit.

As regards the political level, the establishment of the inter-ministerial Committee of Major Works in 1996 (Decision of the Prime Minister 3307) reflects not only the wider political and economic significance of public works in Greece but also the importance that Prime Minister Simitis attached to the co-ordination of formulation and implementation of government policy. Chaired by the Minister of the Environment, Spatial Planning and Public Works, its membership included the Ministers of Development, Transport and Communications, junior ministers from the ministries of National Economy, Environment, Spatial Planning and Public Works, and three advisers to the Prime Minister.[14] The committee monitored the development of all major public works projects. Unlike other committees that were created while Simitis was Prime Minister, this committee met frequently in order to monitor the development of all major public works (*To Vima* 29 March 1998). In addition, Simitis included (every three to four months) the progress of all major public works projects in the agenda of the Cabinet.

The electoral victory of the conservative ND in March 2004 changed the pattern of government activity yet again. Indeed, the Cabinet met just nine times between March 2004 and the end of 2005. During this period, most discussions were of a general nature and only one of them was devoted to EU-related issues – specifically, the implementation of the third Community Support Framework. By contrast, the Government Committee meets practically every week. Although it appears to rely on single-issue agendas, this inner Cabinet has discussed EU-related issues, such as the preparations for the fourth Community Support Framework and the Common Agricultural Policy – but not major public works projects (Xiros 2006, 174–7).

Learning and the dynamics of implementation in Greece
One of the key claims made in the introductory and the theoretical chapters of this book is that implementation patterns are dynamic. This is demonstrated by the Greek case. The pattern in the early 1980s was one of political conflict underpinned by the persistent pursuit of domestic policy priorities. Change occurred initially in the mid- to late 1980s and accelerated in the 1990s, albeit in a variegated and incremental manner. Variation relates to the pace of change, which is quicker in public works. This has been transformed into a pattern of co-operation with the Commission and broad compliance with EU public procurement policy.

The available data support this view. Indeed, although procurement expenditure as a share of Greek GDP fell between 1987 and 1994 by about 50%, more contracts have been advertised (European Commission. Directorate General XV 1996, 19, 125). This is evidence of the market's increasing transparency, which is a fundamental objective of EU public procurement policy. Between 1993 and 1998, the number of Greek calls advertised in the *OJEC* rose steadily from 922 to 1,680[15] i.e. by more than 82%. Furthermore, between 1995 and 2002 Greece has consistently achieved the highest transparency rate – defined as the value of public procurement contracts published as a percentage of the estimated total procurement value in 2002 figures – among the fifteen member states (European Commission 2004, 7, table 2). In addition, data from Tenders Electronic Daily indicate that between 2001 and 2005 the number of advertised Greek contracts grew from 1,623 in 2001 to 4,390 in 2005.[16]

To what extent do specific attributes of the Greek central government account for change in implementation patterns and, more importantly, how did this change come about? The first five years of Greek membership of the

EU were characterised by the newly elected socialist government's political opposition to trade liberalisation *en bloc* largely, but not exclusively, for ideological reasons. However, significant problems occurred both before and after that period. Therefore, it has been argued that fundamental attributes of the Greek central government account for the patchy nature of implementation in Greece. The process of transposition illustrates clearly that the Greek central government was, and partly remains, dominated by sectoral logics which transform the policy process into a power struggle between ministries and ministers. Repeated calls for a co-ordinated approach to transposition are frequently ignored by major actors, who seem to be more interested in pursuing their narrow goals rather than acting as parts of a larger body. Arguably, this attribute has become a part of the ethos of the Greek central government and mirrors identical problems that have plagued the Cabinet and the Athenian bureaucracy since the 1970s. The Ministry of Environment, Spatial Planning and Public Works has repeatedly acted as a pro-active player by promoting a narrowly-defined sectoral logic which ignores wider policy considerations while considerably weakening the position of the Greek state *vis-à-vis* EU institutions. Thus, problematic co-ordination (or total lack thereof) was associated with ineffective transposition and subsequent implementation.

Problems in administrative implementation initially mirrored difficulties in transposition. The passive role of the administration after transposition largely reflected the view held by many officials that their role ended once EU law had been incorporated into national legislation (Anastopoulos 1988, 250). The capacity (Lundquist's 'can') to use the tools of government in order to steer action *after transposition* largely remained outside the actual remit of the bureaucracy, although it was within its formal powers. The lack of homogeneity and equilibrium in the bureaucracy also contributed to this phenomenon. The bureaucracy is both top-heavy and politicised. Thus it remains unable to develop skills and practices that could improve its effectiveness. As Makridimitris and Passas (1994, 59) put it, every systematic attempt to improve the bureaucracy's own capacity to manage EU affairs is negated or undermined by politicisation. Hence, attempts to change long-established practices and implementation patterns (steering) are either imposed from the top or stem from the EU. Both of these trends account for changes in implementation patterns in Greece.

Change in the field of public works is indicative of the significant role of determined ministers and the Commission. The Commission has provided a major incentive for the acceleration of change because it has enabled the Greek central government to 'understand' what was at stake. In the past the symbolic power of Art. 169/226 procedures and subsequent proceedings in the ECJ (authority) have been unable to foster change by influencing the 'will' of the Greek government. On the contrary, when the Commission threatened to stop the flow of EU funds, change gathered pace. The subtle but significant change observed in the arguments used by government officials in cases that reached the ECJ exemplifies the new approach. Clearly, the choice of the tools of government and the change of attitudes affect each other and it is their cumulative effect that shapes implementation patterns, while both are mediated by key attributes of the Greek central government which affect its ability to learn.

Arguably, learning played a significant role in the evolution of these implementation patterns. The concept of organisational learning outlined in Chapter 1 relies essentially on (a) observations and inferences, (b) the acquisition of new techniques and (c) the improvement of an organisation's performance. Crucially, it has been argued that it involves changes in an organisation's theory of action which is implicit in its activity. Further, the key difference between single-loop and double-loop learning consists in the fact that the latter, unlike the former, entails a change in *values* that underpin this theory of action. Single-loop learning accounts for the changes in Greek implementation patterns in the case examined here, for five reasons.

First, change started from the bureaucracy when officials identified a mismatch between an increasing number of problematic cases raised by the Commission on the one hand, and the gradual abandonment of PASOK's anti-EU rhetoric from the mid-1980s on the other. Thus they resorted to blame avoidance and the gradual adaptation of the domestic legal framework. From the perspective of the bureaucracy, this is a case of single-loop learning because the values, in particular the primacy of the elected government and the passive subordinate role of the bureaucracy, remained stable.

Whether the stance of the government represents a case of double-loop learning, that is, one that involves changes in values, is less clear. It is disputed whether PASOK actually meant to take the country out of the EU in the first place. Indeed, one of the first acts of foreign policy undertaken by the socialist government in early 1982 – only a few months after the general election of October 1981 – was the submission of the memorandum, which focused on the *terms* of membership rather than membership *per se*. Changes in values are much more cumbersome and take place over longer periods of time than changes in strategies. Hence, this change in emphasis from membership *per se* to the terms of membership was tactical and cannot be interpreted as evidence of learning. On the contrary, if one places this shift in a wider context, in particular the involvement of pro-European politicians in the management of European affairs and the gradual discovery of the opportunities offered by the then EC (Pangalos 2000), one can argue that, although the values – that is, the importance attached to the protection of the economic interests of the country – remained unchanged, the strategy was evolving.

Second, learning has been *facilitated* by the approach of the Commission, which has institutionalised contacts with the Athenian bureaucracy during the second half of the 1980s. Indeed, unlike court proceedings that are by definition confrontational, these contacts enabled the Greek administration (and government) to approach issues regarding implementation as a form of problem-solving. The gradual introduction of new techniques, such as the use of copy-out for the transposition of EU legislation and, more importantly, blame avoidance, constitutes evidence of single-loop (instrumental) learning. Blame avoidance has enabled both the government and the administration to divert pressure from the previously protected domestic suppliers, who gradually became exposed to competition.

Third, evidence that single-loop learning, illustrated by the conscious use of new techniques as a result of observations and inferences in the quest for improved performance, rather than a rational institutionalist approach based on the use of the 'stick and carrot' strategy – accounts for the dynamics of the implementation patterns examined here. This includes the fact that change (a) had started *before* the critical event of the Evinos' dam and (b) timid though it was – it occurred first in the field of public supplies, where the Commission did not (and still does not) possess a 'carrot' (conditional funding). More importantly, when the Commission resorted to this strategy, the changes introduced by the Greek government did *not* remain limited to the field of public works.

Fourth, since learning is not always routine (Olsen and Peters 1996, 12), it relies on critical events. One such event was the decision of the Commission in the case of the Evinos dam. This was a branching point that has affected subsequent developments by demonstrating that the Commission was both able and willing to use its powers. This has facilitated learning not only by defining the potential and the limits of alternative strategies – e.g. how far the Greek authorities could go in breaching EU law – but by openly legitimising subsequent changes as well. This was underpinned by the attempt of the Greek government to limit potential losses, which is a typical feature of implementation (Bardach 1977, 42).

Fifth, learning is easier when it is associated with incremental rather than radical change. Marginal adjustments based on trial and error (normally associated with experiential learning) do not generate strong opposition. Such opposition can be overcome when promoters of change draw on the experience generated by critical events. More importantly, strong opposition may not even occur in the first place *because* of critical events. Indeed, the use of fines against (mainly domestic) constructors prior to the case of the Evinos dam would have been opposed by their powerful lobby.

Finally, single-loop learning such as that identified in this case does not lead to the resolution of chronic problems that generated it in the first place. Indeed, the action of the Greek government remained confined to the field of public procurement. In other words, the basic characteristics of the Greek central government initially identified as causes of problematic implementation have been addressed only to the extent that they concern public procurement.[17]

The politicisation of public procurement

One particular aspect of the reform process was the explicit politicisation of public procurement and its direct links to other cardinal issues regarding the Greek political system. This was the result of the explicit strategy of the conservative New Democracy party (in opposition between 1993 and 2004) to make political capital against the socialist governments led by Andreas Papandreou and – especially – Simitis, by turning public procurement into a major component of party politics.[18] The legislation that regulates the links between public procurement on the one hand and mass media ownership on the other is a clear example.

Given that the owners of some Greek construction companies were also major shareholders in mass media companies (especially daily newspapers and television channels) fears arose during the 1990s that (i) the power of the latter might be used in an effort to influence decisions regarding the former and (ii) media power might be concentrated in a handful of powerful organisations. As a result, the socialist government introduced in the mid-1990s new legislation stipulating that companies involved in the award of major[19] procurement contracts had to name their shareholders at the time of the submission of their bid and to do so by means of a certificate obtained from the relevant supervising authority (Koutoupa 1996). As a result, interested firms lobbied the government in an effort to postpone the implementation of this legislation. They also unsuccessfully sought to have this legislation suspended by the Council of State,[20] i.e. the country's highest administrative court (Koutoupa 1996, CS 169).

Moreover, as a result of the revision of 2001, the Constitution stipulates (Art. 14.9) that owners, partners, main shareholders or senior executives of media companies cannot simultaneously be[21] owners, partners, main shareholders or senior executives of media companies engaged in public procurement projects.[22] Although the MPs of the two main political parties ended up voting in favour of the new provision, the intensity of the debate regarding its scope – especially the contentious notion of 'main shareholder' and the specificity of its definition – was indicative of a broader problem that undermined efforts to resolve a real issue whose implications go way beyond the remit of public procurement. Indeed, the prevailing climate of polarisation that resulted from the attitude of the main opposition party (the conservative ND) forced the socialist government to (i) accept a constitutional provision and (ii) endorse the implementing law purely in an effort to avoid allegations regarding favouritism. In that context, the voices of those (including Prime Minister Simitis and senior members of the Cabinet[23]) who claimed – rightly, as it turned out – that the draconian provisions of domestic legislation were (a) in conflict with primary and secondary EU legislation and (b) likely to prove ineffective, were hardly heard. The opposition made political capital by portraying the real problem of compatibility with EU law as a fig leaf[24] covering laxity while the government was simply forced to bide its time until the expected future EU-induced changes to domestic legislation. After its victory in the general election of March 2004 the conservative ND passed a new law (Law 3310/2005) that was meant to enhance the existing national legislation. In the letter of formal notice that it sent to the Greek government in March 2005, the Commission argued that domestic legislation[25] violates both procurement-related directives (in particular the provisions that specify the selection criteria) and the provisions of the Treaty regarding 'the exercise of almost all the fundamental freedoms acknowledged by the EC Treaty' (European Commission press release IP/05/356).

As a result of the subsequent suspension of Law 3310/2005, Law 3021/2002 (adopted by the socialists) came back into force. Nevertheless, according to the Commission, it too posed the same problem (press release IP/05/855). The sensitivity of the issue and the intensity of the domestic political debate are such that the Commission repeatedly stressed its willingness to collaborate closely with the Greek authorities in order to resolve the problem[26] while, on the domestic front, the two main parties agreed to revise Art. 14.9 in the context of the ongoing constitutional reform that commenced in 2006.

In a narrow sense, the main question concerns the proportionality of the provisions of domestic legislation. The dispassionate analysis of the new legislation introduced in 2005 leads to the conclusion that (in their draft form) these provisions breached key legal requirements regarding the single European market (Hellenic Parliament 2005, 17). At the same time though, both the jurisprudence of the ECJ and the Treaty allow exemptions to the extent that they are either dictated by considerations regarding public order, public safety or public health or are in the public interest. Indeed, the ECJ has accepted the notion that limitations may be placed on the fundamental freedoms enshrined in the Treaty when this is required by the effective handling of services of general interest (Hellenic Parliament 2005, 18). More importantly, the preamble of Directive 2004/18 stipulates that:

> [n]othing in this Directive should prevent the imposition or enforcement of measures necessary to protect public policy, public morality, public security, health, human and animal life or the preservation of plant life, in particular with a view to sustainable development, provided that these measures are in conformity with the Treaty.

Moreover, as regards the substance, politicians were aware of (a) the limits of any legislative measure and (b) alternative means of problem-solving used in other member states, including the enhanced role of national competition authorities (Simitis 2005, 412–3). Thus, the embarrassing situation in which the conservative government put itself could have been avoided if the route of overt political conflict had been replaced by the dispassionate analysis of existing opportunities and constraints. Of course, this requires a more mature understanding of the implications of membership of the EU. Such an understanding appears far from being part of the *référentiel* of the senior ministers involved in the handling of this sensitive case or, if it was present, it was quickly discredited as a result of the requirements of party political competition.

In a more general sense, what is at stake here is the capacity of the Greek politico-administrative system to cope with the exigencies of membership. The preceding analysis regarding learning, and its impact on patterns of implementation ought to be assessed against the recent experience regarding the laws of 2002 and 2005 as well as other changes announced by the conservative government since it took office in 2004. The first announcement concerns the establishment of an independent administrative agency that would be empowered to verify the legality of all public procurement contracts. It is unclear as to whether and how its role would differ from the role that is currently performed by the Greek Court of Auditors. The announcement made in Parliament by the junior Minister of Development in March 2006[27] did not indicate whether the role of the new agency would include guidance on substantive issues (Ministry of Development 2006b).

The second announcement concerns the establishment of a system that will deal with procurement issues in the area of the health service. In response to numerous media reports which indicated that major problems exist in this area,[28] the Minister of Health decided to introduce legislation that centralises the health procurement system. For that purpose, he has decided to create a separate central procurement agency (specific to the health sector) that will unify the existing fragmented system that operates in this particular sector. This seems to maintain the logic of fragmentation and raises the simple issue of continuity: what is so peculiar about procurement in the domain of health that requires a separate system?

France: nodality and authority in competition

The role and limits of the CCM

The action of the CCM, whose economic section took the initiative to open the debate in France on the implementation of the basic principles of the Treaty of Rome in public procurement as early as 1960, took a number of forms (Dillemann 1987). First, it was an important contact point not only for individual bidders but, more importantly, for every part of the administration that deals with public procurement. Using the rich background knowledge incorporated into a number of reports that its sections had produced, the CCM was (until 2004) an inter-ministerial body that ensured a degree of continuity in terms of the guidance that was provided to other parts of the administration. Examples include the definition of the concept of 'awarding authority' and its concrete application on a day-to-day basis,[29] the choice of the correct award procedure, the concept of the concession contract[30] and also the necessary distinctions between services and works contracts. Furthermore, CCM officials provided answers to questions regarding horizontal issues such as the definition of what constitutes a single works project and what can be considered as part of such a project. This function was especially important in cases where a principle had to be established. This is when recourse to the CCM was seen as necessary.

The studies produced by the CCM (especially the prices section, which used to be autonomous) have enabled the administration to specify the content of the most frequently used award criterion, namely 'the most interesting offer', a typical characteristic of the French Public Procurement Code. As a result, a number of elements have to be taken into account during the award procedure.[31] The initial vagueness of this criterion underlines the significance of the role of the CCM in the precise definition of its content on the basis of various elements, including the price, the cost of use, the technical value and the time scale for the execution of the contract. These criteria were subsequently integrated into the Code (e.g. Art. 97 *bis*, 299 *ter*). Clearly, 'the most interesting offer' was the French equivalent of what in other countries became known as 'the most advantageous offer'.

The high profile that the CCM has developed over the years enabled its officials to have direct access to the Minister of Economy and Finance, and more importantly, to the members of his *cabinet* in order to resolve problems relating to day-to-day implementation of EU public procurement policy. This channel worked both ways. Indeed, the efforts to reform the Code in order to further enhance transparency and simplicity in the preparation and the execution of the contracts linked the CCM directly with the political realm within the same ministry and in co-operation with trade and industry organisations (large construction companies, small and medium-sized suppliers etc.), which were an important driving force behind this effort. The CCM maintained close contacts with these organisations, primarily through its economic and technical sections. This, in turn, was a key part of this body's ethos. Indeed, extensive consultation procedures also concerned the wider public administration. In the mid-1980s between 2,000 and 3,000 members of the wider public sector and professional organisations (such as civil engineers) were associated with the work of this body (Dillemann 1987, 100).

This contact was important because it enabled the CCM to take account of many views in the administrative implementation of EU policy. This action included the standardisation of documents used by the administration in award procedures (which facilitated comparisons and the detection of irregularities) and, more importantly, the standardisation of norms and specifications that are necessary for the definition of works, supplies and services and the subsequent award of the corresponding contracts.[32]

The establishment of comparable norms was a function performed by the technical section of the CCM in collaboration with other parts of the administration and covered whole groups of functions and supplies. This function underlined the importance of the role performed by horizontal bodies – such as CCM – which were in a position to develop solutions to problems that are faced by other parts of the implementation structure. Finally, the CCM also performed the role of an educator not only by preparing guides (relating to each phase of the award procedure) for the attention of awarding authorities, but also by organising training schemes (through the *Cellule formation*, i.e. the training unit of its secretariat). These schemes were meant to disseminate expertise on various aspects of public purchasing, including cost limitation and negotiation techniques (Dillemann 1987, 111).

The formal and informal means employed by bidders and trade organisations during the implementation process demonstrate the limits of the role of CCM. The very notion of *précontentieux*, that is pre-judicial review (Gaudemet 1994) is very familiar to French lawyers and it constitutes an important instrument for the preservation of a free market, through the use of three methods namely administrative review, conciliation and transaction.[33] Nevertheless, its existence has not limited the development of important case law that the CCM followed closely.

The increasing French case law on public procurement (Martin 1994a, 1994b, 1996; *Les Echos* 20 March 2001) did not hide a certain timidity of French companies in the implementation process. This timidity is reflected through their unwillingness to attack their clients in court (Bréchon-Moulènes 1990, 164) by way of traditional legal procedures, despite the reinforcement of other relevant institutional structures – such as the Competition Council, an independent administrative authority that has been involved in public procurement cases[34] relating to collusion between bidders (Bazex 1994, 104). French civil servants underlined a correlation between the size of the company and its willingness to pursue a *politique jurisprudentielle*, that is a systematic policy of using judicial review in an effort to promote their interests.[35] Significant market players were (and remain) more able and willing than small and medium-sized companies to afford the high cost of litigation.[36]

Furthermore, there are three reasons why the importance of the aforementioned timidity should not be over-estimated. First, the transposition of the Remedies Directive produced an important innovation in French law, namely the so-called *référé précontractuel* (Valadou 1993, 331; Lichere 2006, 171). This entails recourse to rapid review prior to the conclusion of a contract. More specifically, this procedure enables the state and certain persons to bring before the courts an action relating to the breach of rules regarding publicity and competitive procedures, during the selection or the award stage but in any case *prior* to the conclusion of a contract. The popularity of this procedure with firms has increased over time (Cartron 1997) despite the fact that the CCM considered that the success rate was limited.[37]

These developments ought to be placed in the broader context of the French system. A key component of this system is the legal concept of the *acte détachable* – that is a detachable act, established by the French *Conseil d'État* (Fernández Martin 1996, 231–3). Instead of treating the action that the administration undertakes during the award procedure and the subsequent contract as an indivisible whole, the two are considered as separable. Hence any interested party may attack in court as unlawful the acts that precede the conclusion of the contract, including the decision to award it. This extends their mechanisms for protection without necessarily affecting legal certainty and the contract. Thus, an awarding authority may be compelled to pay compensation as a result of the unlawful award of a contract whilst the latter may remain valid, thereby preserving the rights of the company that won it. This increased the risk of turning public procurement projects into a source of problems for public finances.[38]

In addition to these developments, throughout the late 1980s and the first half of the 1990s a number of significant cases of procurement-related corruption occurred in France (see, for instance, Potet 1998; *Le Monde* 28 March 1994, 9 May 1994, 8 February 1995; *Les Echos* 16 June 1994). These were clear indications of the problems that permeated the French system. Some of these cases were of wider importance since they were linked to the illegal[39] provision of funds to political parties.[40] These developments had two direct implications. On the one hand, the French central government undertook successive reforms including the establishment of the *Mission interministérielle d'enquête sur les marchés* (MIEM – Procurement Inquiry Task Force) and the revision of the Code. On the other hand, this process has been marked by the explicit politicisation of the regulation of public procurement. These issues are discussed in the next sections of this chapter.

Authority and its limits: the role of MIEM
Since its establishment in 1991 (Loi 91–3), MIEM has become a key component of the institutional apparatus dealing with public procurement within the French central government. Composed of magistrates and senior civil servants,[41] it has the power to undertake – at the request of the Prime Minister, the Minister of Economy and Finance[42] and prefects[43] – inquiries into the preparation, award and execution of procurement contracts.[44] Its power of investigation are very significant and extend to the public and the private sector. Indeed, given that unlawful preparation, award and execution of public procurement contracts can falsify competition,[45] MIEM is mandated[46] to inform the French Competition Council when it uncovers indications of violations of domestic competition legislation (Bazex 1994). Its members have a significant degree of operational autonomy when they deal with individual cases, while issues of principle are discussed in plenary sessions (Mission interministérielle d'enquête sur les marchés 1999, annex 1).

The establishment of this body was part of the response to problems that go beyond the domain of public procurement and include corruption, the transparency of financial markets and money laundering (Mission interministérielle d'enquête sur les marchés 1995). The law that created this body also established severe penalties for officials (be they elected or not) involved in the provision of an unjustified advantage to firms involved in public tenders (Art. 7). In its effort to enhance the effectiveness of the new system, the government took action that revealed a problem of co-ordination at the level of law-making. Indeed, when it extended the scope of MIEM's area of responsibility to cover, *inter alia*, concession contracts (Loi 93–122) it did so after the relevant provision (Art. 7) had been abrogated as a result of its introduction into the French penal code (Mission interministérielle d'enquête sur les marchés 1995). In other words, the government ended up extending the scope of a provision that it had abrogated.[47]

MIEM's initial investigations shed light on the types of action that are covered by the aforementioned provision. They include the fragmentation of one project into multiple small procurement projects, the provision of inside information to a candidate, the unclear definition of procurement needs which, in turn, facilitate arbitrary decisions, the definition of technical specifications that limit competition, limited publicity and the non-exclusion of bids that do not correspond to the project (Mission interministérielle d'enquête sur les marchés 1995). MIEM has no power of initiative but once it has started an investigation, it has the power to extend its scope if that is deemed appropriate. Moreover, it collaborates closely with the various units of DGCCRF (*Direction de la concurrence, de la consommation et de la répression des fraudes* – Competition, Consumption and Anti-fraud Directorate) of the Ministry of Economy and Finance (Mission interministérielle d'enquête sur les marchés 1999, annex 1).

MIEM was intended to operate primarily as a deterrent in an otherwise fragmented system. Indeed, as the MIEM acknowledged (Mission interministérielle d'enquête sur les marchés 1998, 3:66) the power of the *Cour des comptes* (the French Court of Auditors, including its regional branches) to examine the lawfulness of procurement procedures used by local authorities entailed controls that took place almost three years after the relevant contract had been signed. In addition, the initial control exercised by the *commissions spécialisées des marchés* at the stage of the preparation of a procurement project was patchy. This is so because their presidents had the power to retain (and then discuss in the plenary session, in the presence of a representative of the relevant awarding authority) only those that appeared to merit this treatment but the commissions drafted their reports on the basis of the information provided by the administration and they had to do so within excessively tight deadlines (30 days). Finally, the lack of staff, the complexity of the subject matter and gaps in the relevant documentation also undermined the capacity of prefects to monitor the legality of award procedures.

However, as the Head of MIEM acknowledged recently, the context – and, as a consequence, the need for its services – changed as a result of the reforms introduced since 2001.[48] These reforms mirrored a shift in emphasis from the detection and repression of irregularities (which was necessary during the 1990s) to the provision of assistance and advice to awarding authorities

(Mission interministérielle d'enquête sur les marchés et les conventions de délégation de service public 2004, 1:5). The data regarding its activity demonstrate that MIEM was very much a product of the 1990s and the problems that occurred in France during that decade. After a slow start (seven cases handled in 1992), its activity peaked in the mid-1990s (thirty-two cases handled in 1994 and thirty-eight in 1995) but during the second half of the same decade it never exceeded eighteen cases. This pattern of decline was confirmed after 2000. Its load fell below ten cases in 2002 and it received no requests for investigation in 2004 (Mission interministérielle d'enquête sur les marchés et les conventions de délégation de service public 2005, 2:36). It is important to note that it would be wrong to ascribe this change in emphasis exclusively to a decision of the government. Indeed, between 1995 and 2004 MIEM received (and responded to) a total of 200 requests for an opinion.[49] Although this was not part of its formal role, various administrative and judicial bodies asked MIEM to give its opinion on various cases. This indicates that the aforementioned shift in emphasis (one of the major changes introduced since 2001) was a response to a growing (and evident) need.

The reforms introduced since 2001: beyond authority?
MIEM, parliamentarians and policy makers in central government explicitly acknowledged the increasing multiplicity and complexity[50] of procurement-related French texts (Ministère de l'Economie, des Finances et de l'Industrie 1999; Mission interministérielle d'enquête sur les marchés 1999, 5; *Les Echos* 15 March 1996). MIEM officials were aware of the fact that this was particularly important for smaller awarding entities since they often did not possess the technical and legal affairs units that would enable them to procure what they need on the one hand, whilst fulfilling EU and national requirements on the other. Nevertheless, this challenge was not limited to these authorities. Rather, it was a systemic necessity.[51] This was a key motive for the simplification of the Code (Décret 2001–210), one of the principal features of the reform introduced by the socialist-led government in 2001 (Fabius 2001). The number of articles included in the revised Code dropped from 399 to 136 in the government's effort to simplify the domestic regulatory framework.[52] The text was structured on the basis of the various stages of the award process (definition of need, award of contract, execution and control) in order to facilitate its use. The distinction between the rules that applied to state authorities and those that applied to local authorities was abolished. Moreover, some important changes stemmed from the government's broader political priorities. Specifically, the new Code (i) explicitly acknowledged the possibility of taking into consideration the social and environmental conditions in which a contract is to be put into effect, (ii) promoted the use of electronic procurement and (iii) simplified formalities in an effort to alleviate the role of elected officials and to promote the involvement of SMEs in procurement projects.

In response to the often acknowledged pressing need for the provision of legal, financial and technical advice and guidance to local authorities, two options (one centralised and one decentralised) were considered (Ministère de l'Economie, des Finances et de l'Industrie 1999) in the context of the two-year consultation that preceded the adoption of the new Code. The government, in the end, opted for a decentralised system.[53] Moreover, given the weaknesses of some centralised procurement practices[54] and advice provided by the CCM (*Les Echos* 10 December 1997; *Le Monde* 18 February 1999), the provision of training[55] and technological support to procurement officers was, rightly, seen as an important additional means to improve implementation (*Le Monde* 7 March 2001).

Acting in an effort to improve – at the level of the central government – the timely provision of advice to public purchasers, the government increased the number of CSMs and enabled awarding entities to obtain the opinion of the relevant CSM before the launch of a procurement project (Décret 2001–739). Although this was certainly a step in the right direction, the CSMs examined only the dossiers that appeared to be most problematic and only to the extent that this examination was possible in the light of the operational capacity[56] of each CSM (Commissions Spécialisées des Marchés 2001, 7–8).

In addition, the legal review procedures have been revised so as to facilitate judicial review *prior* to the conclusion of a contract (Loi 2000–597). Acting in an effort to resolve the problem of abnormally low bids that falsify competition, the government limited to 5% the amount that constructors could claim on top of the initial budget of a project and explicitly allowed the exclusion of 'abnormally low offers'.

The efforts of the French government to simplify the domestic legislation – especially the reduced number of articles – inevitably meant that individual provisions would need to be more abstract so as to regulate certain forms of procurement practices. As a result, the Commission[57] objected (press release IP/02/1507) to a number of provisions of the new Code because it felt that they undermined competition. They included those that concerned the thresholds that apply to service contracts,[58] the use of negotiated and restricted award procedures, the provision of prior information and the use of variants, the provisions regarding contracts that are not subject to EU procurement directives and some service-related contracts[59] as well as the evidence that tenderers from other member states ought to provide so as to demonstrate that they comply with domestic legislation regarding tax and social contributions. The Commission raised these issues by means of a reasoned opinion (which is just one step away from the referral of a case to the ECJ). The response of the French government took the form of a revised Code that was adopted in January 2004 (Décret 2004–15).

Six changes ought to be highlighted, namely the use of higher thresholds for the definition of contracts that must be awarded on the basis of formal procedures, the extension of the duty to advertise contracts, the introduction of provisions that allow the exclusion of certain kinds of contracts (such as those that concern security or state interests), the extension of the scope of application of negotiated procedures to the contracts whose value is lower than the EU thresholds, the promotion of recourse to central procurement agencies and the co-ordination of procurement and, finally, the reduction of the documents that tenderers must submit along with their offer.

The Commission referred France to the ECJ (press release IP/04/162; *Le Monde* 6 February 2004) for non-compliance. It alleged, in particular, that the new French legislation failed to resolve the problems regarding some service contracts (such as those that concern legal, health, recreational, cultural, sporting, education, vocational training and placement services) that ought to be advertised and the minimum number of participants to be invited to a restricted procedure. A year later the *Conseil d'État* annulled the provision of Art. 30 of the Code (services) for breach of EU legislation (*Les Echos* 7 March 2005). The substantive issues raised by the Commission and the *Conseil d'État* had an institutional origin. The inter-ministerial consultation that preceded the adoption of the Code of 2004 operated effectively at the political level but it is important to note that (a) it required the direct involvement of Prime Minister Raffarin and (b) this focused on the important (but not sole) issue of the thresholds (*Le Figaro* 3 July 2003, 19 July 2003; *Les Echos* 18 July 2003, 8 January 2004; *La Croix* 21 July 2003, 9 January 2004). On the other hand, other important aspects of the reforms envisaged by Francis Mer (the pro-business then Minister of Economy and Finance of the centre-right government) such as the limitation of the role of the CSMs[60] was problematic. Indeed, Pierre Lelong, president of the CCM that co-ordinated their activity, publicly denounced the lack of co-ordination between the legal affairs directorate of the Ministry and the CSMs and went as far as to state that there was no communication between them (Lelong 2003). In substantive terms, he claimed that, since the French state did not have many good purchasers, it would be a mistake to limit the role of CSMs given the prevalence of 'untidy' procurement dossiers in France (Lelong 2003).

The need for improved co-ordination was at the heart of the establishment of the *Commission des marchés publics de l'État* (CMPE – State Procurement Commission), a result of the reforms introduced in 2004 (Décret 2004–1299; *supra*, Chapter 3). It replaced the CSMs that operated since 1972 but includes approximately only half of their personnel (Commission des Marchés Publics de l'État 2006, 7). It is responsible for assisting ministers and officials involved in procurement in terms of the preparation or the award of major procurement projects by issuing comments, recommendations or reserves. Its role is preventive in the sense that awarding authorities are obliged to consult with it prior to publicising any plans for major[61] procurement projects. However, not all major procurement projects are scrutinised by the CMPE. The dossiers are initially examined by its secretariat general. Acting on its proposal, the president decides (i) whether to retain a given dossier for further scrutiny and (ii) how to handle those that are retained, i.e. provide comments directly to the awarding authority or include in the agenda of the plenary (Commission des Marchés Publics de l'État 2005, 6). Tight deadlines – seven and thirty working days respectively – apply in both cases so as to avoid unnecessary delays but this has an impact on the number of cases that are actually examined.

When dealing with a particular case, the CMPE examines the needs that a procurement project is meant to address, the place that this project occupies in a broader programme or operation undertaken by the awarding authority, the precise content of the procurement project, the way in which the price range has been defined, the provisional calendar for its implementation, the characteristics of the sector (e.g. industrial or other) and the type of company that is likely to respond, the chosen award procedure, the award criteria and their relative importance and particular issues regarding its implementation (e.g. intellectual property rights). Awarding authorities must specify the points or issues on which they need the CMPE's advice. Crucially, once the CMPE has provided its response, its interlocutors are not bound by it. Nevertheless, its president has the right to communicate the response to the relevant minister if the issue warrants it (Art. 4, Décret 2004–1299). Finally, in cases of procurement projects of particular economic significance, complexity or difficulty in terms of the implementation of the relevant legislation, the CMPE has the power to utilise a special assistance procedure so as to guide the activity of the awarding authority.

In contrast to the committees that it replaced – which became involved only in the final stage of decision making and, as a result, could not really provide advice but only criticise actions that had already taken place[62] – the CMPE's guidance is provided at the beginning of the process, even prior to the publication of the call for expressions of interest, but in some cases it can be extended until the stage of the signing of the contract (Commission des Marchés Publics de l'État 2006, 7). Moreover, the composition of the CSM produced unintended consequences in the sense that the financial controller who attended the meetings often used the negative opinion of the CSM in order to block the implementation of procurement projects despite the availability of the monies. Since January 2005, this is no longer the case because the CMPE does not include officials responsible for financial control (Décret 2005–54). Finally, the president of the CMPE has the right to involve ministers if he considers that this would be beneficial, though this facility is used relatively rarely[63] (Commission des Marchés Publics de l'État 2006, 10).

The CMPE's initial findings indicate that its interventions cover the whole of the procurement process, including the definition of the need that a procurement project is meant to satisfy, the form of the project, the choice and the operation of the award procedure, as well as the execution of procurement projects (Commission des Marchés Publics de l'État 2006, 18–35). In addition, as regards supply and works[64] contracts, awarding authorities actively incorporate in their projects the recommendations and opinions issued initially by the CMPE (Commission des Marchés Publics de l'État 2006, 36, 44).

Initially the CMPE did not possess the means to (a) identify cases of dossiers that should have been but were actually not submitted to it for scrutiny and (b) have a clear and systematic view of the use of its work made by awarding authorities (Commission des Marchés Publics de l'État 2006, 50). In response to these problems, two changes were introduced in early 2007. First, senior officials of CMPE have decided to begin scrutinising both the Official Journal and the relevant authoritative website[65] where public contracts are advertised in order to identify the contracts that should have been, but were actually not, submitted to the CMPE. Once a contract of this kind has been identified, the President of the CMPE or the relevant minister sends a letter to the corresponding awarding authority reminding it of its obligations. Second, a new formal arrangement has been put in place whereby all awarding authorities are obliged to submit to the CMPE, once the process has been concluded, the full details of their final decision (Art. 4 IV, Décret 2007–61). This will allow the CMPE to have a more accurate picture of the actual responses given to its observations and opinions.

Nevertheless, one problem that has been noticed concerns the fact that some ministries frequently change their representatives. As a result, the CMPE promotes the designation of one *'Monsieur Marchés de l'État'* in each ministry. This would provide an additional focal point of expertise at the intra-departmental level.

Learning and the impact of politicisation
Arguably, learning played a significant role in the evolution of implementation patterns in France. In the light of the fact that organisational learning entails observations and inferences, the acquisition of new techniques, improvements in an organisation's performance and changes in the theory of action which is implicit in its activity, it can be argued that changes in implementation patterns in France were couched in single-loop learning. This is so for three reasons.

First, the change that occurred in the French system during the 1990s reflects long-standing patterns of institutional evolution, as opposed to a radical change of values. The initial emphasis of the institutional reforms introduced in the early 1990s on the *post hoc* detection of problems by means of a small but powerful body (MIEM) shows growing awareness of the weaknesses of the system as well as an institutionalised emphasis on suppression and punishment as opposed to the *prevention* of problems. The dramatic increase in the number of French calls advertised at the European level between 1993 and 1998 – from 5,773 to 19,691, i.e. by more than 240%,[66] is the direct result of the pronounced emphasis on publicity and competition as well as the presence of MIEM. Nevertheless, this was only part of the changing trend.[67] Indeed, the links between the roles performed by the MIEM and the French Competition Council indicate growing awareness of not only the limits of sectoral regulation but also the implications of the dominant role of one group of companies in two seemingly separate markets (public procurement and media).

Second, although the efforts to simplify the Code indicate growing awareness of the implications of its initial complexity for its users, crucially, this reform was combined with the enhancement of the capacity of the centre to prevent and detect problems. This resulted not only from the significant volume of French case law but also the external pressure exercised by the Commission through the pursuit of infringement cases under Art. 169/226. Third, evidence that learning was taking place is provided by the fact that the aforementioned changes did not remain confined to one sub-sector. Rather, when they were introduced, they were explicitly meant to cover the entire system of public procurement.

There are three reasons why the pace of change (and learning) was slower in France than it was in Greece. First, the absence of a direct link to EU funding deprived the French central government of a powerful additional incentive that was present in reform in Greece. Second, the absence of a critical juncture did not help focus the attention of French policy makers on the reform of the French system. Although the case of the *Stade de France* could have become this juncture (given the magnitude and the public profile of the project) structural weaknesses of infringement proceedings under Art. 169/226 of the Treaty (in particular the length of time required for the completion of the process) and the decision of the Commission to stop the process once the French government had acknowledged its mistakes, prevented this development. Finally, the timing of the politicisation of public procurement in France contributed to the slow pace of the reforms. Unlike the Greek case (where politicisation occurred *after* the most significant reforms had taken shape) politicisation in France occurred during the 1990s, i.e. when the necessity of reform was becoming apparent.

Once the implications of the establishment of the single market began to become apparent in France – in part as a result of the drive to liberalise public procurement – pressure on the conservative government (in power since 1993) grew to protect major French companies involved in public procurement (see, e.g., *Les Echos* 13 June 1994). At the same time, the anti-corruption legislative framework that the socialists had established (Loi 93–122) was beginning to bear fruit, not only in the form of the increased number of corruption cases brought to courts but also in terms of the need to improve transparency, i.e. a pre-requisite for increased competition in public procurement. Caught between these two competing trends, the pro-business conservative government opted for the reduction of the transparency-related legislative requirements at a time when evidence was emerging about the illegal provision of funding to political parties (*Les Echos* 16 June 1994). The combination of these factors created a political opportunity structure that was not conducive to the dispassionate handling of a complex issue.[68] As a result, both the government and the opposition took positions that – despite the appearances – could be, but were not, reconciled. While the former chose to hide behind the *lourdeur* and the unintended consequences of the '*Loi Sapin*', the latter denounced the changes introduced by the government despite the aforementioned unintended consequences (Sapin 1994; Thiriez 2000). The combined effect of politicisation and the absence of a critical event meant that the necessary reforms could only be adopted years later.

The UK: the confirmation of nodality and treasure

The centrality of the Treasury
Administrative implementation of EU public procurement policy in the UK reflects the centrality of the Treasury in the wider transition to the neo-liberal paradigm brought about by the Conservative party after the general election of 1979. During the 1970s the process of administrative implementation was characterised by the use of preferential schemes dating from the immediate post-war period (Turpin 1989, 77). The aim of these schemes was the allocation of contracts to firms based in specific developing regions. While under the General Preference Scheme government departments awarded contracts to firms based in these areas when all else (including price, quality and delivery) was equal, the Special Preference Scheme gave the opportunity to firms based in the areas in question to obtain 25% of the order if no additional cost occurred and if other considerations were equal. Both schemes were running counter to the very philosophy of the EU's policy (as it evolved since then) because of their emphasis on the allocation of contracts to firms located in British regions – a clear way of discriminating against firms from other member states. In addition to the regional element, British procurement policy had a pronounced sectoral element. British governments sought during the 1970s (and even the 1960s) to support the domestic computer industry through a preferential policy which meant that large computers were purchased from a British company through single tender,[69] subject to satisfactory price and delivery. This policy was abandoned in the end of the 1970s not only as a result of the change of government but also because the exemption granted by the then EEC[70] expired (Turpin 1989, 76). In August 1994 the British government abandoned the Priority Suppliers Scheme – implemented mainly by the Ministry of Defence. Under that scheme a degree of preference was given to products of certain workshops for the disabled and prison workshops. The consolidation of the supplies directive in 1993 brought an end to it (Arrowsmith 1994).

Although some reforms had already been adopted in the late 1960s by the Labour government which had decided to contract-out cleaning services in central government departments (Turpin 1989, 72), the first signs of change date from 1972 when the Conservative government led by Heath introduced the Local Government Act 1972. It established compulsory competitive tendering procedures for local authorities in cases of some purchases of goods or the execution of works (Art. 135 § 3). The Department of the Environment, contrary to its previous practice, arranged to issue weekly press releases that included information about notices which had already been sent to the Official Journal of the European Communities for publication. These notices were published in the specialised press in order to enable interested British firms to be informed about forthcoming competitions.

During the 1980s, the implementation process was underpinned by the clear shift towards competitive procedures, the limitation of public expenditure and the predominance of the Treasury. The role of the Treasury in this domain went far beyond the mere transposition of the new policy paradigm and the actions taken in order to bring developments in EC public procurement policy to the attention of British awarding authorities. It was after the Treasury's intervention through the provision of guidance that some authorities abolished the requirement – previously imposed on prospective contractors – to provide information about the composition of their workforce and an indication of plans to use their own or local workforce for the execution of works contracts. Moreover, the Treasury collected data on the award of works contracts before submitting them to the Commission and offered guidance on a number of instances.[71] This guidance included not only the detailed explanation of the public procurement directives but, more importantly, day-to-day advice to awarding authorities. The Treasury's role involved the enhancement of awareness about domestic policy requirements and the directives, especially detailed aspects thereof, such as technical specifications whose role in promoting (or, indeed, undermining) competition is crucial.

This effort to turn the provisions of the public procurement directives into reality took rather diverse forms that reflect the pivotal role of the Treasury in the wider implementation process. In some respects, the role of the Treasury was similar to that of the Commission in the sense that its authority was used in order to convince interested parties about the procedures that had to be followed in the purchasing process. For example, by shifting 'blame'[72] to the Treasury, purchasing officers were able to avoid pressure from users of supplies, works or services. Other, more general, forms of action included the publication of detailed guidance notes addressing particular issues that some awarding authorities faced as a result of lack of experience, and significant practical problems such as the change in the cost of a purchase between the initial and the final estimate, and the handling of the key issue of publicity (see, for example, HM Treasury 1988; 1995; 1996; 1998). The role of the Treasury as a nodal contact point also concerned bidders who occasionally aired their complaints with this department. The role of the Treasury in this case took the form of an informal legal adviser. Its officials drew attention to the rights conferred upon bidders by the directives and the relevant domestic legislation, leaving them to decide as to how to pursue a given issue (see *infra*).

Apart from these procedural aspects, the role of the Treasury was inextricably linked to significant domestic policy developments that were channelled through it. This was more evident in the case of policies that had a horizontal economic dimension. Indeed, the traditional primacy of the principle of 'value for money' in the UK's public procurement policy was channelled through the Treasury. This emphasis led to the primacy of the criterion of the most economically advantageous offer. The Treasury defined this concept as 'the optimum combination of the whole life cost and quality to meet the customer's requirement' (HM Government 1995, 6).

It further sought to promote flexibility by acknowledging that there is no single organisational model for effective procurement and by organising courses (Williams and Smellie 1985, 28) for purchasing officers[73] in order to facilitate the implementation of the core policy principle of 'value for money'. In addition, it identified key factors characterising effective procurement activity including, *inter alia*, central co-ordination of activities ensuring sharing of expertise, and a pro-active approach.[74]

A significant domestic development that affected the implementation process involved the privatisation of central purchasing agencies. This, in turn, is directly linked to the concept of 'untying'. It entailed the abolition of the obligation of central government departments to procure products through central agencies. This meant, in practice, that alternative arrangements could be made by departments for their procurement needs, e.g. through contracts with commercial suppliers (Turpin 1989, 3). Previously, the use of central purchasing agencies[75] meant that they (as opposed to their clients) were responsible for meeting the purchasers' international obligations, in line with the Treasury's guidance. The abandonment of this traditional feature of the UK's procurement policy commenced in 1982 when ministerial departments were formally untied from HMSO. This development has had direct repercussions on the implementation of EC policy in this field.

Untying meant that responsibility for day-to-day implementation of EC policy went back to the relevant users, i.e. individual government departments, if the latter chose not to use central agencies. A significant implication of this development was the proliferation of purchasers within central government.[76] In turn, this led (albeit indirectly) to the reinforcement of the role of the Treasury as well as the view that public procurement is, above all, a matter of public expenditure – i.e. an area in which the Treasury had (at least since 1979) an unchallenged lead within Whitehall. Crucially, the Treasury's public procurement policy staff included not only policy specialists but, crucially, procurement practitioners as well. As a result, this team of officials could understand and deal with both policy and the practical issues regarding public procurement. Moreover, the privatisation of some central purchasing agencies meant that they were obliged to behave as proper market players by becoming more competitive and by aiming at the generation of profit. In cases such as these, guidance from the Treasury emphasised the right of private bodies to advertise contracts in TED and the OJEC when acting as a purchasing agent for one or more departments, while also underlining the need for the latter to ensure that the private body had a contractual responsibility to act in conformity with the directives.

The role of the Treasury in the implementation process, just like every part of public administration for that matter, is conditioned by the action of the target groups, i.e. potential and actual tenderers. One must draw a distinction between their willingness to submit offers and their willingness to protect their rights during or after the award procedure. On the one hand, the UK's local government procurement market constituted an important 'test case' during the 1980s and early 1990s. Indeed, the UK government's policy on compulsory competitive tendering[77] meant that local authorities in the UK were obliged to put out for tender procurement contracts, even when they had the in-house expertise to cover their needs and the value of the contract was below the thresholds stipulated by the directives. In-house units had to be treated as any other tenderer. Nevertheless, very little interest has been generated in the form of 'foreign tenders' (Paddon 1993, 168–72). What has actually happened was a wave of joint ventures and acquisitions of British firms. These two strategies were used by French, German, Dutch and Italian companies, especially during the 1980s. Significantly, Paddon (1993, 172–3) underlined the fact that '[i]t is in these services that the pursuit of Europe-wide development and acquisition strategies by a number of EC-based multinational service companies, with particular targeting of the UK public sector, is most evident', even before the inclusion of the services sector into the European regulatory framework that covers public procurement. The same trend has been observed by Treasury officials who also noted that in a significant numbers of cases foreign companies set up subsidiaries in the UK. These subsidiaries subsequently responded to calls for tenders.[78]

On the other hand, the willingness of firms to contact the Treasury and the European Commission in pursuit of a case in which they considered that their interests had been damaged appears to have been used more readily than formal legal procedures. The existence of limited case law[79] has been noted not only by academics (Birkinshaw 1990, 303) but also by the administration itself as well as the Confederation of British Industry (Department of Trade and Industry 1994, § 104). British officials attribute this phenomenon to the fact that – although companies actually bring to the attention of public authorities the alleged irregularities that they face, the pursuit of these cases in the courts is not part of the prevailing business ethos.

Finally, the Private Finance Initiative (Clark 1996, CS87), which aims to attract private capital to public works and services, has been streamlined through the Treasury which provided both a 'carrot' (relaxation of rules relating to free-standing projects and the provision of services to the public sector) and a 'stick' (the refusal to authorise expenditure for projects that have not been PFI-tested) to public bodies. The issue of the right of public authorities to use the competitive negotiated procedure[80] has been settled (Clark 1997, CS28) by means of Treasury guidance. In it the Treasury (i) stipulated that the onus for the proof of the need to use it rests with the relevant public authority and (ii) suggested ways of putting it into practice. Between 1993 and 1998, the number of British calls that were advertised at the European level grew from 7,340 to 11,061 (*Single Market News* 2000, 12–13). Significantly, the pace of change in Britain (50.69%) was slower than it was in Greece and France (see Conclusion).

The domestically-driven increasing policy congruence and a business ethos that avoids the pursuit of alleged breaches of legislation through the courts may appear to obscure not only the existence of a small number of cases of conflict, but also the centrality of the institutions that are involved in the implementation process (this book's central argument). Both deserve to be discussed explicitly. As regards infringement cases, it is important to note that the aforementioned prevailing business ethos should not be considered as a determining factor. This is so for two reasons. First, it does not affect the autonomy of the European Commission in that area; rather, both the credibility of the EU's public procurement regime and that of the Commission as guardian of the Treaty are at stake. Second, non-UK based actual or potential tenderers are not unlikely to have a completely different business ethos.

An economically significant case with a high public profile (though not for reasons that concerned the EU directives) involved the construction of the building that houses the new Scottish Parliament. Although the infringements took place in the late 1990s, i.e. prior to the full implementation of the devolution-related arrangements, the Commission raised the issue in March 2005 (press release IP/05/314), i.e. after the completion of the building work and, more importantly, after Lord Fraser had completed his inquiry (Fraser 2004). The Commission argued that the process used for the award of the contracts regarding the design and the construction of the new building breached Directive 92/50 (services) as well as the principle of equal treatment that underpins the Treaty. In his report Lord Fraser stated that familiarity with EU requirements was lacking from the individuals who appeared before his inquiry (Fraser 2004, 259). In their response to the Commission, the British government acknowledged that the procedure had violated both the aforementioned directive and the principle of equal treatment enshrined in the Treaty. Crucially, acting in direct response to recommendations made by Lord Fraser, the Scottish Executive put in place not only new detailed guidelines but also new training programmes regarding the implementation of EU requirements by officials involved in procurement projects. As a result, the Commission decided to close the case (press release IP/06/1376). Despite its profile and economic importance, this case is not reflective of the actual operation of the post-1999 arrangements that involved organisation reform within Whitehall – namely the establishment of the OGC (*supra*, Chapter 3) – and the full implementation of the devolution-related arrangements. Rather, the capacity of the centre to steer implementation has remained unaffected. Indeed, devolution and the establishment of a separate body within the Treasury have, in fact, confirmed the integrated nature of the system. These developments are discussed in the next section.

The advent of the OGC and devolution
The establishment of the OGC was directly linked to the priorities of the new Labour government that took office in May 1997. After eighteen years in opposition, the Labour party had to establish its credentials as a reliable manager of the British economy in a manner that would not conflict with the interests of the electoral coalition that brought it to power. In that sense, the Gershon report (1999) that preceded the establishment of the OGC reflected an effort to improve the management of public finances as part of Labour's pre-electoral pledge to match the spending plans of the Conservative Party, whilst preparing the ground for the significant increases in public spending that followed the general election of 2001. It is in that context that one must place both some of Gershon's findings and the ambitious objective of saving one billion pounds as the expected consequence of the implementation of Gershon's recommendations by the end of the 2001–2 fiscal year (Gershon 1999). He argued that, as a result of the policy pursued by previous governments – whereby procurement practice was decentralised to each government department – greater coherence was required in how public funds are spent and, based on the views of suppliers, he identified divergence in procurement practices used by various government departments as a key issue. More importantly, his recommendations placed emphasis on changes in terms of organisational arrangements – through the establishment of the OGC – as well as manpower.

As regards the former, Gershon saw it as an organisation capable of maintaining the role of the Treasury in public procurement, mainly through the formulation of an integrated procurement policy and the involvement in all relevant international bodies – including the EU and the WTO, but with a remit that was to be extended to managerial issues including the management of the supplier base (including the strategic management of key suppliers), ownership of the generic procurement process, benchmarking of procurement performance across government, the identification and promotion of best practice and undertaking of procurement on behalf of the government where aggregation[81] was likely to lead to better results in terms of obtaining value for money (Gershon 1999, annex 1). As regards the latter, Gershon pointed out the strategic importance of the development of skills and qualifications. In other words, the establishment of the OGC was the result of renewed domestic policy priorities and not EU-specific requirements. Nevertheless, since institutional change may lead to unintended consequences, it is important to examine the OGC's actual operation and its involvement in the implementation of the EU public procurement directives, in conjunction with the Scottish Executive, itself the result of another major change introduced since the late 1990s, namely devolution.

One of the core characteristics of the transition from the previous institutional arrangement to the OGC and devolution was the transfer of officials who previously dealt with public procurement policy in the Treasury and the Scottish Office to the OGC and the Scottish Executive[82] respectively. This was a major step in the direction of (i) providing continuity (which is always a major issue in organisational reform) and (ii) concentrating expertise, which was one of the key objectives of the recommendations contained in the Gershon report. More specifically, this ensured the preservation and diffusion of the ethos of collaboration and sharing of information and expertise among officials who have worked closely together in the past. This serves as an important basis for problem-solving. After all, the UK remains one market[83] and problems that arise north of the border are not unlikely to arise south of the border too (and vice versa).

The OGC relies on the systematic use of nodality for the pursuit of its objective of moulding the behaviour of awarding authorities. This involves the use of centres of expertise[84] and regional centres of excellence[85] (themselves linked to the Treasury's efficiency savings targets), the direct provision[86] of horizontal guidance on key areas[87] (especially when new directives are transposed), guidance based on infraction proceedings and new jurisprudence of the ECJ[88] as well as contributions[89] to seminars, often in conjunction with private sector firms. Although the OGC is part of the Treasury, whose authorisation is required if expenditure that arises from the award of a contract falls outside a department's 'delegated limits'[90] (HM Treasury 2000, 22.1.3), its role is to a large extent couched in its position at the heart of a network of organisations. Instead of simply enabling it to dictate policy, this position allows the OGC to play a broader range of, often subtle, roles.

Its Chief Executive has a procurement advisory group composed of procurement experts both from central government departments (such as the Home Office and the departments of transport, health and defence) and the broader public sector (such as the police service). Coupled with the presence of the OGC's own trading arm and the links with purchasing bodies that operate on behalf of individual awarding authorities,[91] the OGC's nodal position (i) facilitates the collection of information about current and new market practices, (ii) shortens the length of the 'chain' that links the OGC's policy makers with individual awarding authorities, (iii) promotes the common understanding of policy challenges and priorities and, above all, (iv) spreads expertise[92] beyond Whitehall in a policy area with a pronounced technical facet. Given that legal provisions that stem either from the directives or domestic legislation may appear to be complex and technical, the guidance that is provided by the OGC is a supplement to domestic legislation. The latter is used to (i) steer awarding authorities in making sense of the rules or (ii) at a minimum, give them confidence in their use of the rules, especially in complex areas such as the Private Finance Initiative[93] (Arrowsmith 2006, 88).

The regional centres of excellence are involved in the implementation process both in tactical and strategic terms (Regional Centres of Excellence n.d.). They help individual councils transfer[94] their existing procurement projects to more efficient arrangements. In this task they are assisted by the OGC, which maintains a database that allows public sector organisations to identify deals on commodity goods and services of which they can take advantage on the basis of existing framework agreements regarding regularly purchased items. They also promote the better use of existing procurement expertise that is spread unevenly across the country. As a result, procurement officers in small awarding authorities that may not possess the required expertise – for example regarding the EU directives – can obtain it without incurring additional costs. Moreover, the OGC sponsors the new public sector facility launched in June 2006 by the Chartered Institute of Purchasing and Supply. This facility offers access to bespoke continuous professional development programmes and specialist training events[95] (Department for Communities and Local Government 2006, 20–21).

This was preceded by the establishment in April 1999 of the Government Procurement Service, which brings together the government officials[96] who are involved in public procurement projects in their respective departments. As a result, procurement now has the status of a recognised specialism[97] within the civil service, just like, for example, the Government Accountancy Service (National Audit Office 1999, 45). This development mirrors the widely perceived need to enhance the status of the procurement function within the civil service and the importance of the choice of the appropriate level of appointment for government procurement officials noted by the Gershon Report.

The practice north of the border mirrors the increasing emphasis on training as well as the systematic provision of guidance (Scottish Procurement Directorate 2004; 2005). A thriving market exists in which companies provide training to subscribers.[98] The provision of training (occasionally with the participation of procurement policy staff of the Scottish Executive) is very much driven by the awarding authorities[99] themselves but attendees often also include representatives of private firms. The importance of training is reflected in the recommendations of the McClelland report published in 2006. In addition to ensuring the appropriate level of staffing (for example by means of recruiting new personnel), the report indicated that awarding authorities should promote the enhancement of existing skill levels through extensive professional training and development, including a formal programme of EU-related workshops to be repeated annually (McClelland 2006, 24, 33).

In more general terms, although the OGC is acknowledged by Scottish Executive officials to be close to a larger set of customers and, as a result, it is more likely to face more practical issues, shared practice and the prevailing ethos of collaboration support the harmonious operation of the system since the advent of devolution.[100] This is demonstrated by the fact that no party has had to invoke the concordat to make the other party comply with it. The concordat is seen as a resource or a safety net rather than a barrier.[101] The coherence and consistency of the approach taken north and south of the border extends to the reluctance of the public procurement policy staff at the OGC and Scottish Executive to systematically rely on the European Commission for the provision of guidance on difficult cases regarding implementation. This may reflect awareness of the fact that the officials of the European Commission may provide an answer with which their UK-based counterparts may disagree but it is also an indication of (i) the significant amount of expertise and experience that has been accumulated in these two bodies, (ii) the absence of significant problems – which is demonstrated by the rarity (unlike the cases of France and Greece) of 'package meetings' involving national and EU officials – and (iii) the fact that the OGC tends to take a restrictive approach to interpretation within the UK.[102]

Despite these commonalities, the McClelland Report published in 2006 indicates that some of the issues that had to be addressed in the institutionalised context of Whitehall merit attention north of the border as well, i.e. in the less mature institutional context of the Scottish Executive. Four of McClelland's recommendations indicate this, namely the emphasis on greater and better use of collaborative procurement,[103] ensuring that compliance with EU legislation is a subject of focus for all internal and external audits performed in awarding authorities and the need for the establishment of a single point of enquiry, within Scotland, to which suppliers can address their concerns and obtain substantive and procedural clarifications (McClelland 2006, 24, 34, 47).

Despite these changes, data from Tenders Electronic Daily indicate that between 2002 and 2006 the number of advertised British contracts[104] remained quite consistent (14,427 in 2002, 15,415 in 2006 with a peak of 15,747 in 2005).

The concluding chapter discusses from a comparative perspective the main themes of the book and the broader implications of this study.

Notes

1 Nevertheless, it does affect the enforcement of contracts indirectly in that it excludes actual or potential bidders who do not meet criteria whose aim is to enable the assessment of their professional conduct and financial credibility.
2 One good example of the credibility of this commitment was the cancellation (in 1995) of a contract (in line with the complaints submitted by the European

Macro-implementation

Commission) for the construction of a waste water treatment facility in Thessaloniki (European Commission press release IP/95/810).
3   The use of a mathematical model for the award of works contracts was a temporary solution. It was designed to operate until the establishment of a robust framework entailing reliable plans, accurate tender documents and effective control mechanisms that would subsequently be combined with the use of the lowest price as the main criterion for the award of works contracts (Simitis 2005, 262). After the introduction by the socialists of the important changes discussed in this section of the chapter, the conservative government introduced new legislation that shifts the emphasis of the system to the lowest price (Law 3263/2004).
4   It has the status of a formal advisor to the Ministry of National Economy.
5   In case of the submission of a complaint, this unit may also represent the relevant awarding authority in discussions with the European Commission.
6   The awarding authorities are only compelled to provide a draft summary and detailed tender documents (and the relevant advertisement), the draft announcement regarding the award of a contract and the main contract. As a result, quite a lot depends on their willingness to co-operate with MOPADIS. This is monitored by the Ministry of Economy and Finance through the monthly reports submitted to it by MOPADIS, with a view to taking the required measures if the awarding authorities prove to be unwilling to co-operate.
7   The threshold was defined by the Secretary General of the Cabinet after consultation with the Court of Auditors in an effort to ensure that the latter would be able to cope with the corresponding workload.
8   Former Prime Minister Simitis acknowledged that when he took office in 1996 each ministerial department and awarding authority had knowledge of its 'own' works projects but the central government was not in a position to provide an accurate overall picture covering the entire country. In turn, this prevented the adoption of *systemic* measures. This is why he introduced an electronic network which – after its full implementation in 2000, collected information from approximately 7,500 awarding entities (Simitis 2005, 464–5).
9   Although this is perceived to be a successful but limited reform, it has been argued (Lalioti 2002, 131–2) that the role of this unit in the implementation of the Community Support Framework that covered the period between 1994 and 1999 would have been even more positive if the attitude of some of its staff was less dismissive *vis-à-vis* the Greek administration.
10 Greek construction companies, too, strongly opposed it because they thought it was an attempt to limit their 'freedom'.
11 Although the use of the second instrument was likely to lead to the imposition of a heavy fine on Greece, thus constituting a rather significant incentive for implementation, the first possibility did not seem to be very likely at that point in time, given the past experience of suppliers (Spathopoulos 1990, 126) despite the fact that the Council of State has used the so-called 'detachable act doctrine' (Spathopoulos 1990, 121; Koutoupa-Rengakos 1993, 395).
12 In December 2006 it comprised four officials.
13 Officials involved in public procurement in the three countries examined in this book almost invariably avoid this practice because of the potential legal implications of the views expressed in their written responses.

14 Simitis wanted to be better informed about the progress of major works projects. For that purpose he recruited a technical adviser in the PM's office and also met regularly with the Minister of Environment, Spatial Planning and Public Works (Simitis 2005, 251).
15 The data concern all types of contracts and awarding entities (*Single Market News* 2000, 12–13).
16 The search covered the entire period between 2001 and 2005 for works, supplies, service and combined contracts, and included contracts awarded on the basis of accelerated negotiated procedures, open procedures, open procedures with recurring quantities, restricted procedures, accelerated restricted procedures, negotiated procedures, competitive dialogue procedures, design contests, calls for expressions of interest and prior information or periodic indicative notices.
17 For example, the errors that MOPADIS has identified would not normally have escaped the attention of appropriately trained civil servants. The most important errors that have been identified by MOPADIS include major omissions such as the absence of reference to the awarding criterion, the publication of summary notices in the Greek press prior to the announcement in the *Official Journal of the European Union*, divergence between the summary documents published in the Greek press and the OJEU as well as practical errors regarding the contact details of the awarding authority or the location of a works project, the non-publication of the indicative budget, the duration of the contract or the deadline for the provision of services, the conditions for and the origin of funding, provisions regarding alternative bids, the date, time and place for the opening of bids, details regarding bank deposits, the documents that tenderers must submit in order to prove their financial and technical standing (Ministry of National Economy 1999). It is important to note that as a result of the establishment of MOPADIS some tenders have been cancelled and then re-advertised, once errors had been corrected (MOPADIS 2004).
18 The socialist government led by C. Simitis re-activated the provision which ensured that major supplies contracts and those that entail the transfer of major technological importance are awarded by committees that include observers of the major political parties. Twenty-three such committees operated between 1996 and 2004 but in 1997 the conservative ND withdrew – as part of its strategy of tension – its representatives and refused to replace them (Simitis 2005, 371). After its electoral victory of March 2004, the same party retained the aforementioned system and asked the opposition parties to appoint their representatives.
19 These were worth more than 3.3 million ECU.
20 As former Prime Minister Simitis noted, in the course of the preparations for the Athens Olympics of 2004 (which entailed large scale construction, supplies and services contracts), in some cases tenderers used legal proceedings as a way of exerting pressure on the government in their effort to win other contracts. However, the government won 58 of the 60 cases brought to the Council of State (Simitis 2005, 441).
21 This prohibition also concerns their consorts, relatives and firms or individuals who are financially dependent on them.
22 Law 3021/2002 was subsequently adopted on the basis of this constitutional provision.

Macro-implementation

23 See, for example, the comments made by E. Venizelos on behalf of the majority in Parliament on 7 February 2001 in the context of the debate on the reform of the Constitution.

24 See, for example, the statement made by Prokopis Pavlopoulos, an academic lawyer and (then) leading opposition MP, in Parliament on 7 February 2001 in the context of the debate on the reform of the Constitution.

25 This concerns both the Constitution and the implementing law of 2005.

26 Of course, it too runs the risk of being seen to promote the economic logic enshrined in the Treaty but in a manner that is detrimental to other legitimate concerns.

27 Nine months later (December 2006) this had not materialised.

28 For example, the price charged for the purchase of the same product has been found to vary by as much as 405% across public hospitals (*To Vima* 17 September 2006, A14). Others allegations concern discrepancies between the advertised contracts and the quantity and quality of the purchases (*To Vima* 9 October 2006, A39).

29 This function is more important in the case of the so-called *sociétés d'économie mixte* (semi-private companies).

30 This was particularly important in the run-up to the establishment and introduction of the single currency and has remained so after its introduction to a large extent because of the budgetary implications of membership of the euro zone.

31 Nevertheless, the quasi-mythical dimension of the lowest price remained present (Gohon 1991, 106).

32 The importance of this aspect of the implementation process was illustrated by the frequent complaints of French firms about the treatment of their offers in other European countries. Although the principle of mutual recognition – which was established by the ECJ (case 120/78) and stipulates that products that are legally produced and marketed in one member state (for example, in compliance with its rules regarding public health) must be allowed to circulate freely within the EU irrespective of differences regarding national regulations – resolved the problem in legal terms, the question of the comparability of offers could only be resolved through the creation of comparable standards which would then constitute the basis for the assessment of these offers.

33 These review procedures allow the administration and the tenderers to save time and money by not having recourse to traditional judicial review procedures.

34 Anti-competitive behaviour in the domain of public procurement has become an area of significant concern for the French Competition Council (see, for example, Conseil de la Concurrence 2005). In a recent example, in March 2006, it imposed fines worth 48.5 million euros on thirty-four French construction companies for participating in agreements that falsified competition between 1991 and 1997 (Conseil de la Concurrence 2006; *Le Monde* 23 March 2006).

35 This was encouraged by the fact that, in cases of unlawful award of contracts, firms operating in France could (since the 1930s) reclaim the costs of their bids and (since 1970) any profit lost (Lichere 2006, 171).

36 The fact that large companies were also those that use an active acquisition policy in order to obtain a part of the market in other member states further underlines the significance of this point.

37 Indeed 59% of the *référés* introduced between 1992 and the beginning of 1997 were rejected, half of them for substantive reasons (Commission Centrale des Marchés 1997).
38 It must be noted that informal and formal measures for the protection of the interests of companies complement rather than exclude each other. This is illustrated by a case brought to the *Conseil d'État* (Maljean-Dubois 1997) by two trade organisations, namely the *Fédération nationale des travaux publics* (National Federation for Public Works) and the *Fédération nationale du bâtiment* (National Federation of Building Constructors) in 1994. The case concerned an interministerial circular of December 1993 adopted in an effort to implement a decision of the *Comité interministériel pour la ville* (Inter-ministerial Committee for Urban Affairs) in July 1994. The objective was to insert to contract notices a clause relating to the local impact of the execution of public works projects upon unemployment and the development of professional skills. Although it is not clear from the text of the circular whether this would become an additional award criterion (in which case it would contradict the logic in which EU public procurement policy is couched), the two organisations contacted informally the Minister of Economy and Finance. It was only when they considered the lack of a response as a rejection of their view, that they took the case to the *Conseil d'État* demanding the annulment of the texts in question. Although the *Conseil d'État* rejected their demand because it considered that the circular was devoid of any regulatory effect (since it was a simple declaration of intent) this example is important because it shows the complementary nature of legal and informal/political means of implementation and the willingness of the market players to use both of them. Furthermore, the fact that the conservative government followed-up on these developments with a much more strongly-worded circular even before the election of a socialist government in a French context of high unemployment, highlights not only the significant economic dimension of public procurement but also its potential for politicisation (see *infra*).
39 This is so despite the reinforcement of the legislative framework regarding party financing (Loi 93–122).
40 Coverage in the French press has been extensive (see, for example, *Le Monde* 26 May 1995, 13 December 2000, 25 July 2001, 7 November 2001, 4 March 2002, 3 July 2004; *Le Figaro* 11 April 1997, 31 October 1998, 15 December 2000; *Les Echos* 16 June 1994, 11 April 1997, 10 September 2001, 27 October 2005; *Libération* 7 June 2001).
41 The inter-departmental, financial, administrative and judicial aspects of its work (and public procurement) are mirrored by the composition of the non-permanent members of this body which ensures a significant degree of operational autonomy (Mission interministérielle d'enquête sur les marchés 1999, annex 1).
42 Other ministers can ask MIEM to undertake inquiries of the same kind but only for bodies for which they are responsible.
43 During the first twelve years of its operation (1992–2004) prefects have been, by far, the most intensive users of this system (Mission interministérielle d'enquête sur les marchés et les conventions de délégation de service public 2005, 2:36).
44 Since 1995 the *Cour des comptes* has the same powers (Loi 95–125).
45 It has long been considered that an oligopoly of large French construction companies had a policy of falsifying competition by segmenting the domestic market (*Le Monde* 16 November 1994).

46 Although it is an autonomous body, MIEM was initially supported in administrative terms by the secretariat general of the CCM but since 2004 this role has been performed by the legal affairs directorate of the Ministry of Economy and Finance (Décret 2004–15).
47 The issue was resolved in 1995 (Loi 95–127).
48 MIEM officials repeatedly argued that this body should have its own power of initiative (see, for example, Mission interministérielle d'enquête sur les marchés 2002, 4:226–7; Mission interministérielle d'enquête sur les marchés et les conventions de délégation de service public 2004, 4:111). This proposal was rejected.
49 This compares with a total of 186 requests for formal investigation submitted between 1992 and 2004 (Mission interministérielle d'enquête sur les marchés et les conventions de délégation de service public 2005, 2:36).
50 This was, in part, due to the EU's procurement directives which were, themselves, in need of simplification (*supra*, Chapter 3).
51 When Laurent Fabius, then Minister of Economy and Finance, presented the new Code he reportedly said that, whilst in the past a mayor would simply consider whether a procurement decision was good or not, they would now have to call their lawyer first (*Le Figaro* 10 September 2001).
52 It was felt that this would increase competition which, in turn, would prevent corruption.
53 This entails the provision of legal advice by the CIJAP (*Cellule d'information juridique aux acheteurs publics* – Legal information unit for public purchasers), a unit of the Public Accounting Directorate General of the Ministry of Economy and Finance, created in Lyon in 2001 (Ministère de l'Économie, des Finances et de l'Industrie 2001). As part of the reforms introduced in 2001, it covered the entire metropolitan territory (*Les Echos* 10 September 2001).
54 This concerned the consistent use of negotiated award procedures by UGAP. This ended in 1997 as a result of the intervention of the ministers of Finance and Education of the socialist-led government (*Les Echos* 2 March 1999).
55 This exercise took place at the sub-regional level (*département*) and involved about 27,000 officials (*Les Echos* 10 September 2001).
56 An internal quarterly publication entitled *CSM Actualité* was used for the purposes of co-ordinating the various CSM through the dissemination of comments and observations on horizontal issues (Commissions Spécialisées des Marchés 2002, 10).
57 Throughout the 1990s the Commission – acting in its capacity as guardian of the treaty – maintained its pressure for reform (*Single Market News* 1995, 1996). One case of both symbolic and substantive importance concerned the construction of the *Grand Stade de France* in the Parisian suburb of Saint Denis. In a decision issued in July 1996 the Administrative Tribunal of Paris annulled the Prime Minister's decision to award the contract. The European Commission challenged the French government which held the view that this was a concession contract. European Commission officials argued that, although the *intention* of the awarding authority was to award a *concession* contract containing the essential requirements for the exploitation of the stadium, they *actually* awarded a contract concerning the construction of the stadium, i.e. a *works* contract (European Commission press release IP/97/33). This is so because both the final bid that was

chosen and the contract that was signed effectively eliminated the risk for the winning tenderer. The Commission also held the view that the principle of equal treatment had been violated because the winning tenderer has been allowed to modify substantially its offer during the consultation procedure. It also accused the French authorities of breaching Art. 59 of the Treaty of Rome (freedom to provide services) and Directives 92/50 (services) and 93/37 (works) by (i) allocating additional important works projects to the winning tenderer without the use of any competitive procedure and also (ii) reserving a part of the related services and works contracts for local companies. French officials argued that the whole issue emanated from the unclear definition of concession contracts that had been included in the directives and that the appropriate procedures had been followed. After the referral of this case to the ECJ (and shortly before the inauguration of the stadium) the French government amended the contract so as to eliminate the local preference clause that it initially contained and – more importantly – the French Minister for European Affairs acknowledged in writing that the infringement had occurred and undertook a commitment to comply with EU legislation in the subsequent stages of the implementation of the project in question. As a result – and in the light of the fact that the stadium had almost been completed, the Commission closed the infringement proceedings (European Commission press release IP/98/345).
58 The French provisions used only the higher of the two thresholds stipulated in Directive 92/50.
59 The Code did not specify the procedure that would apply to them.
60 On the origin and role of CSM see Chapter 3.
61 Ministers or officials involved in procurement also have the right to ask for the CMPE's advice in particularly complex projects whose value does not exceed the aforementioned threshold.
62 The reports of the CSM for 2000, 2001, 2002 and 2003 indicate that between one fifth and one third of its opinions on the dossiers that it examined were negative.
63 This happened only once in 2006 in a case that concerned the Ministry of Defence.
64 CMPE officials working in the sector of public works have noticed that answers given to queries submitted (often informally) by purchasing officers in one case, are often used verbatim by other officers working on other cases.
65 www.achatpublic.com/
66 Calculated by the author on the basis of data published in *Single Market News* (2000, 12–13).
67 Data from Tenders Electronic Daily indicate that between 2002 and 2006 the number of advertised French contracts remained high (58,379 in 2002, 51,125 in 2006 with a peak of 62,630 in 2003). The search covered works, supplies, service and combined contracts and included contracts awarded on the basis of accelerated negotiated procedures, open procedures, open procedures with recurring quantities, restricted procedures, accelerated restricted procedures, negotiated procedures, competitive dialogue procedures, design contests, calls for expressions of interest and prior information or periodic indicative notices.
68 Indeed, dissent appeared within the ranks of the majority (*Le Monde* 10 December 1994).
69 This method involved the direct negotiations between the relevant user and one supplier chosen on the basis of pre-defined criteria. The selection that precedes

Macro-implementation

these negotiations has a restrictive effect on competition. Various degrees of this restriction can be envisaged.

70 This exemption could only have been based on Art. 92 § 3 of the Treaty which concerns competition policy. Also, this exemption had to be limited in terms of time.

71 In one case local protesters attempted to use the EC's procurement policy in order to oppose plans relating to Ipswich airport.

72 In another case mentioned by civil servants, an academic was exerting pressure on his university's purchasing officer to purchase an important piece of equipment necessary for his work, without taking account of the directives. It was only when the purchasing officer asked for and obtained an official letter from the Treasury detailing the procedure that had to be followed and thereby confirming the view of the purchasing officer that the academic's pressure ceased.

73 This activity has become an important feature of the Treasury's action (HM Government 1995, 31).

74 Market testing (the recourse to the market in order to determine the best option for a particular need) is one of the basic elements of the Treasury's approach which exemplifies pro-activeness.

75 Five 'horizontal' purchasing agencies (Gohon 1991, 116) were being used until then for the procurement of stationery (HMSO), computers and telecommunications material (CCTA), land and buildings (PSA), fuel and electrical equipment (CS) and information services (COI).

76 Until well into the 1990s the Treasury advised purchasers to rely on departmental lawyers for legal advice in the first instance (HM Treasury 1998, 13). This enabled the Treasury to concentrate on a more strategic role and to deal with issues of wider significance.

77 It was enhanced in 1980 through the Local Government, Planning and Land Act 1980 and subsequently extended to cover more aspects of public procurement through the Local Government Act 1988 and the Local Government Act 1992.

78 The Wood report confirms this trend (Wood 2004, 41).

79 As an exception one can mention a case (Arrowsmith 1996) in the Queen's Bench Division, where Portsmouth City Council was found to have failed to advertise a contract whose initial value did not exceed the threshold, although both the value and the time length had subsequently been altered in a substantial manner, and the subsequent proceedings in the Court of Appeal (Kunzlik 1997) by some of the aggrieved tenderers.

80 This is an important issue in the sense that public authorities need a margin for negotiation in order to maximise the contribution of private funds. At the same time though, this needs to be managed in a way that does not violate the directives which place emphasis on open procedures.

81 This is an important difference *vis-à-vis* the policy pursued by the Conservatives during the 1980s and 1990s, despite the fact that the British government's procurement policy guidelines have remained unchanged in principle since they were first published in 1981 (HM Treasury 2000). While the Conservative government reduced the purchasing power of the state by disaggregating demand, Labour sought to enhance it by promoting demand aggregation in an effort to achieve economies of scale. For that purpose, an executive agency of the OGC – OGCbuying.solutions – acts as its trading arm and provides procurement services

to public sector organisations. Its significant buying power is a major instrument of its activity.
82 Public procurement is a devolved area for Scotland while Whitehall has retained responsibility for EU affairs (*supra*, Chapter 3).
83 Senior officials of the OGC meet annually their counterparts from Scotland, Wales and Northern Ireland. In addition, the Central Procurement Directorate (CPD) of the Department of Finance and Personnel in Northern Ireland is represented in working groups convened by the OGC on issues such as e-procurement, legal issues and collaborative opportunities. The latter is of strategic importance to a large extent due to the size of the UK market and the possibilities for economies of scale (Central Procurement Directorate 2003, 6.2, 6.3).
84 A similar approach has been followed in Northern Ireland since devolution. Although individual awarding authorities continue to have access to framework agreements and contracts established under the auspices of the OGC, they also carry out procurement projects through service level agreements concluded with either the CPD (which often acts as a central purchasing body on behalf of smaller organisations) or one of the existing (subject-specific) centres of procurement expertise that have been identified and assessed on the basis of formal and explicit criteria (Department of Finance and Personnel 2002, 10). In addition, these (currently six) centres and the CPD are responsible for policy implementation in Northern Ireland. Indeed, as of March 2005, all public sector procurement in Northern Ireland is channelled through these centres (Central Procurement Directorate 2004, 5; 2005, 36). Their representatives sit in the Procurement Practitioners' Group which identifies and shares best practice (Central Procurement Directorate 2003, 3.7). Between the establishment of the CPD in April 2002 and March 2006 only two complaints have been made regarding compliance with EU legislation for contracts awarded in Northern Ireland. Both concerned contracts that had been advertised through the Official Journal of the European Union (Central Procurement Directorate 2003, 2.4; 2004, 14; 2005, 13; 2006, 28). One of them was subsequently withdrawn (Central Procurement Directorate 2006, 6.1).
85 In 2003 the Office of the Deputy Prime Minister (now Department for Communities and Local Government) established nine such centres in partnership with the Local Government Association, initially as Centres of Procurement Excellence whose aim was to support local authorities in the implementation of the National Procurement Strategy for local government in England (Office of the Deputy Prime Minister 2003).
86 This is done by means of a 'cascade approach'. The OGC provides guidance to each department's Head of Procurement and they relay the information to purchasing officers in the bodies that are under each department's responsibility.
87 The guidance on competitive dialogue and central purchasing bodies (Office of Government Commerce 2006c) are two good examples.
88 One example is the guidance provided by the OGC (Office of Government Commerce 2006b) about the implications of the ECJ's ruling in the *Alcatel* case (C-81/98) regarding the mandatory standstill period between (a) the decision to award a contract and (b) the conclusion of that contract. The ECJ ruled that when a contract is covered by the directives, the decision to award it must, in all cases, be open to review before its conclusion. As a result, national courts can set aside

an award decision when a breach of rules has prejudiced the interests of a bidder – irrespective of the fact that the latter retains the right to seek damages. This guidance (which was published in March 2006) followed the inclusion of the corresponding legal clause in the transposing regulations of January 2006. The note describes in detail the requirements regarding the announcement to unsuccessful bidders of an awarding authority's decision to award a contract, the process for the debriefing of these bidders (including the deadlines) and the scope of exceptions. This guidance was issued after a separate consultation organised by the OGC in the run-up to the adoption of the aforementioned regulations.
89 For example, this entails the preparation of training modules with detailed case study material.
90 Indeed, '[n]o resources can be properly committed or expenditure incurred without the approval of the Treasury' (HM Treasury 2000, 2.4). On the Treasury's role in the planning and control of public expenditure see Thain and Wright (1995).
91 The OGC's own trading arm and the central or regional purchasing bodies that operate on behalf of individual awarding authorities facilitate not only the achievement of economies of scale but also compliance with national and EU legislation. Individual purchasers do not have to comply as long as the central purchasing body (that, unlike many of their clients, actually possesses the required expertise) has done so.
92 This includes EU-specific expertise.
93 For examples of the 'political steer' (i.e. guidance) provided by the Treasury on issues regarding the compatibility of PFI with EU rules, see Braun (2003, 581–2).
94 This is done, in part, through the production of 'on the money' guides for specific products. The first such guide (on postal services) was published in 2006.
95 This is part of a wider intensive strategy of improving procurement services by means of encouraging procurement officials to attend courses that lead to professional qualifications such as the Local Government Certificate of Competence (Department for Communities and Local Government 2006, 21). In addition, the National School of Government – the successor to the Civil Service College – offers training (including EU-specific) programmes for procurement professionals.
96 They were approximately 1,500 in 1999 (National Audit Office 1999, 45).
97 A similar strategy is currently pursued in Northern Ireland as part of the Procurement Board's strategic priorities for 2005–8 (Central Procurement Directorate 2006, 34).
98 At least one of them is based in Glasgow, the city that hosts the Procurement Policy Directorate of the Scottish Executive.
99 In one case a contract was signed with a law firm that subsequently provided training to approximately 200 officials involved in procurement projects.
100 Although in a small number of cases firms sought to engage in 'venue-shopping', officials of the OGC referred them to the Procurement Policy Directorate of the Scottish Executive.
101 Thus Henderson's initial assessment is confirmed (2003, 179).
102 This is precisely what its officials have come to expect from the Commission.
103 This also applies to the Welsh context, where better collaboration between local authorities that engage in public procurement projects is one of the priorities of

the Welsh Local Government Association (2005). The Welsh Local Government Procurement Support Unit was established in an effort to support local authorities in Wales. In addition to a programme of procurement awareness training sessions for elected members and senior local government officers, the unit provides (a) written guidance on strategic issues and (b) 'procurement fitness checks' whose aim is to highlight good practice and opportunities for further improvement (Welsh Local Government Association n.d.). The more pronounced emphasis on cross-sector procurement collaboration in Wales has been promoted as a direct result of devolution (Henderson 2003, 180).

104 As in the previous two cases, the search covered works, supplies, service and combined contracts and included contracts awarded on the basis of accelerated negotiated procedures, open procedures, open procedures with recurring quantities, restricted procedures, accelerated restricted procedures, negotiated procedures, competitive dialogue procedures, design contests, calls for expressions of interest and prior information or periodic indicative notices.

6
Conclusion

This book has set out to demonstrate that the impact of key characteristics of the institutions of central governments – in particular, the capacity to co-ordinate their activity – extends beyond formulation to the stage of policy implementation. Unlike existing literature that understandably focuses on either success or failure, it has subsequently demonstrated the dynamic nature of patterns of implementation. The cases of Greece and, to a lesser extent, France are particularly illustrative in that respect. Despite initial problems, sector-specific changes have enabled central governments to improve implementation in a manner that a static analysis of either success or failure would not have illuminated. Change was driven by learning and fixing at the national level whilst conditional funding has been found not to have been the powerful mechanism of change that one would have intuitively expected. The remainder of this concluding chapter discusses the link between these findings and our understanding of patterns of implementation in the EU, the literature on the so-called 'Europeanisation' of the nation state and the development of European integration.

The differential dynamics of implementation

The liberalisation of public procurement in the EU entails the transposition and implementation of the EU's directives at the national level. This process is steered (macro-implementation) by the central governments of the member states. In the light of the fact that (a) implementation is inextricably linked to the formulation of policy and, therefore, necessitates a significant capacity to co-ordinate the governmental actors involved therein and (b) the way in which central governments deal with the latter in the context of the EU varies considerably (in a manner that reflects historically defined patterns of institutional development) one can expect implementation to vary accordingly. Nevertheless, the pattern of implementation is political (Dimitrakopoulos 1998) and dynamic – for implementation is not an event but a process – and central governments can play a significant role in steering it. These are the central claims examined in this book.

In Chapter 2 it has been demonstrated that despite facing similar pressures, the Greek, French and British central governments have responded to the challenge of their involvement in EU policy making in ways that reflect pre-existing patterns, in line with the basic premise of historical institutionalism. In other words, accession to the EU has not led to a punctuation, i.e. a significant change, or a branching effect. Despite important similarities (Chapter 2), the three systems differ (again in historically defined ways) in the sense that co-ordination (a key issue that concerns both formulation and implementation) is efficient in the UK, less so in France and even less so in Greece. While the British system does not appear to have been affected by recent changes – at least until the elections of 2007 – stemming from the process of devolution, the operation of the French system mirrors the constant quest for, as opposed to the consistent presence of, co-ordination. Finally, the Greek system is the 'outlier' in the sense that it is lacking in terms of the pro-active attitude that is required at official level for effective lesson-drawing and fixing and, consequently, it relies extensively on the willingness and ability of the political promoters of change to sustain their interest in reform. Furthermore, these differences extend to the transposition of EU legislation: what is routinely achieved in Whitehall, has to be actively sought in Paris, despite successive prime ministerial circulars – while the operation of the Greek system is patchy and mirrors the capacity of the centre to sustain the momentum both at the political and the administrative level. In short, the extent to which a given politico-administrative system is integrated affects its capacity to deal with the exigencies of EU policy making. This leads to the expectation of variegated implementation. Implementation, it is argued, can be expected to be more problematic in countries with fragmented systems than those with integrated systems.

Nevertheless, this is only one aspect of the 'story' in that the patterns of implementation are *dynamic*. They change over time because the institutional actors involved therein have the capacity to learn and this affects their capacity to steer the process. This twofold claim has been examined empirically (Chapters 4 and 5) on the basis of the case study on public procurement (a policy presented in Chapter 3). The empirical analysis confirms both arguments. While the process of implementation was initially problematic in Greece and France, it was much less so in the UK even after the constitutional and institutional reforms (devolution and creation of the OGC respectively) introduced since 1999. At the same time though, change has been most remarkable in Greece and France. In terms of transparency (a key objective of the EU's public procurement policy), both countries have made significant progress despite the problems that they faced initially. The volume of public procurement projects that they advertised via the OJEU has risen dramatically as part of the estimated total value of procurement between 1995 and 2002 (Figure 6.1).

Conclusion

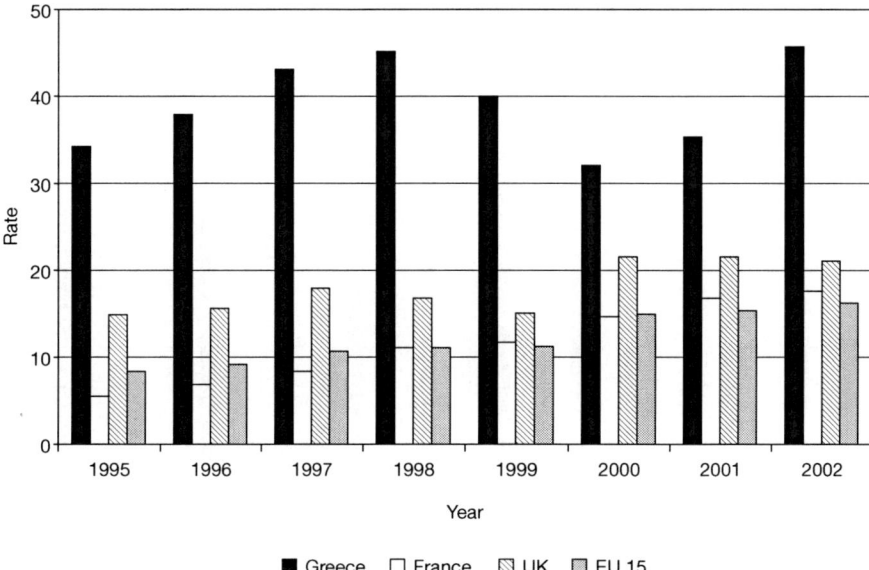

Figure 6.1 Value of public procurement contracts advertised as part (%) of the estimated total public procurement value in 2002 figures, 1995–2002

Source: Compiled by the author on the basis of data published by the European Commission (2004, 7, table 2).

The same argument can be made with regards to the volume of public procurement projects that they advertised via the OJEU measured as part of their respective GDP between 1993 and 2003 (Figure 6.2).

Moreover, between 1993 and 1998 (i.e. a crucial period during which both countries engaged in significant incremental institutional reforms) the pace of substantive change (defined in terms of the number of calls that were advertised at the European level) was much faster in Greece and France (82.21% and 241.09% respectively) than it was in the UK (50.69%).[1] However, implementation was problematic both in Greece and France, but in both cases the pattern changed over time as a result of incremental changes introduced by the two central governments. Although the precise combination of the tools of government used in each case varied from one country to the other, in both cases the reforms affected the extent to which each system is internally integrated.

More specifically, it has been demonstrated that *fragmentation* (construed as the inability to effectively co-ordinate government activity) affects macro-implementation by obscuring or even destroying the clear line that must exist in the process of 'forging links in a causal chain'. The validity of this point is further underlined by the lack of administrative and political co-ordinating

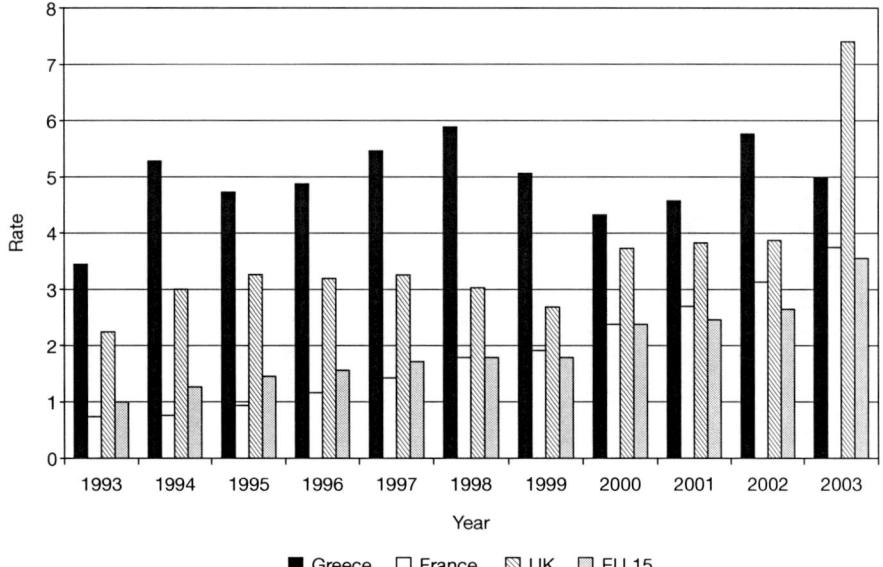

Figure 6.2 Public procurement advertised in the Official Journal as part (%) of GDP, 1993–2003

Source: Compiled by the author on the basis of data published by EUROSTAT.

mechanisms capable of resolving the problem directly or indirectly. Fragmentation affects the predictability of actors' behaviour and, therefore, the stability of the process. Moreover, it has been argued that fragmentation increases the number of decision points thereby undermining effective macro-implementation. Even if co-ordination is achieved within fragmented politico-administrative structures, it is likely to be more costly, at least in terms of time. In addition, the detection of problems is easier in integrated politico-administrative structures. Finally, it has been argued that the implementation of reforms is more difficult in a fragmented politico-administrative structure. Change underlines the need for adaptation which, in turn, requires a certain ability to learn. Lesson-drawing is more difficult in fragmented structures because each actor is confined to limited (sectoral or sub-sectoral) sources of input. This further highlights the need for horizontal (co-ordinating) structures that resolve conflict, promote the diffusion of lessons when systemic problems occur and maintain a sense of the overriding priorities in complex organisations that are necessarily internally differentiated.

The argument about the impact of the integrated (or fragmented) nature of a given politico-administrative structure concerns both transposition and the action taken by central governments in their effort to steer post-transposition activity. The Greek and French central governments have

Conclusion 139

provided similar responses to the part of the problem that concerns *transposition*, namely they have established centralised mechanisms that enhance their capacity to detect and then resolve problems. The Greek case provides two particularly useful illustrations regarding transposition. Indeed, the adoption of two contradictory laws in the space of a few months in 1979, i.e. when the accession of Greece was imminent – illustrates that the same actors may adopt incoherent or even contradictory courses of action in a manner that undermines the ability of other participants to act in a coherent way when they are parts of a fragmented system. What was a purchasing officer of a Greek awarding authority supposed to do in this case? Was she expected to implement the Treaty of Accession – stipulating that domestic suppliers and suppliers from the then EC would have to be treated equally – or the law that followed it which included discriminatory clauses? In another case involving Greece, Directive 89/665 (remedies) was transposed six years after the formal deadline and only after the direct involvement of the Prime Minister and the Secretary General of the Cabinet. Both cases reflect a systemic weakness, namely the need for the systematic operation of a reliable co-ordinating mechanism. The enhanced role of Secretariat General of the Cabinet (now Secretariat General of the Government), the Cabinet and its various committees between 1996 and 2004 in Greece significantly reduced the scope for delays and the non-resolution of conflict between departments and ministers. In the French context, although the system is often regarded as efficient, closer examination reveals weaknesses. Both in public procurement and in other sectors (as revealed by the non-sectoral circulars of successive French Prime Ministers) the core of the central government needs to keep on the institutional agenda the issue of co-ordination and the link between formulation and the subsequent stages of the EU policy process.

Paradoxically, perhaps, this important similarity between the Greek and the French systems subsequently revealed the *fragility* of these reforms. Indeed, in both countries the effectiveness of the reforms – as implemented at the political level – does not appear to have survived their promoters' departure from power.[2] In other words, these reforms do not appear to have taken root[3] despite the fact that they were intimately linked to patterns of learning. By contrast, the procurement-specific reforms introduced at the administrative level appear to have taken root as indicated by the significantly improved transparency rates. Therefore, it is argued that the reforms introduced in Greece and France are examples of *single loop*, i.e. instrumental, learning.[4]

Both in Greece and France the central governments introduced significant incremental reforms aiming to resolve problems that concerned the post-transposition stage. This similarity reflected the common problems faced by the two systems. Their use of the tools of government reveals important similarities in the sense that both governments relied heavily on authority, organisation and nodality. However, it is also indicative of an important difference, namely the role of treasure. In both countries implementation and reform entailed extensive use of authority exemplified by the introduction of new legislation. Moreover, the use of authority also entailed the introduction of new control mechanisms in an effort to minimise deviance from EU policy at the administrative level. This significantly reduced each awarding authority's margin for error. One particular idiosyncrasy of the Greek case concerns the intensive and systematic use of the same tool at the political level (which can be termed *political authority*) under Prime Minister Simitis who provided (directly or indirectly) the required impulse. The need for the involvement of the Greek Prime Minister (and individuals and collective bodies that operate under his authority) is not only policy-related. Rather, it is above all the result of an institutional arrangement, namely the fact that responsibility for public procurement is shared by three ministerial departments.

This was directly relevant in transposition and indirectly relevant (though equally important) in terms of the broad direction of the country's involvement in the process of integration. In that sense, effective implementation was important not only in terms of the country's credibility as an EU partner but also in terms of the economic as well as political implications of public procurement projects. Organisation was also used intensively in both Greece and France in an effort made by central governments to improve each system's capacity for fixing. However, again despite the aforementioned broad similarity, the origin and nature of domestic problems is at the heart of more subtle differences that distinguish the case of Greece from that of France.

Indeed, while the intensity and the political implications of the significant problem of corruption led to the establishment of MIEM in France, anti-corruption measures took the form of the scrutiny of the income of public officials in Greece. Beyond this issue, both sets of reforms entailed the involvement of new (CIJAP and CMPE in France, MOPADIS in Greece) or existing (Court of Auditors in Greece) organisations that utilise preventive[5] measures in an effort to ensure that awarding authorities avoid problems of deviance from EU policy. In other words, efforts to promote what Bardach termed 'fixing' were couched in a dynamic (and therefore appropriate) understanding of procurement as a process, rather than an event.

Finally, both sets of reforms entailed the use of nodality. It took the form of the provision of information and guidance by the aforementioned organisations as well as a more effective personnel policy, especially through the use of training and a more pronounced effort (in Greece) to recruit specialist staff. The use of nodality is much more intensive in the British system. Unlike Greece and France where public procurement was (and still is) often construed as an overtly political issue,[6] in Britain it is construed as an essentially technical (though significant) aspect of public spending. Major institutional developments (such as the establishment of the OGC, centres of expertise and regional centres of excellence) are directly linked to this

Conclusion   141

dominant view of public procurement.[7] They reflect an effort to promote the better use of public funds whereas many of the procurement-related institutional changes introduced in Greece and France focus either on legality or the need to promote the effective implementation of EU policy (or both).

The combination of measures that aim to promote the prevention, detection and suppression of illicit practices is important for an additional reason. It indicates that, although the Greek and the French systems have changed quite significantly since the early 1990s, both sets of changes reflect an integrated understanding of procurement as a process, rather than a set of disjointed events. Although this is more evident in France – where the role of the CMPE includes an examination of the need that a planned procurement project is meant to address (often the origin of many problems that become apparent in subsequent stages), the incremental changes introduced in both countries since the early 1990s did not lose sight of the broader (albeit sectoral) context.

The institutionalist explanation offered in this book can be challenged on the grounds of a (potential) interest-based alternative account. This challenge merits explicit consideration. It is discussed in the next section of this chapter.

Motives, institutions and implementation: the limits of 'Europeanisation'

Given the overtly political nature of the process of implementation, an *interest-based explanation* is intuitively appealing. Such an explanation would highlight the important role of conditional funding as the key origin of the reforms introduced in Greece (i.e. the 'outlier'). However, it would be wrong to ascribe these reforms to interests (specifically, the need to ensure the provision of EU funding) not only because the process of change had started prior to the landmark case of the Evinos dam but also because reform did not remain limited to the sub-sector (i.e. public works) where conditional funding applied. Rather, it was also evident in the two sub-sectors (supplies and services) where the 'carrot' of EU funding (or, conversely, the 'stick' of its withdrawal) was absent.

There are two additional reasons why the interest-based alternative explanation ought to be rejected. First, significant parts of the extensive institutional reforms undertaken mainly by the socialist governments led by Costas Simitis were not directly required for the continuing provision of EU funding not least because EU public procurement policy does not cover the execution of public contracts. Second, even if one were to ascribe overwhelming power to an interest-based explanation of change in Greece, this argument could not be extended to the other case where change occurred, namely France. Although it would be wrong to ignore the significance of EU funding in the case of Greece, it is arguably more appropriate to consider the role of the EU as the source of change in the light of wider significant domestic realities in the three countries examined here. Indeed, arguing that conditional funding was the veritable origin of the observed changes in implementation patterns would obscure the fact that Simitis' entire tenure was characterised by a sustained effort to improve the pattern of the country's participation in the process of integration and to turn membership of the EU into a key plank of his government's policies across the board. In other words, one of the core problems of an interest-based explanation would be the focus on the narrow definition of 'interests' exclusively on the basis of conditional funding, as opposed to – for example – a country's ability to contribute credibly to the operation and the development of the EU.

In addition, significant aspects of the reforms introduced in France went far beyond the requirements of the implementation of the directives. A good case in point is the role of the CMPE in examining the needs that a procurement project is meant to address and its place in a broader programme or operation undertaken by the awarding authority. This indicates that, although the exigencies of implementation may highlight weaknesses in the domestic institutional structure, the motivation for reform is – at least in this case – directly linked to essentially domestic considerations that exceed the limits of ensuring either the flow of funding from Brussels or compliance with EU directives. For example, the Greek administration had to resolve problems – such as the need for specialised staff and better monitoring and control mechanisms – even prior to the emergence of conditional funding as a major political issue. In other words, an interest-based explanation would place undue emphasis on one factor to the detriment of others in a manner that would ignore the centrality of institutions.

One important such factor concerns the link between institutional reform and the extent of politicisation of public procurement. Unlike the case of the UK, public procurement has become overtly politicised in both Greece and France. Although politicisation occurred in both countries, its timing varied: it occurred once most of the key reforms had been adopted in Greece but in France it occurred during the 1990s, i.e. just as the necessity of reform was becoming apparent. This is important for two reasons that are linked to the impact of learning on patterns of implementation. The timing of the overt politicisation of the issue allowed the most significant reforms to be implemented in the Greek system, which was in greater need of institutional change. By contrast, politicisation slowed the pace of change in France and contributed to it being 'locked' in a path of institutional development that placed greater emphasis on suppression and punishment as opposed to the prevention of problems.

This is not the only reason why the issues of politicisation, learning and institutional development are intimately linked. The national paths of institutional development affect the way in which policy issues are conceptualised and subsequently handled. Although the problem of the link between media ownership and public procurement exists both in Greece and in France, it has

Conclusion   143

been handled in rather different ways. The presence of the Competition Council in France facilitated the use of competition rules as the means to fight against efforts to falsify competition in public procurement. It is this kind of uncompetitive behaviour that often gives undue power to major firms that are present in both sectors. By contrast, when the issue arose in Greece, the central government was in the process of establishing a wide range of autonomous regulatory authorities which had not yet managed to become part of the state's repertoire (or 'toolkit'). The rhetoric of the main opposition party simply obscured this lacuna. The ensuing climate of polarisation further undermined reform as it locked it in a path that led (the same party) to an embarrassing procedural, as well as substantive, climb-down after its electoral victory of 2004.

This has significant implications for the literature on the so-called 'Europeanisation' of the nation state (construed as the consequences of membership of the EU for the member states). It indicates that the precise meaning of the 'pressure' that results from involvement in the EU policy process (as well as European integration more generally) is *not* given. Rather, this meaning can be (indeed, often is) politically contested *within* the nation state. As a result, the notion that members states 'adapt' to pressure from 'Brussels' (i.e. the policies that are made *collectively* at the level of the EU) is problematic – to say the least. Neither its precise meaning nor its capacity to lead to change can be taken for granted.

This is not to deny that membership of the EU in general and involvement in the EU policy process in particular has the capacity to challenge domestic arrangements (policies and institutions). Indeed, one form of this challenge is the diffusion of institutional models. In the area of public procurement the European Commission has, in the past, recommended that member states consider the idea of promoting the successful implementation of EU policy through the establishment of independent national enforcement authorities that would play an important role especially with regards to jointly-funded (i.e. works) projects (Commission of the European Communities 1996, 17). Similar arguments have also been put forward at the national level (*supra*, Chapter 5). They reflect a broader effort to 'de-politicise'[8] public procurement. The involvement of appropriately-trained non-partisan officials can certainly contribute to the solution of the problem of corruption. Appropriately trained and numerically sufficient professional staff can help handle public procurement projects in a manner that is consistent with the letter of the law, despite pressure from interested parties (such as local providers etc).

However, it would be wrong to portray – as some politicians have done at the national level – this arrangement as panacea since it cannot resolve many of the other significant problems that are associated with public procurement, including the need for expertise that ensures the better definition of needs, increased awareness of market practices, controls during (rather than after) the execution of works projects etc., many of which touch on core characteristics of national politico-administrative structures. The exigencies of these reforms go way beyond the remit of the sectoral logic that dominates individual segments of large, complex and internally differentiated organisations. This is precisely why co-ordination is a systemic issue.

Efforts to 'de-politicise' public procurement have also been hampered by market practices that are also indicative of (i) the weaknesses of sectoral regulation and, more importantly, (ii) the need for greater horizontal co-ordination both at the national and the European level. One significant case in point concerns the link between media regulation on the one hand, and public procurement on the other. Major firms that make significant profits from public procurement subsequently use them to play a political role via the media market – since they often own major television channels and newspapers. This ought to be handled as a *single* set of issues whose implications for democratic politics can be very significant. Nevertheless, the overwhelmingly sectoral patterns of integration are not conducive to cross-sectoral co-ordination at the European level. In the absence of effective co-ordination at the European level, the need for co-ordination is rendered both more necessary and more difficult at the national level.

Since the meaning or, more accurately, the perception of the pressures that stem from membership of the EU is contested at the domestic level, what are (if any) the implications of this study for another key aspect of the literature on 'Europeanisation', namely institutional convergence (Knill 2001)? The aforementioned analysis of the similarities of the cases of Greece and France (where the problems that were expected and were subsequently identified have also been, to a large extent, resolved) may give the impression of a gradual institutional convergence stemming from the exigencies of the implementation of the directives examined here. Such an impression would be misleading for three reasons. First, it would ascribe undue causal influence to the exigencies of the implementation of the directives examined in this book. The procurement-specific reforms introduced in Greece and France in an effort to improve the implementation of the directives, in fact, correspond to *pre-existing* lacunae, rather than weaknesses *created* by the directives and they did not appear to challenge key aspects of domestic institutional arrangements such as the centralisation of responsibility for public procurement in France and Whitehall and its dispersal in the Athenian bureaucracy. Put in a different way, even in the absence of the directives, both the Greek and the French systems would still need to, for example, (i) monitor plans for major procurement projects prior to their announcement to interested parties so as to ensure not only that illicit practices are avoided but also the better use of public monies and (ii) provide training to staff involved in public procurement. Second, as it has been argued in the analysis of the manner in which national parliaments deal with the exigencies of scrutinising the policy making activities of ministers when the latter operate at the level of the EU (Dimitrakopoulos 2001a), membership of the EU *highlights* patterns, issues or lacunae that exist in domestic politico-administrative structures. Member states deal with these issues in ways that reflect historically defined patterns of institutional development. This is demonstrated by the *fragility* of some of the reforms introduced in Greece and France (see *infra*). For example, if the impact of membership is so overwhelming, what accounts for the problems encountered in Greece in the case of the regulation of the activity of owners of mass media organisations who are also active in the area of public procurement? Even more importantly, if the reforms introduced by the Greek and the French governments in an effort to improve implementation at the domestic level were exogenously-induced, why did they extend to functions or areas of activity that had nothing (or little) to do with 'pressure' from Brussels? Finally, it would be wrong to ascribe to membership of the EU a causal impact in the area of public procurement because there is no reason to believe that the political preferences that led to the aforementioned institutional reforms were totally exogenous to the governments that introduced them, i.e. that the promoters of these reforms did not actually share the views that led to these reforms. In other words, contrary to what some politicians would like citizens to believe, national governments are not the passive recipients of 'mandates' emanating from the EU. They shape policies along with a number of other important actors like the European Commission and Parliament. Ignoring this fact would have perilous implications for the accuracy of the analysis of implementation at the domestic level.

This has additional important implications for the argument regarding the so-called 'worlds of compliance', i.e. a 'world of law observance', a 'world of domestic politics' and a 'world of neglect', defined not in terms of outcomes[9] but as standard modes of dealing with implementation duties (Falkner *et al.* 2005, 320). The empirical material presented in Chapters 4 and 5 indicates that in the two problematic cases (namely Greece and France) the pattern of operation of the two central governments is dynamic (since it has changed over time) rather than static as implicitly suggested by the argument regarding the aforementioned 'worlds'. Indeed, the same argument applies to the UK as indicated by the switch from circulars to hard law and the procedural failings that led to the problems encountered in the case of the building of the new Scottish Parliament. As a result, it would be misleading to suggest (and to do so only on the basis of evidence from one sector) that each of the countries examined here exemplifies one of the aforementioned 'worlds of compliance'. Moreover, if the 'world of neglect' exists and it is, as the exponents of this typology claim, characterised by inertia and bureaucratic failure, significant (though low profile) reforms[10] in both Greece and France would be in stark contrast with the key characteristics of the 'world' which they are supposed to exemplify.

In more general terms, the analysis of the dynamics of implementation leads to two broader conclusions regarding the impact of European integration on the nation state. First, since involvement in the process of integration entails challenges to patterns of domestic governance, this contributes to the gradual development of these patterns by highlighting weaknesses, lacunae and capability deficits in domestic politico-administrative systems. Far from being led (exclusively or even primarily) by EU 'fixers' such as the European Commission, domestic actors have a defining role in shaping the responses to these challenges. Second, this argument can be extended from the domain of institutional development to policy content. The example of public procurement – a core aspect of the single European market – indicates that EU policies do not eliminate the margin of manoeuvre of national governments. National governments retain the capacity to make crucial choices (e.g. to choose between the lowest price and most economically advantageous offer as the key criterion for the award of public contracts) when they implement the policies that have been formulated collectively at the level of the EU. This is much more than a merely technical arrangement. Rather, it exemplifies a key political choice. The notion of *Vollzugsföderalismus* found in federal polities (or those with a federal orientation) also permeates crucial choices made by the 'founding fathers' of the EU. It combines *de facto* a certain respect for the histories of the individual state machineries that give meaning to EU policies on a daily basis, with a degree of faith in the gradual nature of reform. If the example examined here is anything to go by, they were right.

Implementation and integration

There are two ways in which the study of implementation can shed light on the process of integration. The first concerns its impact on the legitimacy of the process while the second concerns the nature of one set of influential actors, namely central governments. Discussing the policy making process from the perspective of theories of integration Webb (1983, 30) argued that 'governments will be far less likely to agree common policies and rule-making while there are doubts over the extent to which these will be observed uniformly throughout the Community area'.

In other words, patterns of implementation may have systemic implications for the wider integration process. Indeed, irrespective of the theoretical perspective that one adopts in order to explain the emergence and development of European integration as a political phenomenon, the belief that the EU can be an effective problem-solving arena is common. At the same time, effectiveness is also a key source of legitimacy. The EU risks being watered down or even abandoned if it does not produce at least some of the expected results. This argument is reinforced by the dominant policy type – that is regulation, which is used within the EU. The pursuit of policies that are dominated by the spirit of competition means that the main focus is on the establishment of a 'level playing field'. Systematic distortion of competition may produce increased pressures for the re-nationalisation of policy, thus initiating a process which may lead to the limitation or abandonment of the

Conclusion 147

whole endeavour. This is particularly important at a time when a significant part of the motives (namely, peace in Europe) that led to the establishment of the initial European Communities begins to fade in the distant past.

The implications of this study are not limited to the traditional Community method. Rather, they extend to the utilisation by the EU of new modes of governance including the open method of co-ordination, co-regulation and self regulation that entail the use of tools such as the 'new approach directives', indicators, benchmarking, voluntary agreements, minimum standards, partnerships, incentives and market-based instruments.[11] As Passas rightly argues, in addition to high levels of planning capacity and the ability to monitor procedures, the utilisation of these new arrangements requires a significant degree of co-ordination of the relevant administrative units (often both within and across sectors) as well as the capacity to assess (and then draw lessons from) their own experience both in an effort to improve their own performance and as a means of contributing to better policy making at the level of the EU (Passas 2008).

The study of implementation and the role of central governments therein also reveal the limits of the theoretical work which assumes that governments are unitary actors. Intergovernmentalists initially saw the state as a single decision making unit which was in a position to make rational decisions on the basis of more or less specific conceptions of its own interests, with the national government being the central actor in this process. This study has illustrated that national governments are multi-faceted complex organisations whose operation is, at least up to a certain extent, subject to internal tensions as well as change. Consequently, as in the case of preference formation (Dimitrakopoulos and Kassim 2004), it is important to problematise, instead of taking for granted – their operation or their capabilities, in an effort to achieve a more accurate understanding of European integration.

Notes

1 Author's calculations based on data published in *Single Market News* (2000, 12–13).
2 This trend is more evident in the French case but it is also present in the developments that occurred in Greece since the general election of March 2004.
3 The same trend was observed in the early 1980s when the challenge of the involvement in the formulation of EC policy was beginning to emerge (*supra*, Chapter 2).
4 Whether these reforms will eventually lead to a new theory of action remains to be seen.
5 However, as regards public works projects undertaken in Greece, these mechanisms also included controls used during the construction process.
6 For a discussion of the impact of politicisation see the next section of this chapter.
7 It is important to note that they operated in the shadow of the exigencies of domestic rules on public accounting.

8 This notion is in and of itself problematic because, although the use of public funds for procurement purposes has a clear technical dimension – it also involves major choices that reflect values and priorities; this is why it is political *par excellence*.
9 However, it is worth noting that the 'world of neglect' is construed by its exponents as one where 'compliance with EU law is not a *goal* in itself' (Falkner *et al.* 2005, 323 – added emphasis).
10 Two examples can be mentioned here, namely (i) the recent informal changes within the CMPE that will allow it to identify contracts that ought to have been but were actually not examined by it and (ii) the fact that civil servants in the Greek Ministry of Economy and Finance are willing to provide written comments regarding problematic cases of public procurement in services (*supra*, Chapter 5).
11 For a discussion of the impact of such policy instruments on closing the implementation gap in the EU's environmental policy see Knill and Lenschow (2000).

Bibliography

Books, documents and articles

Achard, Pierre. 1972. Rapport. In *Les Communautés européennes et le droit administratif français*, edited by Faculté de Droit de Strasbourg, 23–61. Paris: LGDJ.

Alberton, Ghislaine. 1995. L'article 88-4 de la Constitution ou l'avènement d'un nouveau Janus constitutionnel. *Revue du Droit Public et de la Science Politique* 111 (4):921–50.

Anastopoulos, J. 1988. Grèce. In *Making European policies work/L'Europe des administrations?* edited by H. Siedentopf and J. Ziller. Vol. II: National reports/ Rapports nationaux, 232–75. Bruxelles: Bruylant.

Argyris, Chris, and Donald A. Schön. 1996. *Organizational learning II: Theory, method and practice*. Reading, MA: Addison-Wesley.

Arrowsmith, Sue. 1993. Enforcing the public procurement rules: Legal remedies in the Court of Justice and the national courts. In *Remedies for enforcing the public procurement rules*, edited by S. Arrowsmith, 1–90. Winteringham: Earlsgate.

—— 1994. Abolition of the United Kingdom's procurement preference scheme for disabled workers. *Public Procurement Law Review* 3 (6):CS225–9.

—— 1996. Interpretation of the procurement directives and regulations: A note on R. v. Portsmouth City Council, ex p. Bonaco Builders. *Public Procurement Law Review* 5 (3):CS90–6.

—— 2000. Implementation of Directive 97/52 and obligations under the Government Procurement Agreement in the United Kingdom. *Public Procurement Law Review*. 9 (6):NA151–3.

—— 2006. Implementation of the new EC procurement directives and the Alcatel ruling in England and Wales and Northern Ireland: a review of the new legislation and guidance. *Public Procurement Law Review* 15 (3):86–136.

Assemblée nationale. Délégation pour l'Union européenne. 2003. *L'état de transposition des directives européennes*. Rapport d'information no. 1009. Paris: Assemblée nationale.

—— 2004. *La transposition des directives européennes*. Rapport d'information no. 1709. Paris: Assemblée nationale.

Athanassopoulos, Dimitris. 1986. *Government and government institutions* [in Greek]. Athens: Ant. N. Sakkoulas.

Bagehot, Walter. [1867] 1963. *The English Constitution*. Introduction by R.H.S. Crossman. Repr. London: Fontana.
Bailey, Ian. 2002. National adaptation to European integration: institutional vetoes and goodness-of-fit. *Journal of European Public Policy* 9 (5):791–811.
Bardach, Eugene. 1977. *The implementation game: What happens after a bill becomes a law*. Cambridge, MA: MIT Press.
—— 1980. On designing implementable programs. In *Pitfalls of analysis*, edited by G. Majone and E.S. Quade, 138–57. Chichester: John Wiley & Sons.
Barrett, Susan, and Colin Fudge. 1981. Examining the policy-action relationship. In *Policy and action. Essays on the implementation of public policy*, edited by S. Barrett and C. Fudge, 3–32. London: Methuen.
Barrett, Susan, and Michael Hill. 1984. Policy, bargaining and structure in implementation theory: towards an integrated perspective. *Policy and Politics* 12 (3):219–40.
Bates, T. St. John N. 1991. European Community legislation before the House of Commons. *Statute Law Review* 12 (2):109–34.
Bazex, Michel. 1994. Le Conseil de la concurrence et les marchés publics. *L'Actualité Juridique – Droit Administratif* (7–8):103–8.
Berlin, Dominique. 1991. Commentaire de la directive no 90/531 CEE du Conseil du 17 septembre 1990 relative aux procédures de passation des marchés dans les secteurs de l'eau, de l'énergie, des transports et des télécommunications. *L'Actualité Juridique – Droit Administratif* (1):13–22.
Berman, Paul. 1978. The study of macro- and micro-implementation. *Public Policy* 26 (2):157–84.
—— 1980. Thinking about programmed and adaptive implementation: Matching strategies to situations. In *Why policies succeed or fail*, edited by H.M. Ingram and D.E. Mann, 205–27. Beverly Hills/London: Sage.
Bernitsas, P. 1987. Greek infringements of EC legislation 1981–1985 [in Greek]. In *Greece in the EC: The first five years*, edited by P. Kazakos and C. Stephanou, 163–201. Athens: Sakkoulas.
Bertram, Christoph. 1967. Decision-making in the EEC: The management committee procedure. *Common Market Law Review* 5 (3):246–64.
Birkinshaw, Patrick. 1990. Application in the member states of the directives on public procurement: United Kingdom. In *Rapports pour le 14e congrès: L'application dans les États membres des directives sur les marchés publics*, edited by FIDE, 287–307. Madrid: Ministerio de Justicia.
Blanquet, Marc. 1994. *L'article 5 du Traité CEE: Recherche sur les obligations de fidélité des États membres de la Communauté*. Paris: LGDJ.
Blumann, Claude. 1993. Comitologie. In *Dictionnaire juridique des Communautés européennes*, edited by A. Barav and C. Philip, 188–98. Paris: PUF.
Börzel, Tanja A. 2001. Non-compliance in the European Union: pathology or statistical artefact? *Journal of European Public Policy* 8 (5):803–24.
—— 2002. *States and regions in the European Union: Institutional adaptation in Germany and Spain*. Cambridge: Cambridge University Press.
Bovis, Christopher. 1998. The regulation of public procurement as a key element of European economic law. *European Law Journal* 4 (2):220–42.
Braun, Peter. 2003. Strict compliance versus commercial reality: the practical application of EC public procurement law to the UK's Private Finance Initiative. *European Law Journal* 9 (5):575–98.

Bréchon-Moulènes, Christine. 1990. L'application dans les États membres des directives sur les marchés publics – France. In *Rapports pour le 14e Congrès: L'application dans les états membres des directives sur les marchés publics*, edited by F.I.D.E., 145–67. Madrid: Ministerio de Justicia.

Browne, Angela, and Aaron Wildavsky. 1984. Implementation as exploration. In *Implementation: How great expectations in Washington are dashed in Oakland*, edited by J.L. Pressman and A. Wildavsky, 3rd edn, 232–56. Berkeley: University of California Press.

Bulmer, Simon and Kenneth Armstrong. 2003. The UK: between political controversy and administrative efficiency. In *Fifteen into one? The European Union and its member states*, edited by W. Wessels, A. Maurer and J. Mittag, 388–410. Manchester: Manchester University Press.

Bulmer, Simon, and Martin Burch. 1998. Organizing for Europe: Whitehall, the British state and European Union. *Public Administration* 76 (4):601–28.

Bulmer, Simon, Martin Burch, Patricia Hogwood and Andrew Scott. 2006. UK devolution and the European Union: a tale of cooperative asymmetry? *Publius* 36 (1): 75–93.

Burdeau, Georges, Francis Hamon, and Michel Troper. 1993. *Droit constitutionnel*. 23rd edn. Paris: LGDJ.

Burnham, June, and G.W. Jones with Robert Elgie. 1995. The parliamentary activity of John Major, 1990–94. *British Journal of Political Science* 25 (4):551–63.

Butt Philip, Alan. 1985. United Kingdom: National survey. In *L'application du droit communautaire par les États membres*, edited by G. Ciavarini Azzi, 93–100. Maastricht: EIPA.

Butt Philip, Alan, and Christina Baron. 1988. United Kingdom. In *Making European policies work/L'Europe des administrations?* edited by H. Siedentopf and J. Ziller. Vol. II: National reports/Rapports nationaux, 637–713. Bruxelles: Bruylant.

Carnelutti, Alexandre. 1988. L'administration française face à la règle communautaire. *Revue Française d'Administration Publique* (48):7–23.

—— (table ronde animée par). 1992. L'administration française face aux nouvelles echéances européennes. *Revue Française d'Administration Publique* (63):459–71.

Cartron, Joël. 1997. Note on *SARL Entreprise générale d'électricité Noël Béranger*. Conseil d'État, Section, 2 October 1996. *L'Actualité Juridique – Droit Administratif* (5): 469–72.

Central Procurement Directorate. 2003. First annual report to the Procurement Board, April 2002 – March 2003. Belfast: CPD.

—— 2004. Second annual report to the Procurement Board, April 2003 – March 2004. Belfast: CPD.

—— 2005. Third annual report to the Procurement Board, April 2004 – March 2005. Belfast: CPD.

—— 2006. Fourth annual report to the Procurement Board, April 2005 – March 2006. Belfast: CPD.

Charrier, Carmenza. 1996. La Communauté de droit, une étape sous-estimée de la construction européenne. *Revue du Marché Commun et de l'Union Européenne* (400):521–33.

Chayes, Abram and Antonia Handler Chayes. 1993. On compliance. *International Organization* 47 (2):175–205.

Ciavarini Azzi, Giuseppe, ed. 1985. *L'application du droit communautaire par les États membres*. Maastricht: EIPA.

Clark, Brian. 1996. Public procurement and private finance initiative. *Public Procurement Law Review* 5 (3):CS87–9.

—— 1997. The private finance initiative in the United Kingdom: 'Treasury guidance on EC procurement procedure'. *Public Procurement Law Review* 6 (1):CS28–9.

Clarke, Michael. 1992. *British external policy-making in the 1990s.* London: Macmillan.

Cohen, Michael D., James G. March, and Johan P. Olsen. 1972. A garbage can model of organizational choice. *Administrative Science Quarterly* 17 (1):1–25.

Collins, Lawrence. 1990. *European Community law in the United Kingdom.* 4th edn. London: Butterworths.

Commission Centrale des Marchés. 1997. Le contexte européen des marchés publics. Manuscript. Paris.

Commission des Communautés européennes. 1996. Treizième rapport annuel sur le contrôle de l'application du droit communautaire (1995). COM (96) 600 final. 29 May. Bruxelles.

Commission des Marchés Publics de l'État. 2005. Présentation des dossiers en CMPE. Instruction CMPE/RG/2005. Paris: Ministère de l'Economie, des Finances et de l'Industrie.

—— 2006. Rapport d'activité 2005. Paris: Ministère de l'Economie, des Finances et de l'Industrie.

Commission of the European Communities. 1987. Guide to the Community rules on open government procurement. *Official Journal of the European Communities*, C358, 31 December.

—— 1988. Communication from the Commission on a Community regime for procurement in the excluded sectors: Water, energy, transport and telecommunications. COM (88) 376 final. 11 October.

—— 1989a. Notice C(88) 2510 to the member states on monitoring compliance with public procurement rules in the case of projects and programmes financed by the structural funds and financial instruments. *Official Journal of the European Communities*, C22, 28 January.

—— 1989b. Public procurement: Regional and social aspects. COM (89) 400 final. 24 July.

—— 1990. Seventh annual report submitted by the Commission to the European Parliament on the control of the application of Community law (1989). COM (90) 288 final. 22 May.

—— 1995. Twelfth annual report on monitoring the application of Community law (1994). COM (95) 500 final. 7 June. Brussels.

—— 1996. Co-operation between administrations for enforcement of internal market law: A progress report. COM (96) 20 final. 29 January.

—— 2001a. Interpretive communication on the Community law applicable to public procurement and the possibilities for integrating environmental considerations into public procurement. COM (2001) 274 final. 4 July.

—— 2001b. Interpretive communication on the Community law applicable to public procurement and the possibilities for integrating social considerations into public procurement. COM (2001) 566 final. 15 October.

Commissions Spécialisées des Marchés. 2001. Rapport d'activité 2001. Paris: Commissions Spécialisées des Marchés.

—— 2002. Rapport d'activité 2002. Paris: Commissions Spécialisées des Marchés.

Conseil de la Concurrence. 2005. Rapport annuel 2004. Paris: Documentation française.
Cot, Jean-Pierre. 1980. Parliament and foreign policy in France. In *Parliamentary control over foreign policy: Legal essays*, edited by A. Cassese, 11–24. Aalpen aan den Rijn: Sijthoff & Noordhoff.
Cottereau, Gilles. 1982. Les délégations parlementaires pour les Communautés européennes. *Revue du Droit Public et de la Science Politique* 98 (1):35–63.
Craig, Paul, and Gráinne de Búrca. 1995. *EC law: Text, cases and materials*. Oxford: Clarendon Press.
Délégation du Sénat pour l'Union européenne. 2001. La transposition des directives communautaires. Rapport no. 182. Paris: Sénat.
—— 2002. L'amélioration des procédures de transposition des directives communautaires en droit français. Rapport d'information no. 250. Paris: Sénat.
Department for Communities and Local Government. 2006. National procurement strategy for local government – two years on. London: DCLG.
Department of the Environment/Welsh Office. 1996. Joint circular 5/96–11/96. 2 April. London.
Department of Finance and Personnel. 2002. Public procurement policy. May. Belfast: Department of Finance and Personnel. http://www.cpdni.gov.uk/pdf-public_procurement_policy.pdf
Department of Trade and Industry. 1994. Public procurement review. London: DTI.
Derthick, Martha. 1972. *New towns in-town: Why a federal programme failed*. Washington, DC: The Urban Institute.
De Smith, Stanley, and Rodney Brazier. 1994. *Constitutional and administrative law*. 7th edn. London: Penguin.
Dewost, Jean-Louis. 1990. Le contrôle de l'application du droit communautaire: Un exemple de coopération entre administrations nationales et administration communautaire. *Administration* (149):78–9.
Dillemann, Christian. 1987. *Les commandes publiques*. Notes et Études Documentaires no. 4827. Paris: La Documentation française.
Dimitrakopoulos, Dionyssis G. 1998. Beyond transposition: A comparative inquiry into the implementation of European public policy. Doctoral dissertation, Department of Politics, University of Hull.
—— 2001a. Incrementalism and path dependence: European integration and institutional change in national parliaments. *Journal of Common Market Studies* 39 (3):405–22.
—— 2001b. Learning and steering: changing implementation patterns and the Greek central government. *Journal of European Public Policy* 8 (4):604–22.
—— 2001c. The transposition of EU law: 'Post-decisional politics' and institutional autonomy. *European Law Journal* 7 (4):442–58.
Dimitrakopoulos, Dionyssis G., and Hussein Kassim, eds. 2004. *Preference formation and EU Treaty Reform*. Special issue of *Comparative European Politics*, 2 (3).
Dimitrakopoulos, Dionyssis G. and Jeremy J. Richardson. 2001. Implementing EU public policy. In *European Union: Power and policy-making*, edited by J.J. Richardson, 335–56. 2nd edn. London: Routledge.
Drago, Roland. 1975. Les incidences communautaires sur le droit des marchés publics et des marchés des entreprises publiques. In *La France et les Communautés*

européennes, edited by Joël Rideau, Pierre Gerbet, Maurice Torrelli and Roger-Michel Chevallier, 859–72. Paris: LGDJ.
Drewry, Gavin. 1995. The case of the United Kingdom. In *National administrative procedures for the preparation and implementation of Community decisions*, edited by S. Pappas, 453–77. Maastricht: European Institute of Public Administration.
Duina, Francesco. 1997. Explaining legal implementation in the European Union. *International Journal of the Sociology of Law* 25 (2):155–79.
—— 1999. *Harmonizing Europe: Nation-states within the Common Market*. Albany, NY: State University of New York Press.
Dunleavy, Patrick and George W. Jones with Jane Burnham, Robert Elgie, Peter Fysh. 1993. Leaders, politics and institutional change: The decline of prime ministerial accountability to the House of Commons, 1868–1990. *British Journal of Political Science* 23 (3):267–98.
Dunsire, Andrew. 1978. *Implementation in a bureaucracy: The execution process*. Vol. 1. Oxford: Martin Robertson.
Ehlermann, Claus-Dieter. 1987. Ein Plädoyer für die dezentralle Kontrolle der Anwendung des Gemeinschaftsrechts durch die Mitgliedstaaten. In *Du droit international au droit de l'intégration: Liber amicorum Pierre Pescatore*, edited by F. Capotorti, C.-D. Ehlermann J. Frowein, F. Jacobs, R. Joliet, T. Koopmans and R. Kovar, 205–26. Baden-Baden: Nomos.
Elmore, Richard F. 1978. Organizational models of social program implementation. *Public Policy* 26 (2):187–228.
European Commission. 1996. Green paper – public procurement in the European Union: Exploring the way forward. Brussels.
—— 2004. A report on the functioning of public procurement markets in the EU: benefits from the application of EU directives and challenges for the future, 3 December. http://ec.europa.eu/internal_market/publicprocurement/docs/public-proc-market-final-report_en.pdf#search=%22A%20report%20on%20the%20 functioning%20of%20public%20procurement%20markets%20in%20the%20EU %3A%20benefits%20from%20the%20application%20of%20EU%20directives %20and%20challenges%20for%20the%20future%22
—— Directorate General XV. 1996. Public procurement: Final report. July. Manuscript.
European Council. 1993. Copenhagen European Council – Presidency conclusions. 21–22 June. Doc. SN 180/1/93 REV 1. Brussels.
—— 1995. Madrid European Council – Presidency conclusions. 15–16 December. Brussels.
European Court of Justice. 2005. Statistics of judicial activity of the Court of Justice. http://curia.europa.eu/en/instit/presentationfr/index.htm
European Union. 2000. General report on the activities of the European Union. Luxembourg: OPOCE.
Fabius, Laurent. 2001. Présentation de la réforme des marchés publics. http://www.minefi.gouv.fr/fonds_documentaire/archives/discours/lf010306.htm
Falkner, Gerda, Miriam Hartlapp, Simone Leiber, and Oliver Treib. 2004. Non-compliance with EU directives in the member states: Opposition through the backdoor? *West European Politics* 27 (3):452–73.
Falkner, Gerda, Oliver Treib, Miriam Hartlapp, and Simone Leiber. 2005. *Complying with Europe: EU harmonisation and soft law in the member states*. Cambridge: Cambridge University Press.

Fernández Martin, José M. 1996. *The EC public procurement rules: A critical analysis*. Oxford: Clarendon Press.

Flamme, Maurice-André, and Philippe Flamme. 1988. Vers l'Europe des marchés publics? *Revue du Marché Commun* (320):455–79.

—— 1990. Le droit européen des commandes publiques: Après leur réglementation, voici les recours. *Journal des Tribunaux* 109 (5548):317–26.

Fournier, Jacques. 1987. *Le travail gouvernemental*. Paris: Dalloz/FNSP.

Fraser, Rt Hon The Lord of Carmyllie QC. 2004. Report on the Holyrood Inquiry. September 2004. http://www.holyroodinquiry.org/FINAL_report/report.htm

Gaudemet, Yves. 1994. Le précontentieux: Le règlement non juridictionnel des conflits dans les marchés publics. *L'Actualité Juridique – Droit Administratif* (7–8):84–90.

Georgopoulos, A. 2000. The system of remedies for enforcing public procurement rules in Greece: A critical review. *Public Procurement Law Review* (2):75–93.

Gerbet, Pierre. 1969. La préparation de la décision communautaire au niveau national français. In *La décision dans les Communautés européennes*, edited by P. Gerbet and D. Pépy, 195–208. Bruxelles: PUB.

—— 1975. L'élaboration des politiques communautaires au niveau national français. In *La France et les Communautés européennes*, edited by J. Rideau, P. Gerbet, M. Torrelli and R.-M. Chevallier, 379–98. Paris: LGDJ.

Gershon, Peter. 1999. Review of civil procurement in central government. http://www.hm-treasury.gov.uk/documents/enterprise_and_productivity/ent_pep_gershon.cfm

Giannakourou, Georgia. 1996. *The implementation of European environmental policy in Greece: Trends towards the europeanisation of national policy-making*. European Policy Process Occasional Papers. Colchester: Department of Government/University of Essex.

Gohon, Jean-Pierre. 1991. *Les marchés publics européens*. Paris: PUF.

Greenwood, John, and David Wilson. 1989. *Public administration in Britain today*. 2nd edn. London: Routledge.

Gunn, L.A. 1978. Why is implementation so difficult? *Management Services in Government* 33 (4):169–76.

Haas, Enst. 1968. *The uniting of Europe: Political, social, and economic forces 1950–1957*. Repr. Stanford, CA: Stanford University Press.

Hargrove, Erwin C. 1975. *The missing link: The study of the implementation of social policy*. Washington, D.C.: The Urban Institute.

Harmsen, Robert. 1999. The Europeanization of national administrations: A comparative study of France and the Netherlands. *Governance* 12 (1):81–113.

Haverland, Markus. 2000. National adaptation to European integration: the importance of institutional veto points. *Journal of Public Policy* 20 (1):83–103.

Hayward, Jack, ed. 1995. *Industrial enterprise and European integration: From national to international champions in Western Europe*. Oxford: Oxford University Press.

Hayward, Jack, and Vincent Wright. 2002. *Governing from the centre: Core executive co-ordination in France*. Oxford: Oxford University Press.

Hellenic Parliament. 1990. Decision Nr. 3076/2008 of the President of the Hellenic Parliament regarding the establishment of a European Community Affairs Committee [in Greek]. 13 June. http://www.parliament.gr/organwsh/comments.asp

—— 2005. Report of the Scientific Support Service on the draft law entitled 'Measures for transparency and the prevention of violations in the context of the conclusion of public procurement contracts' [in Greek]. 16 January. Athens: Hellenic Parliament.
Henderson, Phinella. 2003. The impact of devolution on public procurement in the United Kingdom. *Public Procurement Law Review* 12 (4):175–80.
Hjern, Benny, and David O. Porter. 1981. Implementation structures: A new unit of administrative analysis. *Organization Studies* 2 (3):211–27.
HM Government. 1995. Setting new standards: A strategy for government procurement. Cm 2840. May. London: HMSO.
HM Treasury. 1988. Guidance notes on public sector purchasing international obligations: Supplies contracts. December.
—— 1995. Introduction to EC procurement rules. Central Unit on Procurement note 51. July.
—— 1996. An introduction to the EC procurement rules: Note by the Treasury. January.
—— 1998. Procurement policy guidelines. Procurement Policy Unit. November.
—— 2000. Government accounting. Amendment 4/05. Online edition. http://www.government-accounting.gov.uk/current/frames.htm
—— 2001. The Government's Expenditure Plans 2001–02 to 2003–04 and Main Estimates 2001–02. Departmental Report of the Chancellor of the Exchequer's Departments. Cm 5116, April. London: HM Treasury.
Hogwood, Brian W., and Lewis A. Gunn. 1984. *Policy analysis for the real world.* Oxford: Oxford University Press.
Hood, Christopher C. 1976. *The limits of administration.* London: John Wiley & Sons.
—— 1983. *The tools of government.* London/Basingstoke: Macmillan.
House of Commons. *Parliamentary Debates.* Various years.
House of Lords. *Parliamentary Debates.* Various years.
Jeanrenaud, Claude. 1984. Marchés publics et politique économique. *Annales de l'Économie Publique, Sociale et Coopérative* 72 (2):151–8.
Joerges, Christian. 1996. Das Recht im Prozeß der europäischen Integration: Ein Plädoyer für die Beachtung des Rechts durch die Politikwissenschaft und ihre Beteiligung an rechtlichen Diskursen. In *Europäische Integration,* edited by M. Jachtenfuchs and B. Kohler-Koch, 73–108. Opladen: Leske + Budrich.
Jones, Charles O. 1984. *An introduction to the study of public policy.* 3rd edn. Belmont, CA: Wadsworth Publishing Company.
Jordan, Andrew. 1997. 'Overcoming the divide' between comparative politics and international relations approaches to the EC: What role for 'post-decisional politics'? *West European Politics* 20 (4):43–70.
Kassim, Hussein. 2000. The United Kingdom. In *The national co-ordination of EU policy: The domestic level,* edited by H. Kassim, B. Guy Peters and V. Wright, 22–53. Oxford: Oxford University Press.
—— 2001. Representing the United Kingdom in Brussels: the fine art of positive co-ordination. In *The national co-ordination of EU policy: The European level,* edited by H. Kassim, A. Menon, B. Guy Peters and V. Wright, 47–74. Oxford: Oxford University Press.

Kassim, Hussein, Anand Menon, B. Guy Peters, and Vincent Wright, eds. 2001. *The national co-ordination of EU policy: The European level.* Oxford: Oxford University Press.
Kassim, Hussein, B. Guy Peters, and Vincent Wright, eds. 2000. *The national co-ordination of EU policy: The domestic level.* Oxford: Oxford University Press.
Knill, Christoph. 2001. *The Europeanisation of national administrations: Patterns of institutional change and persistence.* Cambridge: Cambridge University Press.
Knill, Christoph, and Andrea Lenschow, eds. 2000. *Implementing EU environmental policy: New directions and old problems.* Manchester: Manchester University Press.
Kosmidis, S. 1997. Political responsibility and the management of public funds [in Greek]. *To Vima* (Athens), 5 October.
Koutoupa. Lia. 1993. Implementation in Greece of the European Community procurement rules on public works and on remedies. *Public Procurement Law Review* 2 (4):CS88–9.
––– 1995. The Greek law 2229/1994 on public works. *Public Procurement Law Review* 4 (4):CS97–9.
––– 1996. The new decree on the naming of shareholders. *Public Procurement Law Review* 5 (6):CS169.
Koutoupa-Rengakos, Evangelia. 1993. Enforcing the public procurement rules in Greece. In *Remedies for enforcing the public procurement rules*, edited by S. Arrowsmith, 387–99. Winteringham: Earlsgate.
Kovar, Robert. 1973. L'effectivité interne du droit communautaire. In *La Communauté et ses États membres*, 201–34. La Haye: Martinus Nijhoff.
Krasner, Stephen D. 1984. Approaches to the state. Alternative conceptions and historical dynamics. *Comparative Politics* 16 (2):223–46.
Kunzlik, Peter. 1997. Interpretation of the procurement directives and regulations: A note on the Court of Appeal judgment in R. v. Portsmouth City Council, ex p. Peter Coles and Colwick Builders limited and ex p. George Austin Limited. *Public Procurement Law Review* 6 (2):CS73–87.
Labayle, Henri. 1989. Le contrôle de la réglementation communautaire en matière de marchés publics. *Revue du Marché Commun* (332):625–36.
Laffan. Brigid. 2006. Managing Europe from home in Dublin, Athens and Helsinki: a comparative analysis. *West European Politics* 29 (4):687–708.
Lalioti, Barbara. 2002. *The management unit for the Community support framework: An example of the Europeanisation of public administration* [in Greek]. Athens: Ant. N. Sakkoulas.
Lane, Jan-Erik. 1983. The concept of implementation. *Statsvetenskaplig Tidskrift* 86:17–40.
Laporte, Jean. 1981. Un nouveau mode de contrôle: Les délégations parlementaires. *Revue Française de Science Politique* 31 (1):121–39.
Lascoumes, Pierre, and Patrick Le Galès. 2007. Introduction: understanding public policy through its instruments – from the nature of instruments to the sociology of public policy instrumentation. *Governance* 20 (1):1–21.
Le Vigan, Thomas. 1990. Les Finances et Bruxelles. *Pouvoirs* (53):73–88.
Lelong, Pierre. 2003. Interview, *Journal de l'Achat Public*, octobre, semaine 5. http://www.achatpublic.com/news/2003/10/5/AchatPublicBreveInviteDuJeudi.2003-10-30.2900

Lequertier, Daniel. 1994. L'outil diplomatique français. *Revue Française d'Administration Publique* (69):17–33.
Lequesne, Christian. 1987. L'adaptation des administrations nationales à l'existence des Communautés européennes: Le cas des ministères français. *Revue Française d'Administration Publique* (42):275–92.
—— 1992. L'appareil politico-administratif central de la France et la Communauté européenne: mai 1981-mai 1991. Thèse de doctorat en science politique, 2 vols., Institut d'Études Politiques, Paris.
—— 1993. *Paris-Bruxelles: Comment se fait la politique européenne de la France.* Paris: FNSP.
Lichere, François. 2006. Damages for violation of the EC public procurement rules in France. *Public Procurement Law Review* 15 (4):171–8.
Lipsky, Michael. 1971. Street-level bureaucracy and the analysis of urban reform. *Urban Affairs Quarterly* 6 (4):391–409.
—— 1980. *Street-level bureaucracy: Dilemmas of the individual in public services.* New York: Russell Sage Foundation.
Louis, J.-V. 1990. *L'ordre juridique communautaire.* 5th edn. Bruxelles: OPOCE.
Loverdos, Andreas. 1991. *Government: Collective operation and political responsibility* [in Greek]. Athens: Ant. N. Sakkoulas.
Lowi, Theodore J. 1964. American business, public policy, case-studies, and political theory. *World Politics* 16 (4):677–715.
—— 1972. Four systems of policy, politics and choice. *Public Administration Review* 32 (4):298–310.
Lundquist, Lennart. 1972. The control process: Steering and review in large organizations. *Scandinavian Political Studies* 7 (5):29–43.
—— 1987. *Implementation steering: An actor-structure approach.* Bromley, UK: Chartwell-Bratt.
McClelland, John F. CBE. 2006. *Review of public procurement in Scotland. Report and recommendations.* Edinburgh: Scottish Executive.
Majone, Giandomenico. 1980. Policies as theories. *Omega* 8 (2):151–62.
Majone, Giandomenico, and Aaron Wildavsky. 1984. Implementation as evolution. In *Implementation: How great expectations in Washington are dashed in Oakland*, edited by J. L. Pressman and A. Wildavsky, 3rd edn, 163–80. Berkeley: University of California Press.
Makridimitris, Antonis. 1992. *The organisation of the government: Issues of cohesion and differentiation* [in Greek]. Athens: Ant. N. Sakkoulas.
Makridimitris, Antonis and Argyris Passas. 1994. *The Greek government and the co-ordination of European policy* [in Greek]. Athens: Ant. N. Sakkoulas.
Maljean-Dubois, Sandrine. 1997. Note on *Fédération nationale des travaux publics, Fédération nationale du bâtiment.* Conseil d'État, 10 May 1996. *L'Actualité Juridique – Droit Administratif* (2): 196–202.
March, James G. 1988. *Decisions and organizations.* Oxford: Basil Blackwell.
March, James G., and Johan P. Olsen. 1979. *Ambiguity and choice in organizations.* 2nd edn. Oslo: Scandinavian University Press.
—— 1989. *Rediscovering institutions: The organizational basis of politics.* New York: Free Press.
March, James G., Martin Schulz, and Xueguang Zhou. 2000. *The dynamics of rules: Change in written organizational codes.* Stanford, CA: Stanford University Press.

March, James G., and Herbert A. Simon. 1958. *Organizations*. New York: John Wiley & Sons.
March, J.G., L. Sproull and M. Tamuz. 1999. Learning from samples of one or fewer. In J.G. March, *The pursuit of organizational intelligence*, 137–55. Oxford: Blackwell.
Marinos, Yannis. 1997. More transparency in state procurement and public works [in Greek]. *Ekonomikos Tachydromos*, 28 August.
Marks, Gary, Liesbet Hooghe, and Kermit Blank. 1996. European integration from the 1980s: State-centric *v.* multi-level governance. *Journal of Common Market Studies* 34 (3):341–78.
Martin, Pascal. 1994a. Public and private contracts in French public contract law: Recent case law. *Public Procurement Law Review* 3 (4):CS141–2.
—— 1994b. Recent developments in French procurement law. *Public Procurement Law Review* 3 (1):CS25–8.
—— 1996. A round-up of recent developments in public procurement in France. *Public Procurement Law Review* 5 (3):CS69–70.
Mayntz, Renate. 1980a. Einleitung: Die Entwicklung des analytischen Paradigmas der Implementationsforschung. In *Implementation politischer Programme: Empirische Forschungsberichte*, edited by R. Mayntz, 1–17. Königstein: Athenäum, Hain, Scriptor, Hanstein.
——, ed. 1980b. *Implementation politischer Programme: Empirische Forschungsberichte*. Königstein: Athenäum, Hain, Scriptor, Hanstein.
—— 1980c. Die Implementation politischer Programme: Theoretische Überlegungen zu einem neuen Forschungsgebiet. In *Implementation politischer Programme: Empirische Forschungsberichte*, edited by R. Mayntz, 236–49. Königstein: Athenäum, Hain, Scriptor, Hanstein.
—— 1983. Zur Einleitung: Probleme der Theoriebildung in der Implementationsforschung. In *Implementation politischer Programme II: Ansätze zur Theoriebildung*, edited by R. Mayntz, 7–24. Opladen: Westdeutscher Verlag.
Mazmanian, Daniel A., and Paul A. Sabatier. 1983. *Implementation and public policy*. Glenview, IL: Scott, Foresman & Co.
Mbaye, Heather A.D. 2001. Why national states comply with supranational law: explaining implementation infringements in the European Union, 1972–1993. *European Union Politics* 2 (3):259–81.
Mendrinou, Maria. 1994. European Community fraud and the politics of institutional development. *European Journal of Political Research* 26 (1):81–101.
—— 1996. Non-compliance and the European Commission's role in integration. *Journal of European Public Policy* 3 (1):1–22.
Menon, Anand. 2000. France. In *The national co-ordination of EU policy: The domestic level*, edited by H. Kassim, B. Guy Peters and V. Wright, 79–98. Oxford: Oxford University Press.
Metcalfe, Les. 1987. Comparaison des systèmes de coordination des politiques: De l'importance des différences? Paper presented at Agir ou réagir? Le rôle des administrations nationales dans le processus décisionnel européen. Cinquième colloque Erenstein, 30–31 octobre, Kerkrade, Pays-Bas.
—— 1988. Institutional inertia versus organizational design: European policy co-ordination in the member states of the European Community. Paper presented at ECPR joint sessions, 5–10 April, Rimini.

Miers, David R., and Alan C. Page. 1990. *Legislation.* 2nd edn. London: Sweet & Maxwell.

Ministère de l'Économie, des Finances et de l'Industrie. 1999. Document d'orientation de la réforme des marchés publics. 26 April. http://www.finances.gouv.fr/marches_publics/

——— 2001. Réforme du code des marchés publics. 6 March. http://www.finances.gouv.fr/fonds_documentaire/archives/dossiersdepresse/2001/dpcode_marches.htm

Ministry of National Economy. 1997a. Circular 521: national system for the provision of technical support regarding public works and services contracts [in Greek]. 8 January. Athens.

——— 1997b. Circular 10543 [in Greek]. 31 March. Athens.

——— 1999. Circular 5527 [in Greek]. 11 February. Athens.

Ministry of Development. 2006a. Circular P1/1105, Implementation of Directive 2004/18 on public supplies contracts [in Greek]. 2 March. Athens. http://www.gge.gr/

——— 2006b. Press release regarding the response of junior minister Yannis Papathanasiou to a parliamentary question submitted by PASOK MPs, 13 March [in Greek]. http://www.gge.gr/7/sub.asp?1508

Ministry of Economy and Finance. 2006. Circular 14873/395, Conclusion of public services contracts [in Greek]. 4 April. Athens.

Ministry of the Environment, Spatial Planning and Public Works. 2006. Circular D17g/09/9/F_ 417, Implementation of Directive 2004/18 on public procurement of works, supplies and services [in Greek]. 18 January. Athens.

Mission interministérielle d'enquête sur les marchés et les conventions de délégation de service public. 2004. Onzième rapport d'activité – année 2003. 4 vols. Paris: Mission interministérielle d'enquête sur les marchés et les conventions de délégation de service public.

——— 2005. Douzième rapport d'activité – année 2004. 3 vols. Paris: Mission interministérielle d'enquête sur les marchés et les conventions de délégation de service public.

Mission interministérielle d'enquête sur les marchés. 1995. Le délit d'octroi d'un avantage injustifié: étude sur le délit d'octroi d'un avantage injustifié. http://www.minefi.gouv.fr/mission_marches/

——— 1998. Cinquième rapport d'activité – année 1997. 4 vols. Paris: Mission interministérielle d'enquête sur les marchés.

——— 1999. Sixième rapport d'activité – année 1998. Paris: Mission interministérielle d'enquête sur les marchés.

——— 2002. Neuvième rapport d'activité – année 2001. 4 vols. Paris: Mission interministérielle d'enquête sur les marchés.

MOPADIS. 2004. The establishment of MOPADIS. http://mopadis.cieel.gr/about.jsp;jsessionid=84E5D6C7D5A0F4A978334521C5D8D4A2?extLang=

——— N. d. Statistical data. http://mopadis.cieel.gr/statistics.jsp?extLang=

Moravcsik, Andrew. 1993. Preferences and power in the European Community: A liberal intergovernmentalist approach. *Journal of Common Market Studies* 31 (4):473–524.

——— 1998. *The choice for Europe: Social purpose and state power from Messina to Maastricht.* Ithaca, NY: Cornell University Press.

National Audit Office. 1999. *Modernising procurement – report by the Comptroller and Auditor General.* HC 808, 20 October. London: Stationery Office.

Bibliography

Neyer, Jürgen, and Dieter Wolf. 2005. The analysis of compliance with international rules: definitions, variables and methodology. In *Law and governance in postnational Europe: Compliance beyond the nation-state*, edited by M. Zürn and C. Joerges, 40–64. Cambridge: Cambridge University Press.

Northern Ireland Executive Committee. N.d. Concordat on co-ordination of EU, international and policy issues on public procurement. http://www.nics.gov.uk/pubs/niconcor.pdf

Norton, Philip. 1995. The United Kingdom: political conflict, parliamentary scrutiny. *Journal of Legislative Studies* 1 (3):92–109.

Office of Government Commerce. 2004a. Consultation document: the approach to implementation of the new public sector procurement directive. http://www.ogc.gov.uk/procurement_policy_and_application_of_eu_rules_european_procurement_directives.asp

—— 2004b. Response to consultation on the new procurement directives. 27 October. http://www.ogc.gov.uk/procurement_policy_and_application_of_eu_rules_european_procurement_directives.asp

—— 2005a. Consultation document: draft regulations implementing the new public sector and utilities procurement directives. June. London: OGC.

—— 2005b. Response to consultation: draft regulations implementing the new public sector and utilities procurement directives. December. London: OGC.

—— 2006a. Domestic, EU and International Policy Development. http://www.ogc.gov.uk/procurement_policy_and_practice_domestic,_eu_and_international_policy_development.asp

—— 2006b. OGC guidance note on the 10-day mandatory standstill period for public sector contracts. March. http://www.ogc.gov.uk/documents/Policy_guidance_10_day_period.pdf

—— 2006c. OGC guidance on Central Purchasing Bodies in the new Procurement Regulations. January. http://www.ogc.gov.uk/documents/Guide_central_purchasing.pdf

—— 2006d. Procurement policy. http://www.ogc.gov.uk/procurement_policy_and_the_eu.asp

—— 2006e. Procurement policy and application of EU rules. http://www.ogc.gov.uk/procurement_policy_and_practice_procurement_policy_and_application_of_eu_rules.asp

Office of the Deputy Prime Minister. 2003. National procurement strategy for local government. London: ODPM.

Olsen, Johan P., and B. Guy Peters. 1996. Learning from experience? In *Lessons from experience: Experiential learning in administrative reforms in eight democracies*, edited by J.P. Olsen and B.G. Peters, 1–35. Oslo: Scandinavian University Press.

O'Toole, Laurence J. 1986. Policy recommendations for multi-actor implementation: An assessment of the field. *Journal of Public Policy* 6 (2):181–210.

O'Toole, Laurence J., and Robert S. Montjoy. 1984. Interorganizational policy implementation: A theoretical perspective. *Public Administration Review* 44 (6):491–503.

Paddon, Michael. 1993. EC public procurement directives and the competition from European contractors for local authority contracts in the UK. In *The political economy of privatization*, edited by T. Clarke and C. Pitelis, 159–84. London: Routledge.

Page, Edward C., and Dionyssis Dimitrakopoulos. 1997. The dynamics of EU growth: A cross-time analysis. *Journal of Theoretical Politics* 9 (3):365–87.
Page, Edward C., and Linda Wouters. 1995. The Europeanization of the national bureaucracies? In *Bureaucracy in the Modern State*, edited by J. Pierre, 185–204. Aldershot: Edward Elgar.
Pangalos, Th. 2000. From hesitant accession to active participation [in Greek]. *To Vima* (Athens), 12 March.
Pappas, Spyros, ed. 1995. *National administrative procedures for the preparation and implementation of Community decisions*. Maastricht: European Institute of Public Administration.
Passas, Argyris, G. 1993. The organisational and functional adaptation of the Greek administration to its Community obligations [in Greek]. In *National administration and Community law: The implementation of EC law by the national administration under the guidance of ECJ precedent*, edited by N. Frangakis, A.D. Papayannides, S. Vodina and M. Souriadakis, 243–54. Athens: Ant. N. Sakkoulas.
—— 2008. The national administration in the institutional and political system of the EU [in Greek]. In *National administration and European integration: the Greek experience*, edited by A.G. Passas. Athens: Papazissis.
Peters, B. Guy. 1997. The Commission and implementation in the European Union: Is there an implementation deficit and why? In *At the heart of the Union: Studies of the European Commission*, edited by Neill Nugent, 187–202. Basingstoke: Macmillan.
—— 1998. Managing horizontal government: the politics of co-ordination. *Public Administration* 76 (2):295–311.
—— N.d. The capacity to co-ordinate. Unpublished manuscript. University of Pittsburgh.
Pierson, Paul. 1996. The path to European integration. An historical institutionalist analysis. *Comparative Political Studies* 29 (2):123–63.
Pisani, Edgard. 1956. Administration de gestion – administration de mission. *Revue Française de Science Politique* 6 (2):315–30.
Pollack, Mark A. 2003. Control mechanism or deliberative democracy? Two images of comitology. *Comparartive Political Studies* 36 (1/2):125–55.
Potet, Frédéric. 1998. Luttes d'influence et querelles d'argent. *Le Monde*, 27 January, 23.
Pressman, Jeffrey L., and Aaron Wildavsky. 1973. *Implementation: How great expectations in Washington are dashed in Oakland*. Berkeley, CA: University of California Press.
—— 1984. *Implementation: How great expectations in Washington are dashed in Oakland*. 3rd expanded edn. Berkeley: University of California Press.
Puchala, Donald. 1975. Domestic politics and regional harmonization in the European Communities. *World Politics* 27 (4):496–520.
Quermonne, Jean-Louis, and Dominique Chagnollaud. 1991. *Le gouvernement de la France sous la Ve République*. 4th edn. Paris: Dalloz.
Raffarin, Jean-Pierre. 2002. Déclaration de politique générale. http://www.premier-ministre.gouv.fr/information/les_dossiers_actualites_19/declaration_politique_gen erale_jean_177/declaration_politique_generale_action_34606.html
Rees, Peter. 1994. Public procurement in the construction industry. In *1993: The European market – myth or reality?* edited by D. Campbell and C. Flint, 169–88. Deventer: Kluwer.

Regional Centres of Excellence. N.d. *The national procurement programme.* http://www.rcoe.gov.uk/rce/core/page.do?pageId=22886
Rein, Martin, and Francine F. Rabinovitz. 1977. *Implementation: A theoretical perspective*: Cambridge, MA: Joint Center for Urban Studies of MIT and Harvard University.
République Française. 1990. Circulaire du 25 janvier 1990 relative à la procédure de suivi de la transposition des directives communautaires en droit interne. *JORF*, 1.2.1990.
—— 1994a. Circulaire du 21 mars 1994 relative aux relations entre les administrations françaises et les institutions de l'Union européenne. *JORF*, 31.3.1994.
—— 1994b. Circulaire du 19 juillet 1994 relative à la prise en compte de la position du Parlement français dans l'élaboration des actes communautaires. *JORF*, 21.7.1994.
—— 1998. Circulaire du 9 novembre 1998 relative à la procédure de suivi de la transposition des directives communautaires en droit interne. *JORF*, 10.11.1998.
—— 1999. Circulaire du Premier ministre du 13 décembre 1999 relative à l'application de l'article 88-4 de la Constitution. *JORF*, 17.12.1999.
—— 2004. Circulaire du 27 septembre 2004 relative à la procédure de transposition en droit interne des directives et décisions-cadres dans le cadre des institutions européennes. *JORF*, 2.10.2004.
—— 2005. Circulaire du 22 novembre 2005 relative à l'application de l'article 88-4 de la Constitution. *JORF*, 25.11.2005.
—— Conseil des Ministres. 2002. Compte rendu de la réunion de 6 novembre. http://www.archives.premier-ministre.gouv.fr/raffarin_version1/fr/ie4/contenu/36629.htm
Rideau, Joël. 1972. Le rôle des États membres dans l'application du droit communautaire. *Annuaire Français de Droit International* 18:864–903.
—— 1987. La comitologie. *Annuaire Européen d'Administration Publique* 10: 739–58.
—— 1994. *Droit institutionnel de l'Union et des Communautés européennes.* Paris: LGDJ.
Risse, Thomas, Maria Cowles, Jim Caporaso. 2001. Europeanization and domestic change: introduction. In *Transforming Europe: Europeanization and domestic change*, edited by M. Green Cowles, J. Caporaso, Th. Risse, 1–20. Ithaca, NY: Cornell University Press.
Rizzuto, Francesco. 2004. European integration and the French parliament: From ineffectual watchdog to constitutional rehabilitation and an enhanced political role. *Journal of Legislative Studies* 10 (1): 123–49.
Sabatier, Paul, and Daniel Mazmanian. 1979. The conditions of effective implementation: A guide to accomplishing policy objectives. *Policy Analysis* 5 (4):481–504.
—— 1981. The implementation of public policy: A framework for analysis. In *Effective policy implementation*, edited by D.A. Mazmanian and P.A. Sabatier, 3–35. Lexington, MA: Lexington Books.
—— 1983. Policy implementation. In *Encyclopedia of policy studies*, edited by S.S. Nagel, 143–69. New York/Basel: Marcel Dekker.
Sapin, Michel. 1994. Les accusations contre les deux grandes compagnies d'eau et le débat sur la repression et la corruption: le gouvernement baisse la garde. *Le Monde*, 11 June.

Sasse, Christoph. 1975. *Regierungen, Parlamente, Ministerrat: Entscheidungsprozesse in der Europäischen Gemeinschaft*. Bonn: Europa Union.
Sauron, Jean-Luc. 1995. *L'application du droit de l'Union européenne en France*. Paris: La Documentation française.
Schaefer, Guenther F. 1996. Committees in the EC policy process: A first step towards developing a conceptual framework. In *Shaping European law and policy: The role of committees and comitology in the political process*, edited by R.H. Pedler and G.F. Schaefer, 3–23. Maastricht: European Institute of Public Administration.
Scharpf, Fritz W. 1978. *Politikformulierung und Implementierung als Forschungsgegenstand am IIMV: Fragestellungen und Ansätze*. Discussion paper no. 78–22. Berlin: Internationales Institut für Management und Verwaltung/Wissenschaftszentrum Berlin.
Scheinman, Lawrence. 1966. Some preliminary notes on bureaucratic relationships in the European Economic Community. *International Organization* 20 (4):750–73.
Schindler, Peter. 1971. The problems of decision-making by way of management committee procedure in the European Economic Community. *Common Market Law Review* 8 (2):184–205.
Schwarze, J., I. Govaere, F. Hélin, and P. Van den Bossche, eds. 1990. *The 1992 challenge at national level: Reports and conference proceedings 1989*. Baden-Baden: Nomos.
Schwarze, Jürgen, Ulrich Becker, and Christiana Pollak, eds. 1991. *The 1992 challenge at national level: Reports and conference proceedings 1990*. Baden-Baden: Nomos.
——, eds. 1993. *The 1992 challenge at national level: Reports and conference proceedings 1991/2*. Baden-Baden: Nomos.
Scottish Executive. N.d. Concordat on co-ordination of EU, international and policy issues on public procurement. http://www.hm-treasury.gov.uk/documents/public_spending_and_services/devolve/pss_devolve_scottconc2.cfm
Scottish Procurement Directorate. 2004. Training module on the new public procurement directives. SPPN 07/2004. Glasgow: SPD.
—— 2005. EU procurement rules on non-discrimination in technical specifications. SPPN (1)2005. Glasgow: SPD.
Selznick, Philip. [1949] 1966. *TVA and the grass roots: A study in the sociology of formal organization*. Repr. New York: Harper and Row.
Siedentopf, Heinrich, and Jacques Ziller, eds. 1988a. *L'Europe des administrations?* Vol. I: Synthèses comparatives. Bruxelles: Bruylant.
——, eds. 1988b. *Making European policies work/L'Europe des administrations?* Vol. II: National reports/Rapports nationaux. Bruxelles: Bruylant.
Simitis, Costas. 2005. *Policy and politics for a creative Greece, 1996–2004* [in Greek]. Athens: Polis.
Simon, Herbert A. 1976. From substantive to procedural rationality. In *Method and appraisal in economics*, edited by S.J. Latsis, 129–48. Cambridge: Cambridge University Press.
—— 1997. *Administrative behavior: A study of decision-making processes in administrative organizations*. 4th edn. New York: The Free Press.
Singh, Robert, ed. 2003. *Governing America: The politics of a divided democracy*. Oxford: Oxford University Press.
Single Market News. 1995. Marchés publics: enquête dans le monde du foot. November, 4.

——— 1996. Marchés publics: procédures d'infraction contre sept états membres. October, 18–19.
——— 2000. Measuring the impact of public procurement policy. March, 12–13.
Skocpol, Theda. 1985. Bringing the state back in. strategies of analysis in current research. In *Bringing the state back in*, edited by P.B. Evans, D. Rueschemeyer, Th. Skocpol, 3–43. Cambridge: Cambridge University Press.
Snyder, Francis. 1993. The effectiveness of European Community law: Institutions, processes, tools and techniques. *Modern Law Review* 56 (1):19–54.
Sorg, James D. 1983. A typology of implementation behaviors of street-level bureaucrats. *Policy Studies Journal* 2 (3):391–406.
Sotiropoulos, D.A. 2004. Southern European public bureaucracies in comparative perspective. *West European Politics* 27 (3):405–22.
Spanou, Calliope. 2000. Greece. In *The national co-ordination of EU policy: the domestic level*, edited by H. Kassim, B. Guy Peters and V. Wright, 161–81. Oxford: Oxford University Press.
Spathopoulos, Photis. 1990. Rapport national héllenique. In *Rapports pour le 14e congrès: L'application dans les États membres des directives sur les marchés publics*, edited by FIDE, 101–32. Madrid: Ministerio de Justicia.
Spence, David. 1993. The role of the national civil service in European lobbying: The British case. In *Lobbying in the European Community*, edited by S. Mazey and J. Richardson, 47–73. Oxford: Oxford University Press.
Stack, Freida. 1983. The imperatives of participation. In *Dilemmas of government: Britain and the European Community*, edited by F.E.C. Gregory, 124–52. Oxford: Martin Robertson.
Stephanou, Constantin. 1992. Administration centrale et intégration européenne: Le cas de la Grèce. Paper presented at conference, Administrative Modernisation in Western Europe, organised by the EUI and Nuffield College, 12–13 June, Aquasparta/Italy.
Sverdrup, Ulf. 2004. Compliance and conflict management in the European Union: Nordic exceptionalism. *Scandinavian Political Studies* 27 (1):23–43.
——— 2005. Implementation: a review essay. ARENA working paper No. 25. Oslo: ARENA.
Tallberg, Jonas. 2003. *European governance and supranational institutions: Making states comply*. London: Routledge.
Taylor, John. 1975. British membership of the European Communities: The question of parliamentary sovereignty. *Government and Opposition* 10 (3):278–93.
Thain, Colin, and Maurice Wright. 1995. *The Treasury and Whitehall: The planning and control of public expenditure, 1976–1993*. Oxford: Oxford University Press.
Thiriez, Frederic. 2000. Moralisation ou demoralisation? *Le Monde*, 10 February.
Thomas, Béatrice. 1991. Infractions et manquements des États membres au droit communautaire. *Revue du Marché Commun et de l'Union Européenne* (353): 887–93.
Timsit, Gérard. 1987. *Administrations et états: Étude comparée*. Paris: PUF.
Toonen, Theo A.J. 1985. Implementation research and institutional design: the quest for structure. In *Policy implementation in federal and unitary systems. Questions of analysis and design*, edited by K. Hanf and T.A.J. Toonen, 335–54. Dordrecht: Martinus Nijhoff.

Tsatsos, Dimitris. 1993. *Constitutional law.* Vol. B: *Organisation and operation of the polity* [in Greek]. 2nd edn. Athens: Ant. N. Sakkoulas.
Turpin, Colin. 1972. *Government contracts.* Harmondsworth: Penguin.
—— 1989. *Government procurement and contracts.* Harlow: Longman.
Underdal, Arild. 1998. Explaining compliance and defection: three models. *European Journal of International Relations* 4 (1):5–36.
United Kingdom. Civil Service Department. *List of ministerial responsibilities*, July 1975 – November 1981. London: HMSO.
—— *The civil service year book* 1974–1981. London: HMSO.
United Kingdom Government. 2001. Devolution – Memorandum of Understanding and supplementary agreements between the United Kingdom Government, Scottish Ministers, the Cabinet of the National Assembly for Wales and the Northern Ireland Executive Committee, presented to Parliament by the Deputy Prime Minister by Command of Her Majesty, December 2001. CM 5240.
Valadou, Patrice. 1993. Enforcing the public procurement rules in France. In *Remedies for enforcing the public procurement rules*, edited by S. Arrowsmith, 327–56. Winteringham: Earlsgate.
Van Meter, Donald S., and Carl E. Van Horn. 1975. The policy implementation process: a conceptual framework. *Administration & Society* 6 (4):445–88.
Wallace, Helen. 1973. *National governments and the European Communities.* London: Chatham House.
Webb, Carole. 1983. Theoretical perspectives and problems. In *Policy making in the European Community*, edited by H. Wallace, W. Wallace and C. Webb, 1–41. 2nd edn. Chichester: J. Wiley.
Weiler, J.H.H. 1982. Community, member states and European integration: Is the law relevant? *Journal of Common Market Studies* 21 (1–2):39–56.
—— 1991. The transformation of Europe. *Yale Law Journal* 100 (8):2403–83.
Wellens, K.C., and G.M. Borchardt. 1989. Soft law in European Community law. *European Law Review* 14 (5):267–321.
Welsh Local Government Association. 2005. Local government joint working and the procurement regime. Cardiff: WLGA.
—— N.d. Procurement. http://www.wlga.gov.uk/content.php?nID=158;lID=1
Wessels, Wolfgang. 1985. *Alternative strategies for institutional reform.* EUI working paper no. 85/184. Badia Fiesolana: European University Institute/European Policy Unit.
Williams, Roger, and Rebecca Smellie. 1985. Public purchasing: An administrative cinderella. *Public Administration* 63 (1):23–39.
Wolman, Harold. 1981. The determinants of program success and failure. *Journal of Public Policy* 1 (4):433–64.
Wood, Alan. 2004. Wood review: investigating UK business experiences of competing for public contracts in other EU countries. Report to the Chancellor of the Exchequer and the Secretary of State for Trade and Industry. November 2004.
Woolcock, Stephen. 1991. Public procurement. In *The state of the European Community: Policies, institutions & debates in the transition years*, edited by L. Hurwitz and C. Lequesne, 127–136. Boulder, CO: Lynne Rienner.
Woolcock, Stephen, Michael Hodges, and Kristin Schreiber. 1991. *Britain, Germany and 1992: The limits of deregulation.* Chatham House Papers. London: Pinter for The Royal Institute of International Affairs.

Wright, Vincent. 1996. The national co-ordination of European policy-making: negotiating the quagmire. In *European Union: Power and policy making*, edited by J.J. Richardson, 148–69. London: Routledge.

WS Atkins Management Consultants. 1988. *The 'cost of non-Europe' in public-sector procurement*. Research on the 'cost of non-Europe'. Basic findings, Vol. 5, Part A. Luxembourg: OOPEC.

Xiros, Thanassis G. 2006. Cabinet and Cabinet institutions. *International and European Politics* (3, special issue edited by A.G. Passas, in Greek): 159–78.

Yiombré, Anna and Efthalia Kapitsina. 2008. The transposition of Community law in the internal legal order: legal and administrative dimension [in Greek]. In *National administration and European integration: the Greek experience*, edited by A.G. Passas and T.N. Tsekos. Athens: Papazissis.

Young, Hugo, and Anne Sloman. 1982. *No, Minister: An inquiry into the civil service*. London: BBC.

Zubek, Radoslaw. 2005. Complying with transposition commitments in Poland: collective dilemmas, core executive and legislative outcomes. *West European Politics* 28 (3): 592–619.

Zorbala, Myrto G. 1992. *The Community régime of drafting public procurement contracts and its impact on Greek legislation* [in Greek]. Athens: Ant. N. Sakkoulas.

Zürn, Michael, and Christian Joerges, eds. 2005. *Law and governance in postnational Europe: Compliance beyond the nation-state*. Cambridge: Cambridge University Press.

Legislation

France

Arrêté du 22 avril 1998 modifiant et complétant l'arrêté du 3 février 1994, modifié par l'arrêté du 17 janvier 1996, relatif aux seuils de publicité des marchés publics et de certains contrats soumis à des règles de publicité. *JORF*, 15.5.1998.

Décret 48–1029 du 25 juin 1948 portant organisation des services français en ce qui concerne la participation de la France au programme de relèvement européen. *JORF*, 27.6.1948.

Décret 52–1016 du 3 septembre 1952 fixant la représentation du Gouvernement français au Conseil des ministres de la Communauté européenne du charbon et de l'acier et les relations entre le Gouvernement français et la Communauté. *JORF*, 4.9.1952.

Décret 58–344 du 3 avril 1958 portant attribution de compétence pour l'application des traités instituant les Communautés européennes. *JORF*, 4.4.1958.

Décret 79–98 du 12 janvier 1979 relatif à la mise en concurrence de certains marchés publics de travaux et de fournitures dans le cadre de la Communauté économique européenne. *JORF*, 4.2.1979.

Décret 81–551 du 12 mai 1981 modifiant le décret 79–98 du 12 janvier 1979 relatif à la mise en concurrence de certains marchés publics de travaux et de fournitures dans le cadre de la Communauté économique européenne. *JORF*, 16.5.1981.

Décret 81–665 du 12 juin 1981 relatif aux attributions du ministre délégué auprès du ministre des relations extérieures, chargé des affaires européennes. *JORF*, 14.6.1981.

Décret 83–1135 du 23 décembre 1983 relatif aux attributions du ministre des affaires européennes. *JORF*, 27.12.1983.

Décret 86–1029 du 12 septembre 1986 relatif aux attributions du ministre délégué auprès du ministre des affaires étrangères, chargé des affaires européennes. *JORF*, 13.9.1986.

Décret 88–724 du 27 mai 1988 relatif aux attributions du ministre des affaires européennes. *JORF*, 28.5.1988.

Décret 90–824 du 18 septembre 1990 modifiant le code des marchés publics et pris pour l'application de la directive du Conseil des Communautés européennes 89–440 du 18 juillet 1989 modifiant la directive 71–305 du 26 juillet 1971 portant coordination des procédures de passation des marchés publics de travaux. *JORF*, 20.9.1990.

Décret 90–980 du 31 octobre 1990 relatif aux attributions du ministre délégué aux affaires européennes. *JORF*, 4.11.1990.

Décret 92–311 du 31 mars 1992 soumettant la passation de certains contrats de travaux à des règles de publicité et de mise en concurrence, et modifiant le livre V du code des marchés publics, *JORF*, 1.4.1992.

Décret 92–964 du 7 septembre 1992 relatif aux recours en matière de passation de certains contrats et marchés de fournitures et de travaux et modifiant le nouveau code de procédure civile et le code des tribunaux administratifs et des cours administratives d'appel. *JORF*, 11.9.1992.

Décret 97–724 du 18 juin 1997 relatif aux attributions déléguées au ministre délégué chargé des affaires européennes. *JORF*, 19.6.1997.

Décret 98–111 du 27 février 1998 modifiant le code des marchés publics en ce qui concerne les règles de mise en concurrence et de publicité des marchés de services. *JORF*, 28.2.1998.

Décret 98–112 du 27 février 1998 soumettant la passation de certains contrats de fournitures ou de prestations de services à des règles de publicité et de mise en concurrence et modifiant le décret 92–311 du 31/03/1992. *JORF*, 28.2.1998.

Décret 98–113 du 27 février 1998 relatif aux mesures de publicité et de mise en concurrence applicables à certains contrats de services dans les secteurs de l'eau, de l'énergie, des transports et des communications et portant modification du décret 93–990 du 3 août 1993. *JORF*, 28.2.1998.

Décret 2001–210 du 7 mars 2001 portant code des marchés publics. *JORF*, 8.3.2001.

Décret 2001–739 du 23 août 2001 relatif aux commissions spécialisées des marchés. *JORF*, 24.8.2001.

Décret 2002–908 du 29 mai 2002 relatif aux attributions déléguées au ministre délégué aux affaires européennes. *JORF*, 30.5.2002.

Décret 2004–15 du 7 janvier 2004, portant code des marchés publics. *JORF*, 8.1.2004.

Décret 2004–1299 du 26 novembre 2004 relatif à la commission des marchés publics de l'État. *JORF*, 30.11.2004.

Décret 2005–54 du 27 janvier 2005 relatif au contrôle financier au sein des administrations de l'État. *JORF*, 28.1.2005.

Décret 2005–715 du 28 juin 2005 relatif aux attributions déléguées à la ministre déléguée aux affaires européennes. *JORF*, 29.6.2005.

Décret 2005–1283 du 17 octobre 2005 relatif au comité interministériel sur l'Europe et au secrétariat général des affaires européennes. *JORF*, 18.10.2005.

Décret 2006–975 du 1er août 2006 portant code des marchés publics. *JORF*, 4.8.2006.

Décret 2007–61 du 16 janvier 2007 relatif à la commission des marchés publics de l'État. *JORF*, 18.1.2007.
Loi 57–880 du 2 août 1957 autorisant le Président de la République à ratifier : 1° le traité instituant une Communauté économique européenne et ses annexes ; 2° le traité instituant la Communauté européenne de l'énergie atomique ; 3° la convention relative à certaines institutions communes aux Communautés européennes, signés à Rome le 25 mars 1957. *JORF*, 4.8.1957.
Loi 79–564 du 6 juillet 1979 modifiant l'ordonnance 58–1100 du 17 novembre 1958 relative au fonctionnement des assemblées parlementaires en vue de la création de délégations parlementaires pour les Communautées européennes. *JORF*, 7.7.1979.
Loi 90–385 du 10 mai 1990 modifiant l'article 6 bis de l'ordonnance 58–1100 du 17 novembre 1958 relative au fonctionnement des assemblées parlementaires. *JORF*, 11.5.1990.
Loi 91–3 du 3 janvier 1991 relative à la transparence et à la régularité des procédures de marchés et soumettant la passation de certains contrats à des règles de publicité et de mise en concurrence. *JORF*, 5.1.1991.
Loi 93–122 du 29 janvier 1993 relative à la prévention de la corruption et à la transparence de la vie économique et des procédures publiques. *JORF*, 30.1.1993.
Loi 95–125 du 8 février 1995 relative à l'organisation des juridictions et à la procédure civile, pénale et administrative. *JORF*, 9.2.1995.
Loi 95–127 du 8 février 1995 relative aux marchés publics et délégations de service public. *JORF*, 9.2.1995.
Loi 97–50 du 22 janvier 1997 complétant, en ce qui concerne certains contrats de services et de fournitures, la loi 91–3 du 3 janvier 1991 relative à la transparence et à la régularité des procédures de marchés et soumettant la passation de certains contrats à des règles de publicité et de mise en concurrence et la loi 92–1282 du 11 décembre 1992 relative aux procédures de passation de certains contrats dans les secteurs de l'eau, de l'énergie, des transports et des télécommunications. *JORF*, 23.1.1997.
Loi 2000–597 du 30 juin 2000 relative au référé devant les juridictions administratives. *JORF*, 1.7.2000.
Loi 2001–1 du 3 janvier 2001 portant habilitation du Gouvernement à transposer, par ordonnances, des directives communautaires et à mettre en oeuvre certaines dispositions du droit communautaire. *JORF*, 4.1.2001.
Loi 2003–591 du 2 juillet 2003 habilitant le Gouvernement à simplifier le droit. *JORF*, 3.7.2003.

Greece[i]

Act of the Ministerial Council 288 of 23 December 1996. Modification, completion and codification of provisions for the collective governmental organs. *GGHR*, A285, 31.12.1996.
Decision of the Prime Minister 565. On the transfer of power to the minister without portfolio G. Kontogeorgis. *GGHR*, B1271, 29.11.1977.
Decision of the Prime Minister 3307. Modification, updating and codification of provisions on inter-ministerial committees. *GGHR*, B1189, 31.12.1996.
Law 3215/1955. On preference for domestic industrial products and artefacts. *Gazette of the Government of the Kingdom of Greece*, A108, 30.4.1955.

Law 4226/1962. On the ratification of the association agreement of Greece with the EEC and other issues relating to its application. *Gazette of the Government of the Kingdom of Greece*, A41, 14.3.1962.

Law 445/1976. On the representation of Greece in the European Communities and the organisation of the administrative services in view of the application of the Community régime. *GGHR*, A260, 1.10.1976.

Law 936/1979. On the modification and completion of the provisions 'on foreign trade and the abolition of other relevant provisions'. *GGHR*, A144, 30.6.1979.

Law 945/1979. On the ratification of the Treaty of Accession of Greece to the European Economic Community, the European Atomic Energy Community and the agreement on the accession of Greece to the European Coal and Steel Community. *GGHR*, A170, 27.7.1979.

Law 992/1979. On the organisation of the administrative services for the application of the Treaty of Accession of Greece to the European Communities and other institutional issues. *GGHR*, A280, 21.12.1979.

Law 1104/1980. On the representation of Greece in the European Communities, the establishment of Diplomatic and Consular Authorities and other relevant organisational issues. *GGHR*, A298, 29.12.1980.

Law 1418/1984. Public works and other relevant issues. *GGHR*, A23, 29.2.1984.

Law 1440/1984. Contribution of Greece to the capital, reserve and provisions of the European Investment Bank, the capital of the European Coal and Steel Community and the EURATOM Agency. *GGHR*, A70, 21.5.1984.

Law 1640/1986. Executory type of the decisions of the EC institutions, creation of the special legal service for EC issues. *GGHR*, A122, 11.8.1986.

Law 1682/1987. Instruments of development policy. *GGHR*, A14, 16.2.1987.

Law 1797/1988. Public sector procurement and related issues. *GGHR*, A164, 4.8.1988.

Law 1880/1990. Modification of laws 1262/1982 and 1338/1983 on the competitiveness of the ship-building industry and other provisions. *GGHR*, A39, 21.3.1990.

Law 2286/1995. Public sector procurement and other issues. *GGHR*, A19, 1.2.1995.

Law 2367/1995. New credit and monetary institutions and other provisions. *GGHR*, A261, 29.12.1995.

Law 2372/1996. Establishment of bodies for the promotion of growth and other provisions. *GGHR*, A29, 28.2.1996.

Law 2522/1997. Judicial protection prior to the conclusion of public procurement contracts in accordance with Directive 89/665. *GGHR*, A178, 8.9.1997.

Law 2741/1999. Unified food control agency and other provisions. *GGHR*, A199, 28.09.1999.

Law 3021/2002. Limitations in the conclusion of public procurement contracts with persons involved in media companies and other provisions. *GGHR*, A143, 19.06.2002.

Law 3060/2002. Issues regarding the Ministry of Justice. *GGHR*, A242, 11.10.2002.

Law 3263/2004. Lowest price-based award of public works contracts and other provisions. *GGHR*, A179, 28.09.2004.

Law 3310/2005. Measures for the protection of transparency and the fight against illicit practices in the award of public procurement contracts (main shareholder). *GGHR*, A30, 14.02.2005.

Law 3316/2005. Award and execution of public contracts regarding the preparation of works plans and the provision of other related services, and other provisions. *GGHR*, A42, 22.2.2005.
Presidential Decree 1141/1977. On the appointment of ministers and junior ministers. *GGHR*, A370, 28.11.1977.
Presidential Decree 105/1989. Adaptation of Greek state procurement legislation to Community legislation. *GGHR*, A 5, 10.2.1989.
Presidential Decree 173/1990. Public procurement regulation. *GGHR*, A62, 10.4.1990.
Presidential Decree 137/1991. Modification of PD 173/1990. *GGHR*, A55, 17.4.1991.
Presidential Decree 265/1991. Adaptation of Greek public works legislation to the provisions of Directives 71/304, 71/305, 72/277 and 78/669 of the EEC. *GGHR*, A99, 1.7.1991.
Presidential Decree 304/1992. Abolition of the Secretariat General for State Procurement and establishment of the Directorate of Procurement Policy in the Ministry of Trade. *GGHR*, A151, 9.9.1992.
Presidential Decree 23/1993. Adaptation of the Greek public works legislation to the provisions of EEC Directives 71/304, 71/305, 78/669, 89/440, and 89/665. *GGHR*, A8, 5.2.1993.
Presidential Decree 428/1995. Establishment of the Directorate General of Quality of Public Works in the Secretariat General of public Works of the Ministry of Environment, Spatial Planning and Public Works. *GGHR*, A245, 24.11.1995.
Presidential Decree 166/1996. Establishment of the Secretariat General for Co-financed Public Works in the Ministry of Environment, Spatial Planning and Public Works, definition of its remit and modification and completion of PD 69/1988 and PD 91/1991. *GGHR*, A125, 17.6.1996.
Presidential Decree 346/1998. Adapatation of the Greek legislation on services procurement to EEC Directive 92/50. *GGHR*, A230, 12.10.1998.
Presidential Decree 18/2000. Amendment of PD 346/98. *GGHR*, A15, 3. 2.2000.
Presidential Decree 334/2000. Adaptation of the Greek public works legislation to EEC Directive 93/37 as amended and updated. *GGHR*, A279, 21.12.2000.
Presidential Decree 63/2005. Codification of the legislation on the government and government institutions. *GGHR*, A98, 22.4.2005.

Jurisprudence

European Union[ii]

C-120/78 *Rewe-Zentral AG v. Bundesmonopolverwaltung für Branntwein* [1979] 649.
C-240/78 *Atalanta Amsterdam B.V. v. Produktschap voor Vee en Vlees* [1979] 2137.
C-96/81 *Commission of the European Communities v. Kingdom of the Netherlands* [1982] 1791.
C-84/86 *Commission v. République hellénique*. Conclusions de l'avocat général Jean Mischo présentés à l'audience de la Cour de Justice du 27.2.1991. Not reported.
C-392/93 *The Queen v. HM Treasury, ex parte British Telecommunications plc* [1996] 1631.

C-234/95 *Commission of the European Communities v. French Republic* [1996] 2415.
C-236/95 *Commission des Communautés européennes v. République hellénique* [1996] 4459.
C-311/95 *Commission of the European Communities v. Hellenic Republic* [1996] 2433.
C-81/98 *Alcatel Austria and others* [1999] I–7671.
C-97/00 *Commission v. France* [2001] 2053.

France

Conseil Constitutionnel. 2003. Décision 2003–473 DC du 26 juin 2003. *JORF*, 3.7.2003.
Conseil de la Concurrence. 2006. Décision 06-D-07 bis du 21 mars 2006 relative à des pratiques mises en oeuvre dans le secteur des travaux publics dans la région Ile-de-France. *http://www.conseil-concurrence.fr/pdf/avis/06d07.pdf*

i   All published in Greek. Author's translation of the titles.
ii All published in *Reports of cases before the Court of Justice of the European Communities* except C-84/86. The present list refers to the year of publication and the relevant page number.

Index

administrative ethos 12
administrative systems 18
Athens Olympics 126n.20
authority 25, 105–14, 116–24, 139–40

Bardach, Eugene 3, 17, 19, 27n.12, 28n.14
Berman, Paul 24
BT 90n.24

central governments *see* national central governments
central purchasing bodies 63, 86, 118–19
Chartered Institute of Purchasing and Supply 86, 123
Chirac, Jacques 43, 44
civil servants, mobility 12
comitology 9, 19
common agricultural policy 10, 99
competition 107, 108, 115, 143, 146–7
compliance 7, 12, 145
co-ordination, implementation and 8–13, 17, 18–19, 24–5, 31, 71–2, 135
Copenhagen criteria 4
corruption 63, 97, 108
Couve de Murville, Maurice 39
Cresson, Edith 55n.22, 55n.24, 56n.32
culture, political culture 5

De Gaulle, Charles 39
decision points 18, 85, 88, 138

Derthick, Martha 17, 23
deuterolearning 21
directives
    implementation process 19–20
    regulation by directives 12, 58, 66
    transposition. *see* transposition
double-loop learning 21, 101
Duina, Francesco 6
Dumas, Roland 55n.22

eco-labels 3
electronic signatures 64
energy 61–2
environment 7, 63
EU public procurement
    case study 12, 58
    central purchasing bodies 63
    coercion 65–6
    comparative transposition 87–8
    competitive dialogue 62
    corruption 63
    environmental and social standards 63
    equal treatment 60, 64
    framework agreements 63
    free market model 65, 66–7
    French implementation 105–16
    French institutions 68–9, 71–2
    French transposition 81–3, 87, 88
    Greek implementation 93–105
    Greek institutions 67–8
    Greek transposition 76–81, 87, 88
    importance 64–5

liberalisation objective 58, 59, 60, 63, 66
margins of manoeuvre 146
monitoring 60
national implications 64–7
national institutions 67–71
objectives 84, 86
origins 59, 60–1
principles 59–60, 63, 65
problems 143–4
public interest exceptions 104
public undertakings 61–2
recent developments 62–4
regulation by directives 12, 58, 66
Remedies Directives 62, 66, 67, 107
scope 60–2, 66
selectivity 59–60
services 61
socio-economic objectives 64
thresholds 60
transparency 60, 65, 85, 86
UK implementation 116–24
UK institutions 69–72
UK transposition 83–7, 87, 88
utilities 61–2, 66, 90n.24
European Commission
  French implementation 111–12
  Greek implementation 93–5, 100–1, 101–2, 104
  institutional fixer 9, 22, 146
  Jenkins Commission 20
  monitoring public procurement 60
  public procurement policy 65
  réunions-paquets 22, 93
European Court of Justice
  effet utile 16n.18
  implementation cases 16n.23, 57n.54
  institutional fixer 22
  obligation de diligence 16n.18
  transposition of public procurement 79, 80, 82, 83, 88
European integration
  convergence 26, 144
  debate 6–7
  implementation 3, 146–7
  limits 143–6
  politicisation 10

single market 5, 7, 20, 58, 61, 62, 65, 82, 115
social regulation 3
European Union
  accession criteria 4
  basic principles 59
  direct effect of EU law 59
  indirect administration 9
  policy process 19–20
  public procurement. *see* EU public procurement
Europeanisation 4, 6, 10, 143–6

Fabius, Laurent 129n.51
federalism 17, 23, 146
fixing 22
France
  actes détachables 107–8
  bicephalous executive 16n.22, 39–40
  CMPE 69, 112–14, 140, 142
  Commission Centrale des Marchés (CCM) 68–9, 105–8
  Competition Council 107, 115, 143
  EU constitutional referendum (2005) 40
  EU specific institutions 52
  favouritism 81
  implementation. *see* French implementation
  Inter-ministerial Committee on Europe 40
  Inter-ministerial Committee for European Economic Co-operation 38, 42–3
  Maastricht Treaty 41
  Ministry for European Affairs 38, 39
  Ministry of Economy and Finance 28n.19, 39
  Ministry for Foreign Affairs 39
  money laundering 108
  national champions 64
  précontentieux 107
  public procurement
    Code 68, 69, 81, 83, 106, 110–12
    corruption 108
    institutions 68–9, 71–2, 105–10, 112–14

Index

policies 64
see also French implementation
référé précontractuel 107
SGAE 40, 44, 53
SGCI 38–9, 40, 43–4, 68
SGG 43, 44
Fraser Report 120
French implementation
  case study 12
  co-ordination 38–44, 52, 53, 72, 136
  deficit 2
  organisational reform 38–40, 144
  parliamentary role 41–2
  public procurement 105–16
    bid prices 111
    CCM role 105–8
    central dynamism 145
    CMPE 112–14, 140, 142
    competition 107, 108, 115, 143
    co-ordination 109, 112, 139
    decentralisation 111
    extent of change 136, 139, 141
    fragility of reforms 145
    Grand Stade de France 115, 129n.57
    infringement proceedings 112
    institutions 105–10, 112–14, 141
    investigation mechanisms 108–10
    judicial politics 107
    learning 114–16
    MIEM 108–10, 114–15, 140
    most interesting offer 106
    motivation 142
    politicisation 115–16, 142
    post-2001 reforms 109, 110–14
    services 111, 112
    social and environmental conditions 110
    standardisation 106–7
    statistics 137, 138
    transparency 136
    transposition 81–3, 87, 88, 138–9
  sources 13
  transposition
    infringement proceedings 82, 83
    institutions 42–4
    politics 44

public procurement 81–3, 87, 88, 138–9
Remedies Directive 107

Gershon Report 74n.26, 121, 122, 123
Giannakourou, Georgia 3
Giscard d'Estaing, Valery 39
governance 9, 146–7
Greece
  association agreement 31
  Brussels representation 32
  bureaucracy 12, 52–3, 71, 98, 100
  Cabinet 34, 99
  Community Affairs Unit 78
  Council of Economic Advisers 33
  credibility as EU partner 37–8, 140
  diffused forms of authority 88
  EEC accession 1, 76
  ENYEK 36, 77
  EU specific institutions 52
  European Affairs Legal Service 36, 77
  European Community Affairs Committee 35
  European Co-operation Committee 32
  Evinos dam 95, 102
  Government Committee 34, 99
  implementation. *see* Greek implementation
  inter-ministerial committees 36–7
  media regulation 145
  ministerial advisers 37
  ministerial circulars 34, 37
  Ministry of Co-ordination 32, 36–7
  Ministry of Economy and Finance 32, 34, 38, 98
  Ministry of Environment 67, 79, 88, 95, 96, 100
  Ministry of European Affairs 33
  Ministry of Foreign Affairs 32, 33
  Ministry of National Economy 93, 95–6, 97, 98
  protectionism 76–7

public procurement
  institutions 67–8, 96–9, 105
  policies 64, 77, 94
  see also Greek implementation
Secretariat General for State
    Procurement 78
technical ministries 33
Greek implementation
  case study 12
  co-ordination 32–3, 34, 38, 53
  French and British models 12
  organisational reform 31–5, 144
  parliamentary role 35–6
  public procurement 93–105
    Athens Olympics 126n.20
    authority 140
    bid prices 95
    Committee of Major Works 98
    co-ordination 98–9, 139
    corruption 97
    dynamics 99–102
    enforcement 96
    extent of change 136, 139, 141
    favouritism 103
    fragility of reforms 145
    guidance 96
    health sector 105
    infringement proceedings 79, 80, 93–4
    institutions 96–9, 105, 141
    insurance 96
    learning 99–102
    monitoring mechanisms 96–7
    MOPADIS 95–6, 140
    motivations 141–2
    politics 103–5, 136, 142
    procedures 95
    proportionality 104
    public works 78, 79, 80, 96–7
    quality of work 94
    services 78–9, 80, 97–8
    Services Procurement Unit 98
    statistics 99, 137, 138
    steering 95, 96, 98, 100
    supplies 78, 97
    transparency 96, 136
    transposition 76–81, 87, 88, 138–9

sources of information 13
transition periods 37
transposition
  politics 36
  process 36–8, 100
  public procurement 76–81, 87, 88, 138–9
  techniques 102
unfinished business 1, 31–8
Guigou, Elisabeth 55n.23

Haverland, Markus 6
Heath, Edward 45, 117
Hood, Christopher 18, 25

implementation
  25-year period 12
  comparative evaluation 51–4
  complexities 17–20
  co-ordination 8–13, 17, 18–19, 24–5, 31, 71–2, 135
  credibility test 3
  cultural explanations 5
  deficit 2, 5–8
  departmental attitudes 5
  discretion 22
  dynamics 2–3, 13–14, 20–3, 99–102, 135–41
  European integration and 3, 146–7
  institutionalist explanations 5–6, 142
  interest-based explanations 5, 141–2
  limits of Europeanisation 143–6
  macro-implementation. see macro-implementation
  margin of manoeuvre 2, 146
  micro-implementation 24, 58
  motivations 141–2
  politics 3, 17, 20
  research methodology 13
  role of national central governments 9, 13
  scholarship 4–8
  sectoral approach 10, 19
  significance 3–4
  steering 25–6
  strategies 2–3

Index

terminology 5
theory 19
see also specific countries
institutions
   academic focus on 7–8
   capacities 22–6
   centrality 17, 22
   continuity 17
   convergence 144
   EU accession and 4
   EU specific 52
   French reforms 38–40
   Greek reforms 31–5
   historical institutionalism 11–12, 14, 23, 31, 50–3
   implementation deficit 5–6, 142
   public procurement 67–72
   stasis 31
   transposition 88
   UK reforms 44–7

Jenkins, Roy 20
Johnson, Lyndon 23
joint ventures 119
Jospin, Lionel 56n.37

Kassim, Hussein 52
Krasner, Stephen 31

Laliotis, Costas 96
learning 20–1, 99–102, 114–16, 135
legal certainty 83, 84
Lelong, Pierre 112
liberal intergovernmentalism 9
Lowi, Theodore 26n.2

Maastricht Treaty 20, 41
McClelland Report 123, 124
macro-implementation
   dynamics 99–102, 135–41
   meaning 24–6, 67
   micro-implementation and 24, 58
   public procurement
      France 105–16
      Greece 93–105
      United Kingdom 116–24
Makridimitris, Antonia 100
Marshall Plan 38

media regulation 143–4, 145
Mer, Francis 112
methodology 13
micro-implementation 24, 58
Millan, Bruce 95
Mitterrand, François 39

national central governments
   capacities 8
   co-ordination 8–13, 17, 18–19, 23, 24–5, 26, 31, 135, 137–8
   Europeanisation 4, 6, 10, 143–6
   implementation deficit 4
   importance 9, 13
   integration and fragmentation 11, 30, 136–8, 137–8, 147
   internal operations 7–8
   margins of action 2, 146
   steering 25–6
   see also institutions
N.A.T.O. scheme 25, 93–105, 139–40
Nea Dimokratia 1, 99, 103, 104
neo-functionalism 9
nodality 25, 81–3, 85, 87, 88, 93–124, 140–1
Northern Ireland 64, 70–1, 83, 87, 132n.84, 133n.97

OECD 38
organisation 25

Packaging Waste Directive 6
Pangalos, Theodoros 36
Papandreou, Andreas 103
parliaments
   France 41–2, 81
   Greece 35–6
   role 30–1, 51–2, 88
   United Kingdom 47–9, 85
PASOK 1, 39, 76, 77, 78, 93, 95, 97, 100, 101, 103, 104, 141
Passas, Argyris 100
Pavlopoulos, Prokopis 127n.24
Peters, Guy 3
politics
   depoliticising public procurement 143–4
   European integration 10

French public procurement 115–16, 142
French transposition 44
Greek bureaucracy 27, 33, 52–3
Greek public procurement 103–5, 136, 142
implementation 3, 17, 20
political cultures 5
Pompidou, Georges 39
Pressman, Jeffrey 17, 18
public interest exceptions 104
public policy
  choices 8, 18
  decision points 18, 85, 88, 138
  meaning 3
  scholarship 4
public procurement *see* EU public procurement
public spending 64

Raffarin, Jean-Pierre 44, 112
regional autonomy 6
Remedies Directives 62, 66, 67, 107
research methodology 13

Sapin, Michel 116
Scotland
  Parliament Building 120, 145
  public procurement 123–4
  transposition of EU public procurement 70–1, 87, 92n.27
Simitis, Costas 34, 37–8, 52, 57n.52, 80, 97, 98, 99, 103, 125n.8, 140, 141–2
single-loop learning 21, 101, 102
single market 5, 7, 20, 58, 61, 62, 65, 82, 115
SLIM initiative 62
social standards 7, 63
soft law 27n.6
steering 25–6

tax avoidance 63
telecommunications 61–2, 63, 90n.24
Tenders Electronic Daily (TED) 72n.6
Thatcher, Margaret 48
transport services 61–2

transposition
  administrative measures 83, 84
  choices 24
  delays 87–8
  France
    process 42–4
    public procurement 81–3, 87, 88
  Greece
    process 36–8, 100
    public procurement 76–81, 87, 88
  institutional role in 88
  instruments 87
  legal certainty 83, 84
  national autonomy 84
  parliamentary role 88
  process 19, 31
  public procurement comparisons 87–8
  transparency 83, 85
  United Kingdom
    parliamentary role 85
    process 49–51
    public procurement 83–7, 87, 88
    Scottish public procurement 87, 92n.27
treasure 25

United Kingdom
  Brussels representation 46
  Cabinet 45
  Conservative Party 116, 117
  co-ordination 52
  departmental committees 46
  devolution 47, 70–1, 87, 122
  EU controversies 31
  European affairs minister 45
  European Integration Department 45–6
  European Policy sub-committee 45
  European Secretariat 46–7, 50, 51, 53
  European Union Strategy sub-committee 45
  European Unit 46
  Foreign Office 45
  Gershon Report 74n.26, 121, 122, 123

Index

implementation. *see* United Kingdom implementation
McClelland Report 123, 124
Ministerial Committee for Europe 45
neo-liberalism 116
neutral civil service 53
New Labour 121
Office of Government Commerce (OGC) 70, 72, 86–7, 88, 121–4, 136, 140
privatisations 118–19
public procurement
  central purchasing bodies 86, 118–19
  implementation. *see* United Kingdom implementation
  institutions 69–72
  policies 64
  Scottish transposition 87, 92n.27
  transposition 83–7, 87, 88
Single Market Compliance Unit 50
Treasury 28n.19, 116–21, 121
Wood Report 131n.78
United Kingdom implementation
  case study 12
  co-ordination 46
  organisational reform 44–7
  parliamentary role 47–9
  public procurement 116–24
    Alcatel case 132n.88
    compulsory competitive tendering 117
    decentralisation 118
    devolution 122–4
    equal treatment 120
    General Preference Scheme 116
    Government Procurement Service 123
    guidance 117, 120
    joint ventures 119
    limited case law 119
    local government 119
    objectives 140–1
    Office of Government Commerce (OGC) 70, 72, 86–7, 88, 121–4, 136, 140
    Priority Suppliers Scheme 116
    Private Finance Initiative 119–20
    Scottish Parliament Building 120, 145
    sectoral support 116
    Special Preference Scheme 116
    statistics 124, 137, 138
    steering 123
    training 118, 123
    Treasury role 116–21
    value for money 118
  record 2, 44–51
  research sources 13
  transposition 49–51
United States, federalism 23, 24
utilities 61–2, 66, 90n.24

Venizelos, E. 127n.23
Villepin, Dominique de 40

Wales 83, 87, 133n.103
water supply 61–2
Webb, Carole 146
Wildavsky, Aaron 17, 18
Wilson, Harold 45
Wood Report 131n.78
world of neglect 145
worlds of compliance 145
WTO 121

Lightning Source UK Ltd.
Milton Keynes UK
UKOW03f0441060114

224032UK00001B/71/P